P9-CLF-840

DATE DUE		
OCT 25 '8		
FEB 16		
NOV 16 '81		
APR 2 1 1990		
JUN 0 1 2007		

PUBLIC TRUST, PRIVATE LUST

Sex, Power and Corruption on Capitol Hill

Also by Rudy Maxa

DARE TO BE GREAT

PUBLIC TRUST, PRIVATE LUST

Sex, Power and Corruption on Capitol Hill

Marion Clark and Rudy Maxa

WILLIAM MORROW AND COMPANY, INC.

NEW YORK   1977

FOR

ADA & THE SCOTSMAN

AND

CHRISTINE & THE COLONEL

Printed in the United States of America.

1   2   3   4   5   6   7   8   9   10

Library of Congress Cataloging in Publication Data

Clark, Marion (date)
    Public trust, private lust.

    Includes index.
    1. Corruption (in politics)—United States.
2. Conflict of interests (Public office)—United
States.   3. Politicians—United States—Sexual
behavior.   4. United States. Congress.   I. Maxa,
Rudy, joint author.   II. Title.
JK2249.C56   328.73′07′6   77-4184
ISBN 0-688-03190-0

BOOK DESIGN   CARL WEISS

PREFACE

This book is about Congress in the mid-1970s and, to borrow a line from *Vanity Fair*, it is a book without a hero. Congress in the post-Watergate years has not distinguished itself; the congressional class of '74, which arrived in Washington filled with brio and promise, adjourned in the fall of 1976 under the shadow of scandal. A record number of congressmen * decided not to seek reelection, some quitting their jobs over disgust with Congress' intractability, others forced out of office by revelations of chicanery and malfeasance. It had not been a season for heroism on Capitol Hill.

Only two years before, in the summer of 1974, Congress presided over the final days of Richard Nixon's political career. Senator Sam Ervin's Watergate hearings in the Senate and impeachment proceedings begun in the House cast Congress in the role of protector of the Constitution. Nixon's resignation as President on August 8, 1974, was viewed by many as a triumph by Congress, proof that the system of checks and balances worked, a catharsis that would begin a serene era of post-Watergate morality.

The respite was brief.

Much as some Washingtonians like to think of their town only as a capital blessed with grand avenues, pristine monuments and a precious heritage, it is also, in the end, a city of men and women as subject to human failings as people everywhere. With the resignation of Richard Nixon the executive branch was humbled, new legislation was passed to curb the orgy of secret cash contributions that had funded the political excesses that preceded Nixon's reelection in 1972. But for decades the legislative branch had quietly grown fat and smug: Congress' payroll had expanded to in-

* Throughout this book the term "congressman" refers to both representatives and senators.

clude eighteen thousand employees on a billion-dollar budget, its lack of accountability had permitted it to escape the consequences of its own legislation.

Standing astride the 94th Congress, with seniority, patronage power, and a clout exercised through sheer orneriness, was Wayne Hays, a congressman from a strip-mined corner of Ohio who turned an obscure committee assignment into a power base that rivaled the office of the Speaker of the House. As chairman of the House Administration Committee, Hays effected moves toward bigger congressional staffs, fatter personal allowances and closed government. No one missed the irony of the fact that it was Hays, suddenly caught up in a sex-and-payroll scandal over committee staff aide Elizabeth Ray in May of 1976, who would provide the impetus for what could be the most significant congressional reorganization in recent history. And whether it was a result of heightened press interest in Congress or simply chance, the Hays affair was quickly followed by a multitude of news stories that depicted a Congress which had grown imperial in its actions.

Hays and Ray, of course, did not introduce illicit sex to the nation's capital; they simply focused attention on it. In Washington an attractive woman will come to a man's home or hotel room and perform sex for about seventy dollars; the service is listed in the Yellow Pages and local vice squads know about it. The address book of an experienced political operative contains the names of half a dozen women who can serve as an evening's escort for a lonely legislator. And some women arrive in Washington with the single ambition of landing a congressman or senator in bed, for no reason other than the expected thrill of seducing a powerful politician. Sometimes Washington sex is as harmless as any casual affair in any town. But on occasion, because Washington is a city where a public figure's image and reputation are often his only currency, a dalliance in the wrong bed can sink a career.

* * *

Suspicions of official misbehavior in Washington are as old as the city, and the Hays-Ray affair did nothing to dissuade those Americans who have always believed some congressmen keep mistresses on their staffs. The authors, however, did not set out to prove Capitol Hill is the devil's playground, and it is not their contention that it is. Conscientious congressmen and earnest staffers abound, and some of them are included in this book. But the same institution that has given us the decency of senators such as Philip Hart and representatives such as Les Aspin has also brought us the conniving of Thomas Dodd and Adam Clayton Powell. Some offices boast staffs that exist primarily to serve their congressman's personal interests, not the interests of the nation. Some members of Congress long ago settled into an obscure, complacent existence, content with the title of "Congressman" until pried from their comfortable seats by death, redistricting or defeat.

A definitive catalog of congressional sins could keep a team of investigative reporters at work for years. Part of this book is the personal story of the two *Washington Post* reporters who conducted the unorthodox journalistic investigation that led to the first news of Wayne Hays's affair with Elizabeth Ray. (For the sake of clarity, the authors refer to themselves in the third person.) Already some of the quotes in that original *Post* story seem a quaint part of American history: "I can't type, I can't file, I can't even answer the phone," Elizabeth Ray told Marion Clark and Rudy Maxa. "Hell's fire!" Wayne Hays exclaimed when confronted with questions about his sexual involvement with Ray, "I'm a very happily married man."

She was the ambitious, voluptuous blond who dreamed of fame and was attracted to Hays partly because "he was the sharpest dresser I ever saw." He was the crotchety congressman with a wandering eye who harbored hopes of running for the Ohio governorship after he completed thirty years in Congress in 1978. Together they ignited a fire storm of publicity about Capitol Hill sex when Ray charged her fourteen-thousand-dollar-a-year salary was only meant to guarantee Hays a bed partner.

Beyond the question of lust for the flesh, the Hays-Ray scandal prompted congressional critics to consider the greater question of lust for power. Much of the extracurricular sex in which Washington's public figures indulge is the result of the pursuit of power, there being no shortage of power's trappings in Congress. The first day a congressman takes office he has an array of fringe benefits and privileges at his command. Capitol Hill police will stop cars for him on busy Pennsylvania Avenue should he choose to cross against the traffic. Special interest groups woo him, staffers adore him. As his length of service increases, so do his perquisites. Even if his career is undistinguished, longevity may bring him recognition and honor of a sort. For example, when one sixteen-year House veteran, Georgia Democrat Robert Stephens, retired in 1976, his colleagues in the House recommended a government building in Athens, Georgia, be named the Robert G. Stephens, Jr., Federal Building. The reason: "In his capacity as chairman of the Subcommittee on Historic Preservation and Coinage, [Stephens] was the driving force behind meaningful legislation designed to assist the entire country."

Such puffery has made it difficult to remain both a congressman and humble.

Ironically, Congress is often the institution to which Americans look for relief—"there oughtta be a law" is an American cliché. Now Congress is faced with the task of considering rules that might put its own house in order, a chore that has been urged on Congress by a liberal minority for at least a decade. Neither Wayne Hays nor Elizabeth Ray could have predicted that they would someday spur such efforts; Hays, after all, never hid his contempt for the reform-minded and Ray went to Congress with far more modest designs. Should the news of their liaison lead to a more efficient and honorable Congress, they just might be remembered as two of America's more curious heroes.

ACKNOWLEDGMENTS

FROM THE DAY we first spoke with "secretary" Elizabeth Ray about her peculiar liaison with her boss, Wayne Hays, Benjamin Bradlee, executive editor of *The Washington Post,* counseled us, cautioned us and kept us on the right investigative track. Without his day-to-day guidance and meticulous editing of the initial Hays-Ray articles, the liaison might still be only a faint rumor in the back halls of Congress. Without Ben Bradlee and the fine news judgment of *The Post*'s managing editor, Howard Simons, the majority of the stories on congressional corruption in the summer of '76, from which this book is drawn, may never have been written.

We are also grateful for the energy and understanding of so many people that it would be impossible to single out Shelby Coffey, Chris Little, Mary Lou Beatty, Morris Udall and Thomas Rees; Capitol Hill experts Nick Curtis, Warren Nelson, Jay Jaffee, Daniel Rapoport and Lois Romano; title-writing wizard Henry Allen and Washington historian Dr. Fred Aengst; the librarians at *The Washington Post, Columbus Dispatch* and the *Greenville Piedmont* and *News;* friends, chefs and disciplinarians Donnie and Annie Abram, Tom Zito and Joel Swerdlow; William Morrow & Company's fine copy editors and workers Bonnie Donovan and Abby Schaefer; a secretary who can (and did) type, Mary Catchings; and our agent, David Obst, who proved he can interest a good publisher in a book by telephone from the Polo Lounge.

This is not to mention Martin Mull (a Buckeye Bonus). And Kathleen and Sarah Maxa.

This is also not to mention the names—though we know and you know who you are—of the many congressional staffers and Library of Congress employees who risked the displeasure of their bosses to help our research.

We *can* mention, but not enough times, Hillel Black, our book editor. More than thanks, he deserves a Guinness Book of Records' award for patience plus our unending gratitude for enlarging the focus of this book by constantly reminding us to take a broad view of the problems of Congress.

March 1977   MARION CLARK
Washington, D.C.   RUDY MAXA

CONTENTS

ONE

NIGHT TRAIN

HE WAS WEARING a Redskins hat and before the lights dimmed you could see the weariness taking over his eyes like red lace. He looked close to sixty, and silly, the way old men look when they've geared up for a last college hurrah. And drunk too much. And pretended too long that they didn't wish they were home watching the game on TV.

He glanced over to where she sat half-turned away from him. Then the weary eyes turned away and looked out the train windows, not searching for anything really, just settling on the next track, half-closed now.

She had a face that looked like trouble, the kind of face James M. Cain wrote about in *Double Indemnity,* hard and sexy, and the kind of body low-life men could kill for. A California girl out of California too long. A California girl gone sour, crusted before her time. A California girl who didn't know how to swim, who hadn't known much joy. No. Not a California girl at all, just someone who knew what California girls should look like.

She had the long, silver-blond straight hair, the blue eyes, the tan, the baby blue knit pants and button-popping white blouse open to the cleavage. But where was the natural wonder, the Cover Girl-clean makeup? The eyes were hidden with mascara and dark eye shadow, the lips too red.

And, how old? Sixteen? Thirty? Too young for him anyway. So, what was the relationship? Did these things still go on? Young women lured by money to go with old men to something like an out-of-town Redskins game?

Too bad for him, if that were the story. Maybe just too long a date. The gossamer looked like it had been gone for hours, and now it appeared that he'd just as soon be sitting on the train across from his wife. They didn't speak, hadn't spoken for twenty minutes.

There were three other people in the car with Marion Clark. Redskins Hat, the neo-California girl and a man, staring at but not reading *The New York Times,* who looked exactly like Elliott Gould.

It was seven o'clock on a Saturday night, September 14, 1974, the day after the White House had agreed not to give Richard Nixon control of the Watergate tapes, and a day after Nixon had publicly announced he had erred in handling Watergate. It was an hour after Marion Clark had abandoned "Mr. Right," a man she was to marry, in the Penn Station Zum Zum.

She looked around the parlor car again as the Washington Metroliner lurched forward. No one else had gotten on and, as she laid her head against the windowpane, she thought that no one in this car had flexed a muscle when the train had started, that no one seemed quite right. Everyone here, she thought, had brought a lot of baggage. She knew what hers was—two weeks in another town, a long romance down the drain, emotional bankruptcy threatening again.

She ordered dinner and then she ordered one whole bottle of wine for herself, some cheap kind of California rosé, and went over to Redskin Hat's seat.

"You look like you must know who won the Redskins game today," she said. And Redskins Hat said, "You're damn right I do. Who wants to know?"

"I do," she said, "but if you don't want to tell me that's o.k. with me. You probably are a Redskin," she lied, hating herself for the cheap, empty flirt, "and you don't look too happy."

"You a Redskins fan?" he said, and now California Dreaming was glowering. Up close she looked almost haggard and definitely not happy. She hadn't had a great time with Redskins Hat at the game, or before or after, or maybe even ever, hat or no.

"I like Sonny," Marion said.

"You're not from Washington," he said.

"Yes I am," she said.

"Well, if you're from Washington," he said, "I'll tell you who I am and maybe you know me. Ever heard of Duke Zeibert?"

"You're Duke Zeibert?" She asked it like someone who'd just been introduced to Howard Hughes. Duke Zeibert. Of course. The reputation was wide. The Toots Shor of Washington. Knew everyone in sports, knew everyone in politics, knew everyone in Las Vegas too, and owned a Jewish-New York type restaurant on L Street where the dill pickles were as big as cucumbers, the gossip as juicy as the matzo balls.

But Duke Zeibert, she thought, isn't this old. In the floor-to-ceiling murals of himself painted on Zeibert's restaurant walls, he looked about twenty years younger. Black hair, black moustache, thin.

Years ago a man had taken her to Duke Zeibert's for lunch and, over chicken livers, proposed marriage. The whole restaurant had been packed with he-men puffing cigars. The waiters were huge too and knew everyone by name. Now she and the man were old friends, and every once in a while over lunch at Chez Camille, he would laugh about the day he took her to Duke's to try to impress her and then, when he'd popped the question, she'd looked around and said, "Let's get out of this fag place."

"The first time I ever ate in your restaurant," she told Duke, "the man I was with asked me to marry him."

"Well, you said yes, didn't you?"

"No. But the dill pickles were the best I've ever eaten," she said.

Duke told her all about the dill pickles in a long soliloquy, the way restaurant owners are wont to do, as if it didn't matter that they hobnobbed with class people who sat in the front banquettes and squired blonds to sit in the owners' boxes at football games—what mattered was that they got those pickles, or that oil that made the heavenly fettucini, from a friend of their father who owned a little farm up in the hills outside some place like Salerno.

The parlor car waiter cut Duke short; her dinner was getting cold, he said. She excused herself and went back—mostly to the wine.

Where was he now, she wondered? Long gone from the Zum Zum, down in Bed-Stuy talking to their good friends, drinking Irish whiskey, telling them why it hadn't worked out, maybe laughing about it now.

Washington was a few hours away, closer than New York. Marion Clark thought about work, going back to *The Washington Post,* where she was managing editor of the Sunday magazine, and that it would be strange not to have the weekends away. She thought about Duke, the stories he must know, and how she should go back to talk to him to get some gossip for the new column Rudy Maxa was ready to launch.

Maxa's column was a good concept, a fine mixture of gossip and investigative reporting that would spread over two full pages at the front of the magazine. He had been "saving string" for it—gathering contacts and keeping in touch with old friends from his pre-*Post* days on the Hill as a summer intern—ever since he'd signed on full-time at *The Post* in the summer of 1971. When he suggested the column to the magazine's editor, Shelby Coffey, they had both thought it would be a natural.

The contacts were there and the old friends, but in Washington contacts have a way of drying up and old friends of moving away. He needed more contacts to feed him items, and more items that weren't going to bite the pressroom dust after *The Post* lawyers finished with them. They had given the column its name, "The Front Page," because it sounded like the kind of old-fashioned newspaper column hustling reporters used to write before soft news and cushy, carpeted newsrooms took over. Maxa was a hustling reporter, even a wheeler-dealer, thought Marion. In his first winter working at *The Post,* right out of journalism school at Ohio University, he had written a series of investigative stories on Glenn Turner, the pyramid huckster, that won Maxa the John Hancock Award for Excellence in Business and Financial Writing, a plum usually picked off by *Wall Street Journal* veterans. Since then Marion had never stopped reminding Maxa that, but for the luck of having an outlet for his hustling ways in reporting for *The Post,* he could have turned out to be another Glenn Turner himself. Good gamblers make the best businessmen, she'd been told. Maybe hustlers make the best reporters.

The paint factory blew up about nine o'clock. It turned night into day out the left-side windows of Metroliner 123, a great crimson hue brightening steel and rubble, track litter and junked cars. The train stopped dead. No word. No explanation. It took twenty minutes for the passengers to get restless, as if this was just one more Amtrak delay, another in a long succession of lowered expectations. Of course the train was never on time. There was always something. You didn't ask anymore. Kids threw something on the track—that was good for an hour. Another Metroliner coming too fast the other way; your train stopped to wait, maybe half an hour. You didn't ask. And no one ever told. But in the parlor car, up front as it were, during these slight delays you could tell real trouble if the "rider" sauntered through on his way to the engineer.

This night the rider raced through the parlor car, waking Duke. Elliott Gould jumped up and followed the rider through the sliding doors to the engineer. "There's a paint factory on fire," Elliott said when he returned, "and the tracks are blocked. We may never move again."

They did move again though, but this time it took five hours. Five hours of no further word and, sequestered in the exclusive front car, the four people became locked in a minuet of strange tales. What went on in the squalor of coach class with cranky, cramped passengers longing to be free, the parlor car crowd didn't know, or care. The parlor car crowd got drunk. And personal. And even happy to be there. Maybe it was because none of the four had anything to get back to really. And maybe it was because California Dreaming told such good stories.

This time Marion Clark took her bottle of wine and her cigarettes and moved into the seat next to Duke, and this time Duke introduced her to his companion. "This is my fiancée," he said, winking. " 'Lizabeth Ray."

"Pleased to meet you," she said like someone who wasn't at all. Her head jerked forward to a *Glamour* magazine she wasn't reading.

"You going back to school?" Duke asked Marion, and Marion thought, Oh boy, is he blind, or is he doing this on purpose? She had just turned thirty-one and told him so.

" 'Lizabeth," Duke said, "wouldn't you say she looks sixteen, maybe eighteen?" And Elizabeth Ray, who looked, up close, a sunny side of twenty, told everyone she was twenty-four but was really thirty-one years old also, said, "I thought she was about twenty-four, I'd say."

There was something in her mannerisms that spoke too blatantly of fear and eternal hurt. She squeaked when she talked, like a small child who hadn't learned to answer grown-ups' questions. It was more than shy, although that was part of it: It was just askew of hostile. She didn't talk to women, thought Marion. You could see the mental bristles.

Duke wanted to know where Marion worked, if she wasn't in school after all, and Marion thought for a moment of telling him she was a short-order cook at a bar. It looked as if they were stuck together for a long night of it and, God forbid, she thought, she should make an enemy by telling him she was the managing editor of the magazine whose restaurant critic had panned everything he served but the matzo balls. Somewhere she remembered a nasty letter. God forbid she should spend the night sitting alone, rereading the *Times* by the cold window, thinking about Mr. Right.

Then she thought about Rudy Maxa's column and about how it wasn't *Post* policy to use anything in print from someone unless that person knew you were a *Post* reporter. "I work for *The Washington Post*," she said.

Duke Zeibert had a lot of stories to tell then, none of them printable. They were backroom stories, wild stories, stories half believable but spellbinding nonetheless, and they passed a good hour. Liz Ray was not interested. She checked her nails, she brushed her hair, and somewhere along the way she mentioned it was Duke's birthday, and then Marion ordered two bottles of champagne.

Now Duke was talking about *The Post's* restaurant critic and the restaurant business and how the critic had done them wrong, and he was boasting about the Redskins who came to his place and the highlifers and once he said, "Liz'll tell you." And Liz Ray said, "I should write a book."

"I'm trying to help her get a writer," said Duke. "She's got a great book to write. I'm getting her together with Peter Maas and he's going to write it."

"Peter Maas?" Marion said. "That's great." But she was thinking, "Peter Maas? Unbelievable. This woman's life being written about by Peter Maas, who wrote *Serpico?* That has to be hogwash."

"What are you going to write about?" Marion asked Liz, but the shop was closed. No hints, just, "My life."

Much later—after Marion had spilled a long tale about her shattered romance, her last great hours in New York, her two weeks on Fire Island with the ex-fiancé, her fears, her sadness, her history of love—Liz Ray nodded, stopped polishing her nails and said, "If you only knew. If you only knew what I've been through. I've had everything. I've slept with congressmen. I've been out with half of Washington. When this book comes out no one is going to believe it. But it's all true! It's unbelievable but it's true."

She had been used, she said. So used it was criminal. And she had been bumped around. It was so cruel she was going to pour it all out to Peter Maas, and when the book hit the stands half of Washington was going to head for the hinterlands. The lid was going to come off Capitol Hill and land on more marriages than Las Vegas on Sunday morning.

"If Peter Maas doesn't work out," Marion said, "let me know. I've got a few writers who could do it and some publishers I know through work."

"But are they good?" Liz asked. "They have to be good. I mean I tried to write it myself, you know, because I know the story and I want to write it, but I just don't know how to put the words down, you know?"

Get her name, Marion thought. Liz something. Can't ask her now. She looks scared. "Do you work on the Hill?" Marion asked. "Oh yes," she said and then she laughed. It wasn't a pretty laugh. It wasn't even a real laugh, but it was louder than real and just as long. "I work for a congressman," she said. "If you want to call it working." She shot a look at Duke. "Duke'll tell you," she said. "I have a book, right?"

" 'Lizabeth, baby," he said, "you have a great book. And I'm gonna get Peter Maas to write it, too."

"Which congressman?" Marion asked, but it was too late, or too early. The brush came out again and much activity was lavished on hair just fussed with minutes before. "Just a congressman," she said. "I'd rather not say. You'd know who he was."

Know who he was? So what, thought Marion. What kind of woman won't even admit who her boss is? Hurt, scared Liz, the non-California girl gone amok. Strange night. Strange woman. A little gossip item for Rudy. Check her out, get her last name. Salvage something from this night that was slipping away in champagne somewhere outside of Philadelphia on a blocked track. How many people had died in the paint factory? How many people had Liz slept with besides her boss? Did they tell her top-level secrets across the pillow? Talk to Peter Maas. Tell Rudy. Take her to Sans Souci. She looked like she might go for a lunch there in exchange for a small tidbit of constructive dirt. But just a small item. This was a woman who looked street-wise, despite the little girl voice, despite the big talk, despite everything.

The engineer got bored during the next hour and brought more champagne, drinking now along with them, as Duke explained Marion's broken heart to him in jovial details, Liz laughing along. And then Duke said, "Who needs Mr. Right with that good-looking guy sitting over there?" The man who looked like Elliott Gould turned red-faced. "Come on over here," said Duke, "I want you to meet a friend of mine. This is Marion—what's your last name?"

"Clark," said Marion, "and I already know your name. It's Elliott Gould."

"That's right," he said. "Most people don't recognize me when I travel in disguise."

"Have some champagne, Elliott," said Marion, which he did, and then there were four passengers not really caring anymore what track they were on. Elliott had a real name back home, but they never found out what it was and didn't care. What they did find out was that he was a toy salesman from South Orange, New Jersey, and that he had even more trouble than Liz. His marriage was shaky to say the least, his wife didn't trust him, his nights on the road were lonely or they were filled with women whose names he never knew. He was always "in trouble" at home; he was always "in more trouble" away from home.

"Take me," said Duke, in an effort at one-upmanship. "I have two ex-wives. I pay double alimony. And I'll tell you what it's like. It's like feeding oats to two dead mares."

They hardly noticed when the train crept ahead, first jerking along one tie at a time, then speeding up to a full ten miles an hour, creeping by another stopped train so close it rattled the windowpanes. The cards came out. They played poker. Marion lost a bundle. Duke told a long, marvelous, but long since forgotten story about his night of sexual victory in Las Vegas after he'd won big at craps. "I tell you what," he said, "when you get to be my age, you don't need sex appeal anymore. You know why? Because you have all you need. You have *checksappeal.*" Everyone laughed, even Liz, and the train rolled on closer to home.

By the time they'd reached the outskirts of Baltimore, Duke had done it again. Introduced his "fiancée" with a big grin and exaggerated wink, this time to Elliott. Marion was getting the picture, and this time she also got the last name. Ray. R-A-Y. Remember that, she thought. You can forget everything. But remember Liz Ray, the woman who works for a congressman she's too scared to talk about.

By the end of the summer of 1974, unless you lived on a desert island, you didn't want to hear any more about government corruption. You had gone without the summer tan, holed up with a TV watching Sam Ervin and the guys become more and more theatrical as new felons joined the elite ranks. Then you had read the tapes, sometimes acting them out with friends for Saturday night special treats. Finally, late summer, Nixon had resigned. The gridiron fete was over, but the outrage lingered on, a straggling guest too tired to go home. In the newspaper biz, boredom settled like fine mist and, in Washington, what had filled the pages of *The Post* in the form of investigative reporting took a subtle turn. Exposés were out. Gossip was in. The woman on the train, Liz Ray, was a gossip item, thought Marion. She never dreamed there was yet more corruption to come, even from this nobody, this inarticulate, shy woman of the parlor car. But the reason she never dreamed there could be more corruption was because it had been a long summer of political shame, and in September, 1974, you just didn't want to think anymore about deceit, a public duped, or, for that matter anything bad about Congress, the all-American housecleaners, our last hope that democracy still worked.

In Baltimore it was raining so hard it looked like the Metroliner was going through a car wash, and the toy salesman got up to leave. "Where are you going?" Marion asked.

"This is my stop," he said, but they had grown close in confinement, like characters in a high-speed movie, and Marion found herself telling him he couldn't leave. It was out of the question. He had to come with her to Washington.

"If I were sure it would be worth my while to come to Washington with you, I would," he said.

But he was near the door now and the train P.A. system was signaling takcoff.

"Life is full of risks," Marion said.

He stepped down backwards to the bottom step, checked out the platform and took a leap, almost losing his balance. The train was moving now and as Elliott Gould righted himself he gave a wave to Marion.

"Not good enough!" he shouted.

And then he was gone.

Outside Union Station, the riders of Metroliner 123 tried to shoehorn themselves into five late-night taxis at the stand. In the confusion Duke screamed across the street to Marion, "Come eat at my restaurant. I'll buy you lunch. Thanks for a great train ride."

Marion screamed back, "I will. This week. I promise. And bring Liz too." But they didn't hear her.

The next morning when Clark told Maxa about Liz Ray, Maxa put long odds on the tip. Washington, he thought to himself, was filled with women who claim to have slept with politicians. But still, Maxa thought, Clark had a shrewd sense of people.

Ray sounded interesting but she didn't sound like a news story or even a potential item for Maxa's column. Even if she'd been romanced by four Presidents, it wouldn't be the kind of story *The Post* would write. Maybe the *National Enquirer*. But, then again, it never hurt to know someone with entrée to the private lives of public men.

Maxa called Maas, and Maas's voice turned cold when Maxa asked if he and Ray were working on writing a book.

"Who told you that?" Maas barked. Maxa said he'd just heard it around town, just a rumor he wanted to check out.

"What are you doing prying into my personal life?" Maas asked angrily.

Now Maxa was interested. Most authors are only too happy to have their books, or prospective books, mentioned in print. Maas was not only angry, he was threatening.

"Does Ben Bradlee know you're asking me about this?" he asked. No, Maxa said, he generally didn't clear his routine calls with the executive editor of *The Post*. When Maas said he intended to tell Bradlee about the call, Maxa stopped being polite. What the hell is wrong with you? Maxa asked him. He just wanted to know whether Maas was writing a book, hardly an unusual question. Maas, a bit calmer now, said he had met Elizabeth Ray in Washington. Duke Zeibert had introduced them and she seemed like a nice enough girl and they had had a pleasant dinner together. Oh yes, he said, they had discussed some book but he wasn't interested in writing it. They had just had a nice evening, that was all.

Apparently what Ray had thought was a preliminary meeting that would lead to a book had been merely a date to Maas. But he did tell Maxa one fact he and Clark hadn't known: Ray worked for Representative Wayne Hays, an Ohio Democrat.

Maxa had attended college in Ohio and knew of Hays's reputation as the gruff, powerful head of the House Administration Committee, a once-obscure housekeeping post. But Hays had realized the potential power those housekeeping functions gave a chairman when he assumed the job in 1971. He quickly became a tyrant in the House, controlling the payroll, travel, office space and fringe benefits of all 435 House members.

Hays, everyone on Capitol Hill knew, also had a penchant for young, attractive women, and he had staffed his office accordingly.

"She works for Wayne Hays," Maxa said to Clark. "That figures. He's the congressman I was telling you I wanted to write about for the column. He's the guy who has all the stunning-looking women on his staff. He's from Ohio, so I've been hearing about him for a long time and I wanted to do a story on 'The Hays Girls.' If Liz Ray works for him, she must be dynamite."

"Let's take her to lunch at Sans Souci," Clark said. "I'll call her up. Maybe she could be a good source."

"Great," said Maxa.

So they set up a lunch at Sans Souci, in fact a lot of lunches at Sans Souci, but Liz Ray never showed once and Shelby Coffey got tired of signing expense accounts for Maxa and Clark to dine alone in style at Washington's chicest restaurant when he was gobbling burgers at Rothchild's carryout. So the weekly, then monthly, Sans Souci dates stopped, and Liz Ray faded out to California that February, "another vestal virgin," as Procol Harum sang in "Whiter Shade of Pale," "heading for the coast."

But Maxa was right. She must be dynamite. And she was, as they would find out one chilly April afternoon in 1976, almost two years later, when she called Clark to tell all from a phone booth. Yes, she was, in more ways than one.

TWO

IT PAYS TO BE A CONGRESSMAN

OFFICIAL WASHINGTON is a city of political shakers and movers, petty men and great men, most of whom spent years somewhere else in America tending to their political careers, cultivating financial backers and convincing their public they could handle the major league that Washington represents. It is a city to which many come but which few leave. "It's awfully hard to go home again after living here," admitted one who did not go home, Philip Buchen, former counsel to President Ford. "This is a very supercharged atmosphere. When you go back after having a taste of this life and of the challenges—new and different ones every day—it's hard to be content." When his boss failed to win reelection, Buchen looked for private employment in Washington, unwilling to return to the life-style of his hometown, Grand Rapids.

They complain, these transplanted Americans, about the oppressive summer weather in Washington ("It's not the heat," everyone says, "it's the humidity."). They say Washington is too transient, that everyone is from somewhere else, that there are more limousines than children. Dinner invitations are extended on the fickle basis of power; some seasons Republicans are the toast of the town; other times no important Georgetown dinner party is complete without a well-placed Democrat. It depends on who controls Congress, who occupies the White House; and some ask, is that any way to run a social life? And the traffic—all those damn circles, streets that begin and end in one block, broad avenues that at the stroke of four-thirty in the afternoon suddenly become one-way, rush-hour highways filled with commuters hell-bent on beating everyone else to the suburbs of Maryland and Virginia.

Washington is a town of gossip, of unnamed sources and background briefings, a town where inside information is routine luncheon chatter, where no one likes to read a major story in a newspaper without having already heard the *real* story the evening before. In some respects Washington is an established city: There are old-line families whose names span generations of Washingtonians, and there are resident political deans with last names like Alsop and Harriman. In other ways Washington is a frontier town ripe for the taking. A particularly fast gun can shoot up the place and appoint himself sheriff, the way Jimmy Carter managed to do it. An obscure congressman can bide his years in the House and then make a bold play for power. If he is successful, as Wayne Hays was when he took over the chairmanship of the House Administration Committee, he gets noticed and, however grudgingly, respected. For it is not entirely heritage, manners or wealth that determines one's social status in Washington. It is sheer power. If someone with power makes one misstep, he learns the game is played for keeps, that it takes little time for Washington's long knives to carve him up and return him to the place whence he came. The successes and failures seem greater in Washington because so many people are watching; approximately five hundred news organizations employ some seven thousand persons in the nation's capital, although even a well-publicized disgrace does not always pry a Washingtonian from the muddy banks of the Potomac. Former Senate scandal figure Bobby Baker, for example, returned to his Washington home after his stay in jail, and plotted his comeback with a book and possibly a movie about his years spent wheeling and dealing on Capitol Hill.

The hub of power is the White House. The President, by

design or chance, sets the tone of the town. From the style of party-giving to the style of clothes worn by bureaucrats, official Washington reflects the personality of the President. Men's clothiers noted a rush to buy narrower, less flashy ties when Richard Nixon replaced Lyndon Johnson. Booksellers note that their sales improve when a Democrat occupies the White House. The spokes in the Washington wheel are the different arbiters of power: the President's Cabinet, the Supreme Court, the diplomatic corps, the press and the Congress. None acts without consideration for all the others; no segment wields so much clout that it can dominate government.

Sometimes a Washingtonian caught up in the rush for power wonders if it isn't all an illusion, whether the city's machinations would be viewed as absurd and meaningless if one day everyone stopped paying attention. It is not a frequent thought and certainly not one on which many Washingtonians prefer to dwell.

A congressman's life, depending on how much energy he wishes to devote to his work, can be a good one—and not just because, as Robert Dole said of the vice-presidency, "it's indoor work with no heavy lifting." Over the years Congress has granted itself a spate of fringe benefits—some visible, some well-hidden—that have persuaded more than one solon to keep making the sacrifice of serving the public year after year.

To begin with, the salary for a representative or senator isn't bad: $44,625 a year, a figure set in 1975 in a bill that included a clause permitting Congress to share in an annual catch-up-with-industry pay raise that had been granted federal workers. Such a clause promised to spare future congressmen the generally unpopular task of voting themselves a pay raise each term. Congress was aware it was playing with fire; the vote in the House was 214 yeas and 213 nays, and members carefully voted to exempt themselves from the automatic increase for one particular year, 1976, which also happened to be an election year.

Not everyone was delighted with the fatter paychecks. A South Dakota freshman, Republican Larry Pressler, asked the Supreme Court to void the automatic increases. And Representative Charles E. Grassley (R-Iowa) was one of a dozen representatives and six senators who returned their 1975 pay raise to the federal treasury.

"I can, in all honesty, state that the current salary of $44,600 a year is more than adequate to maintain myself and my family—which includes four children and my wife living on a farm in Iowa," Grassley reported to a commission considering salary increases for top government officials in late 1976.* "It is obviously very difficult to determine the productive capacity of an elected official. Whereas one can fairly determine the productive capacity of an individual in private industry by measuring the output of a finished product attributable to him or her, this is not the case with elected officials.

"For instance," added Grassley, whose sarcasm did not win him any friends in Congress, "if one were to measure the amount of printed material generated each year by Congress and its individual members, one might determine that congressmen and senators are grossly underpaid. But if one were to judge their work on the basis of how effective Congress has been in dealing with the nation's major problems, it is clear that our elective representatives in Washington would merit a substantial cut in pay."

One man's healthy salary is another man's poverty wage. Consider part of the financial portfolio of one member of Congress, a twenty-two-year veteran Democrat from Detroit, Charles Diggs, Jr., founder and past chairman of the Congressional Black Caucus. Diggs, a mortician by training, is best known on Capitol Hill for his frequent travels to Africa

* In February, 1977, Congress accepted the commission's suggestion that members of the House and Senate be granted a thirteen-thousand-dollar pay raise. Some members branded their colleagues "coward" as Congress carefully avoided a vote on the raise, which the House leadership promised would be followed later in the year by a strict new code of ethics. The raise set a congressman's annual salary in early 1977 at $57,500.

and his leadership of the House District of Columbia committee that finally granted Washington home rule in the early 1970s.* Despite his two decades of living on a congressional salary combined with the income of his wife, a foreign service officer, Diggs needed money several years ago. He quietly borrowed eight thousand dollars from a Salt Lake City lending firm, Sheraton Gold Crest Service, around Christmas of 1972. By Christmas of 1976 Diggs had paid back only half of the loan, though the total amount was past due. Efforts to collect the balance by a law firm retained by the loan company were met with obfuscation and delaying techniques that "only a congressman could get away with," according to a source close to the case. Diggs simply refused to respond to requests for payment.

In June, 1975, collection efforts began in earnest when a suit was filed against him. Five efforts by U.S. Marshals to serve a subpoena to Diggs were unsuccessful. Finally, in September, Diggs's legislative secretary worked out an agreement that would have permitted Diggs to pay back the remaining portion of the loan in lieu of a messy, public lawsuit. Only one check, the first in what was supposed to have been a series of two years' worth of monthly payments, was received by the lender.

In February, 1976, the suit against Diggs was filed again, and this time a Washington attorney active in Democratic politics called the lender's law firm to plead Diggs's case. The lawyer said he was working gratis for Diggs to help him straighten out his tangled financial situation, a plight he said Diggs would not be in if he wasn't an "honest" politician. By late 1976 the lender was still hoping Diggs would make good without need for a lawsuit, a courtesy one person involved in pursuing repayment said was extended only because Diggs is a congressman.

* Among Washington residents "home rule" has been a bitter subject for decades, ever since Congress in its wisdom decided the District of Columbia was better governed by senators and representatives instead of locally-elected residents. Not until the 1972 election were D.C. residents permitted (thanks partly to the efforts of Diggs) to vote for President.

Another veteran Democrat, Thomas Rees of California, served in Congress for twelve years and finally decided he couldn't afford it anymore. His solution: not to run for re-election in 1976.

"I get forty-four thousand, six hundred dollars a year," Rees said, "and I live in a fifty-thousand-dollar house, drive a Ford. But I find we tend to have unusual expenses. An Easter trip and summer trip to California—there's three thousand dollars' worth of airfare right there. [Rees's figure includes fare for his wife and two children.] Then I pick up constituents' checks at restaurants all the time. I haven't saved any money and with two boys in private school, there's no way I can afford to stay another term."

So Rees returned to his old field of international finance with no apologies for the new, higher congressional salaries: "If I was worth forty-two thousand dollars eight years ago, well, if I'm not worth more than that by 1976, then I shouldn't be here."

But a congressman's lot cannot be measured by salary alone. A vast array of fringe benefits boost congressional salaries by an average of 35 percent, according to a budget watcher on Capitol Hill who prefers to remain unidentified, a curious request that demonstrates congressional sensitivity toward perquisites. While a sharp-eyed accountant or executive in private industry might expect to be rewarded for his diligence in cutting expenses, a congressman who turns a spotlight on waste and padding in Congress can expect to earn only the enmity of his colleagues.

The costs of some of the comforts of Congress are minuscule. To shuttle a congressman from the basement of his House or Senate office building to the basement of the Capitol costs about eighteen cents in electricity. When congressmen leave Washington, however, the price of caring for and feeding them grows more substantial: According to State Department records, it cost $1.7 million in 1975 to send legislators around the globe. Consider the following scenario which illustrates the bill a congressman can run up should he decide to avail himself, in one marathon day, of some of the benefits to which he is entitled.

Congressman Foghorn wakes in the morning in his northwest Washington home. Because he keeps a residence in his congressional district as well as in Washington, the congressman is permitted a three-thousand-dollar tax deduction each year (assuming his tax bracket is about 45 percent) for his living expenses in Washington. In one of the few acts of the day which will not cost the taxpayers money, the congressman eats breakfast at home. If he is one of the eight members of the House or Senate leadership, his limousine and driver will take him to Capitol Hill. Even if his rank does not warrant a limousine, a parking place awaits him at the Capitol, no small luxury in a car-clogged town where commercial parking rates can run as high as five dollars per day.

Our composite congressman decides to begin the day with a haircut at the barbershop in the Capitol basement, an exclusive shopping mall that houses all sorts of services for the nation's legislators. On the way to the barbershop the congressman stops by the frame shop to have a favorite print mounted and framed. And he checks in with the photographer's office to make sure a cameraman will be on hand later in the day when he meets with a constituent. There will, of course, be no charge for the framing or photography services.

The haircut is a bargain, a paltry two dollars, which these days wouldn't buy anyone a trim at a barbers' college. (On the Senate side of Capitol Hill, senators' haircuts were free until 1977.) On his way back to his office, the congressman buys a dictionary for his high school-aged son at the House Stationery Store. While the rest of America pays $12.95 for *The American Heritage Dictionary,* members and staffers of Congress pay $8.57, thanks to a subsidy from the taxpayers. The congressman charges his purchase to his office supply account; he receives seventy-five hundred dollars a year in the form of a stationery allowance, a sum he could withdraw in cash until the rules changed in late 1976.

(Some congressmen withdrew the money at the start of each year and deposited it in an interest-bearing account; others let the allowance accumulate and withdrew the unused portion when they needed some cash or when they left the Congress. In 1975, seventy-seven of the ninety-two departing congressmen withdrew a total of $193,300 in cash from the stationery fund. The biggest share went to a congressman normally known for his tightfisted attitude toward federal spending, Iowa Republican H. R. Gross, who pocketed $23,611 in unused stationery funds.)

As he enters his office, Congressman Foghorn's staff is busy preparing a mailing to his home district. The congressman reassures himself that postage for his newsletter will be an insignificant part of the estimated forty-seven million dollars Congress would pay in 1976 for the privilege of free mail. (The budget gets the biggest jolt when a senator from a populous state decides to mount a mass mailing; when he was senator from California, John Tunney mailed a letter to more than one million households in January of 1976, putting $143,000 on the congressional postage meter all by himself.)

On the way to his private office the congressman may admire the attractive plants sent to him by the Botanical Gardens—each congressman is entitled to one plant a month, most of which end up in the apartments of Hill staffers.

After glancing at the morning mail the congressman rides the private "members only" elevator to the subway that will take him to the bowels of the Capitol. There, down a subterranean hallway that looks as if it leads to the engine room of an ocean liner, the congressman enters the House Recording Studio, where his press secretary is waiting, set to record a message from the congressman that will be sent to his home district for free use by area radio and television stations. The small fee charged the congressman will pay the cost of the recording tape used but not the salaries of the professionals who work in the studio, which explains why in fiscal year 1975 the taxpayers picked up the studio's operating deficit of $316,000.

If important business is being conducted on the House floor (and Congressman Foghorn need not bother looking in himself—his aides will keep him informed), the congressman may choose to play some paddle ball and take a steam bath in the House gym, where the congressman pays annual membership dues of fifteen dollars. Then it's to lunch. Assuming Congressman Foghorn makes an effort to avoid having lobbyists buy him meals and drinks in fancy Washington restaurants, he probably goes to the House member's dining room, where a chef's salad costs $1.90, a twelve-ounce steak costs $6.75. Senate and House restaurants have traditionally been subsidized in varying degrees with public funds. Should he dine with a constituent, the congressman generously picks up the check, perhaps charging it to his reelection committee.

Back at his office the congressman's staff is working to make sure their boss will have no difficulty catching a flight to New York that evening—he must be on time for his airplane to Brussels, where he will join a congressional delegation conferring with the top brass of the North Atlantic Treaty Organization. The congressman's personal secretary dialed for reservations using a special, unlisted VIP telephone number to alert the airlines that a congressman will be aboard one of their flights; the secretary was assured all courtesies would be extended to her boss.

A young staffer will drive the congressman and his wife to National Airport, where convenient parking will be no problem. Hard by the main terminal of that congested airport is a VIP parking lot Congress has ordered the Federal Aviation Administration to maintain; to make sure the hoi polloi do not infringe on any of the seventy free VIP parking spaces, a private police service stands guard at an annual cost to the taxpayers of $48,541. The average Washingtonian pays $1 an hour to park further away from the air terminal. There are five free parking places for severely handicapped persons.

Before he goes abroad Congressman Foghorn stops by the medical office the U.S. Navy staffs in the Capitol and picks up some free medication for his airsickness. By the time the congressman returns to his office an aide has fetched the congressman's wife and luggage from his home; after he has dropped the boss and his wife off at the airport, this same staffer will take the congressman's car to be washed, will pick up some of his dry cleaning and return both to the congressman's house. Then for a few days the congressman will be in someone else's care—the escort officer assigned to accompany the congressional delegation abroad. Working with the American embassy in whatever foreign capitals the congressmen choose to visit, the escort officer will make sure plenty of cash and liquor is on hand for each traveler. In some cases, if a congressman is a rascal, he will demand (and probably be provided with) a prostitute. Until late 1976, when a congressman returned to Washington he was permitted to breeze through customs. A military truck may still deliver his luggage and duty-free souvenirs to his home and a staffer will probably be at the airport to offer his services as a chauffeur.

Nothing in the foregoing scenario is an exaggeration; congressmen avail themselves of those services regularly, although some members observe more of a spartan existence than others. How many ways can a member of the House or Senate enhance his salary? Let us count the ways:

Double Dipping. Thirty-eight members of the 94th Congress fattened their bank accounts by accepting their monthly military retirement pension or Veterans Administration compensation payment in addition to their regular government salary, a practice known in the federal government as "double dipping." Former Speaker of the House Carl Albert did it. So did Senators Barry Goldwater, Strom Thurmond, John Sparkman, Hiram Fong, Robert Dole and Howard Cannon. And even more members of the House.

A Government Apartment. Over a dozen House members live in apartments in a House-owned building where they pay $120 a month for apartments that would rent for at least $400 monthly elsewhere in Washington. On the first floor of the House annex is the National Capitol Democratic Club; upstairs the one-bedroom, furnished apartments, with maid service, security service, and switchboard, are occupied by such House veterans as Dan Flood (D-Pennsylvania). Until his downfall Wayne Hays also lived there.

Free Vacations. Gerald Ford admitted that when he was House Minority Leader he accepted free golfing weekends from a U.S. Steel Corporation executive. For House Minority Leader John J. Rhodes the weekends were provided by the Aluminum Company of America and, on another occasion, Firestone Tire and Rubber Company.

Honoraria. Before Congress set a twenty-thousand-dollar-per-year limit on honoraria, the lecture circuit sometimes paid a congressman more than he earned in his full-time job. In 1970, for example, Senator Birch Bayh (D-Indiana) earned $44,331 in lecture fees. (His salary was then $42,500.) Other top money-makers included Senator Mark Hatfield (D-Oregon), who made $41,955 and Senator Edmund Muskie (D-Maine) who earned $35,626. Most of the cash is from special interest groups, some of whom will pay a congressman $1,000 for an address to a luncheon group in downtown Washington. Not all congressmen pocket the cash. During Christmas recess in 1974 and 1975 the late Representative Jerry Litton (D-Missouri) treated his staff to vacations in the Virgin Islands and in Vail, Colorado, with his honoraria.

Nepotism. Hiring a relative may not put money directly into a congressman's pocket, but it sure helps out the family finances. In 1967 Congress outlawed the hiring of relatives (though those already on the payroll were permitted to stay). The dodge: Trade off with another congressman—you hire one of his relatives, he hires one of yours. The relatives of at least fifteen congressmen have joined the congressional payroll in that manner since the law was passed. Sometimes you just have to be a friend of a relative; sharing Elizabeth Ray's bare office in the House's Longworth Building was the man who lived with Wayne Hays's niece.

No one ever accused Congress of rewarding itself only on a grand scale. Little things count too, like the hideaways in the Capitol where some senior legislators keep private bars. The leadership of the Senate and House parcel the rooms out carefully. Ostensibly the private rooms (with no identifying nameplates on the door) are to allow a solon to relax without having to return to his office. Hill gossip has it that the relaxing is not always done alone.

Should the lawmaker wish to catch some summer sun the doors in the rear of the House Speaker's lobby open to a private, wide balcony where some members of the House strip for a snooze and sun during lunch. An August, 1974, memo posted nearby warns the balcony is off limits to members of the press. Also in the Capitol is a prayer room whose value, one Hill staffer said dryly, "cannot be measured in dollars."

Then there is the *Congressional Record,* the official minutes of the House and Senate, printed overnight at the Government Printing Office. In addition to the transcript of the previous day's proceedings on the floor of Congress, the *Record* is a handy place for legislators to gain some political mileage by inserting small essays and speeches in the section of the *Record* called "extension of remarks." That section is generally devoted to paying tribute to such obscure events as the Woman of the Year contest in Queens, New York, and the Greater Pee Dee Fair in Florence, South Carolina. At a cost of nearly three hundred dollars a page, the *Record* has grown fat with insertions by congressmen who later reprint their flattering comments and send them to grateful constituents. Nothing in the "extension of remarks" section is actually said on the floor of Congress; the remarks are simply given to the printer to be set in type, though the writing style is as fetching as that of a chicken-circuit speech. In February, 1975, for example, Representative Martha Keys (D-Kansas) began an insertion with the sentence, "I speak because I cannot remain silent on this."

Members of Congress find it difficult to remain silent on a number of matters. During a randomly selected week in September, 1976, Representative Charles Carney (D-Ohio) reprinted the dinner program and the names of the debutantes at a testimonial banquet for Mary Grabowski, commissioner of District Nine of the Polish National Alliance in Youngstown, Ohio. Representative Larry McDonald (D-Georgia) offered the taxpayers Parts 21 and 22 of his opus titled "Trotskyism and Terrorism: Socialist Workers Party Fronts." Representative Robert McEwen (R-New York) described his pleasure at meeting the woman Marine who captured the national women's title during a rifle match at Camp Perry, Ohio; she had earned a combined score of 1,935 out of a possible 2,000 points. Representative Gladys Noon Spellman (D-Maryland), who said she has "on more than one occasion, been deeply moved by the performances of the First Baptist Church of Riverdale [Maryland] Choir," saluted the church on its golden anniversary. Representative Matthew McHugh (D-New York) wished the 243rd Field Artillery Battalion "a happy 31 years of memories" on the occasion of their annual reunion in Binghamton, New York. Representative Ed Jones (D-Tennessee) paid tribute to a ninety-one-year-old woman in his district and admitted he didn't know the secret to her longevity except that "I am told that she has drunk one or two Dr. Pepper soft drinks every day since they came on the market." Representative Lester Wolff (D-New York) printed for the edification of his colleagues and country, the entire text of his latest newsletter to his district in Queens and Nassau counties in New York. And Representative Tennyson Guyer (R-Ohio) reprinted a poem written to honor a fellow congressman, Pennsylvania Democrat Thomas "Doc" Morgan. The poem began this way:

In this earthly transient stream,
Few men consummate their dream.

Congress, more than all the rest,
Seldom paints one at his best.

Solons come—some ill-begotten,
Soon are gone, and soon forgotten.

But with us—a rare exception,
Our Doc's a man of true affection.

Generally a congressman's staff clips out the *Congressional Record* insert and has it reproduced with the impressive nameplate of the *Congressional Record* at the top of the page. Copies are then printed and sent to voters in the district who might be thrilled to see their name in the official journal of the proceedings of the House and Senate. At the bottom of the copy a line normally reads "Not printed at government expense." That's only half the story.

Even when they are talking about serious business, members of Congress can fill up a page of the *Congressional Record* quickly with inconsequential words. During a debate on tax reform on August 4, 1976, the Senate engaged in this colloquy as recorded in the next day's *Record:*

MR. ROBERT C. BYRD: I thank the Chair and I thank all Senators, Mr. President, I renew the order for a quorum.

MR. KENNEDY: Regular order, Mr. President. There is obviously a quorum present.

MR. LONG: I suggest the absence of a quorum.

MR. KENNEDY: I ask for regular order, Mr. President.

THE PRESIDING OFFICER: Does the Senator make a point of order?

MR. KENNEDY: Yes, make the point of order. There is obviously a quorum present.

MR. LONG: Mr. President, I suggest the absence of a quorum.

MR. KENNEDY: Regular order, Mr. President.

Mr. Long: I suggest the absence of a quorum, Mr. President.

The Presiding Officer: The quorum call is now in order because business has intervened since the rollcall which showed a quorum was present. So the clerk will call the roll.

(The second assistant legislative clerk proceeded to call the roll.)

Mr. Gravel: Mr. President, may I explain something to the Senate? We had a vote this evening and there were 70 Senators voting, 30 Senators absent. All the Members here, including myself, have played the absentee game before. Obviously—

The Presiding Officer: The time has expired for debate.

Mr. Gravel: I ask unanimous consent to make a one-minute statement.

Mr. Taft: Regular order, Mr. President.

The Presiding Officer: Regular order is called for. The question is on agreeing to the amendment of the Senator from Colorado.

Mr. Tower: Mr. President, I suggest the absence of a quorum.

That exchange in the arcane language of parliamentary procedure continued on as the clock ticked off the dollars and minutes. Obscure extras congressmen enjoy, such as *Congressional Record* insertions, make for titillating reading. But other perks aren't as entertaining. Until recently, for example, congressmen were reimbursed fifteen cents a mile when they drove to their home districts while other government employees received thirteen cents a mile. And Congress sets taxicab fares in the District of Columbia, a cozy arrangement that has given Washington the lowest cab fares in the country. Instead of using meters, D.C. cabs must charge according to a congressionally mandated zone system. Within one inexpensive zone are all the major government buildings, which allows Hill staffers to travel all the way across town to, say, the State Department for $1.10, about a quarter of what a similar trip would cost in New York City. To a Washington hacker, there is nothing worse an embarking passenger can say than "Capitol Hill, please."

But the portion of the congressional budget most important to congressmen is the less entertaining department of jobs, for jobs and staff mean power. A member's payroll allowance is based on the number of constituents he serves. For a senator the top allowance is $751,980; a House member can receive about $250,000 per year. How a member divides his payroll is his choice. Some opt for medium salaries for most staffers, thus allowing for the hiring of more workers. Other congressmen may pay their two or three top aides high salaries and pay their routine office help poorly. As a member accumulates seniority he acquires more hiring power with each subcommittee or committee assignment he garners. Senator Birch Bayh, (D-Indiana), for example, heads a Judiciary subcommittee on constitutional amendments and one on juvenile delinquency, which means he oversees about seventy employees and a $1.4 million budget.

In 1975 the Americans for Democratic Action compiled the cost of the special advantages an incumbent congressman enjoys over a challenger. The total, nearly $500,000 per member, was divided this way:

$333,725 for salaries and office space
$120,791 for communications and travel
$33,989 in miscellaneous benefits

In five years, between 1971 and 1976, Congress has doubled its budget and increased its personnel by 70 percent. The Senate has two office buildings and is constructing a third, while the House is contemplating erecting a fourth office building. For the first time, Congress will spend nearly one billion dollars to function in fiscal year 1977. To be fair, that figure includes such giant appendages as the Library of Congress, the General Accounting Office and the Government Printing Office. But even those departments are open to routine congressional abuse. The Government Printing Office, like it or not, must print the frequently self-serving "extension of remarks" section in the *Congressional Record* every day Congress is in session. And while most Americans think of the Library of Congress simply as a national storehouse for books, Congress thinks of it as its private preserve of researchers. Indeed, a major function of the library is the $20.3-million Congressional Research Service (CRS) whose job it is to respond to inquiries from Hill staffers. Some of the inquiries would be more amusing if the taxpayer wasn't being billed for the time spent answering them:

—One congressional office asked the CRS to determine how the Battle of Gettysburg would have ended had it been fought with nuclear weapons.

—A retiring representative from Michigan requested a detailed report on Irish Catholic voting patterns in the 1890s. "I had the feeling I was contributing toward someone's Ph.D.," said the angry researcher who had to compile the report.

—Before she became notorious, Elizabeth Ray called the CRS to ask a staffer to search for a review of a movie *(Scorpio)* in which she had played a walk-on part.

Among CRS staffers there are legends. There was the congressional office that called to ask how much an ounce of marijuana weighed. The most frequently asked question— and no one seems to know why—is: "What is the name of the 'His Master's Voice' dog that used to be part of the RCA logotype?" And every staffer at the CRS knows the story of the researcher assigned to assist a House probe of pornography in the 1960s. His job: to see how easy it was to obtain pornography and "marital aids." For months he performed his work diligently, much to the amusement of fellow employees. He learned it wasn't too difficult to receive pornography but it was hard to hold onto it; after he gave his booty to the committee chairman no one ever saw the collection again.

For the record, Hill staffers plead that the outlandish requests CRS employees must sometimes answer originate in letters from constituents who view their congressman as the fount of all knowledge. That's why, they say, they sometimes must call to ask how best to remove chocolate stains from corduroy or where the best trout fishing is in the Washington area. CRS employees suspect many of the requests, which sometimes take days to research, are personal. Whatever their origin, the abuse of the Congressional Research Service is as expensive as it is legendary.

"Join Congress and see the world" isn't a Capitol Hill recruiting slogan, but it might as well be. Congress has been labeled the world's most exclusive travel club for good reason: Members of the House and Senate travel abroad in a style to which only emperors were once accustomed. Just across the Potomac River the 89th Military Airlift Wing waits for orders to fly the elite of government wherever they choose to go. The 89th, as it is called in official Washington, maintains the President's planes, including *Air Force One,* and a fleet of medium- as well as long-range jets that can be ordered up by House and Senate committee chairmen for junkets at any time. There is no limit to where congressmen can go, how much they can spend or how long they can stay, save for the guidelines a committee chairman may issue for each individual junket. In the winter, favorite spots for congressional study include Acapulco, South America and warm climes in the Pacific. There is no requirement that a congressman actually produce anything concrete on a junket, though it is considered good form to write a report after returning from an overseas trip.

In 1975, 62 of the 535 members of Congress ordered junket flights, with two well-known Senate figures heading the list: John Stennis (D-Mississippi), chairman of the Senate Armed Services Committee, who ordered twenty-two flights that year, which cost the Air Force about $53,000; and Barry Goldwater (R-Arizona), who was close behind in number of flights—

twenty-one—but far ahead in cost, $102,000. Three hundred congressmen traveled abroad in 1975 at government expense.

Early in 1976 Goldwater sent a "Dear Bill" letter to Senator William Proxmire (D-Wisconsin) telling him what he thought of Proxmire's criticism of the cost of some flights congressional members were taking with the 89th.

"These flights," Goldwater wrote, in reference to his own considerable travel schedule, "were made to speak at meetings of Air Force officers or enlisted men and, at the same time, to investigate problems on bases involving personnel, equipment, etc. You and your cohorts in the Senate and the House who are making, and have been making, such a determined assault on the man in uniform are as responsible for the morale in our troops as any one source. And it's my purpose in traveling to these bases to do what I can do to bring that morale up.

"Now the question, should I give this effort up? If your answer is no, then I'd like you to tell me how in the devil I'm going to visit some of these bases, going out and back the same night to areas that are not, in some cases, near an airline terminal and which would require automotive or other means of transportation. I'd really like an answer from you on this because you have no idea of the problem that you, [Representative Les] Aspin and others are causing our military."

Goldwater invited Proxmire to discuss the matter with him —"please don't send a staff member, I'd like to discuss these things with you man-to-man"—and concluded, "I would suggest that some kind of Golden Fleece Award that you might dream up be given those members of Congress who constantly vote for more staff members, or for more pay for staff members, who continue to put up with the uncalled-for travels all over this world by members of Congress, their families and staffs. That's where your money is going, not in flying a handful of airplanes."

Goldwater was correct in fingering the overseas flights as the biggest drain on the federal travel budget. When he was House Majority Leader in 1976, Representative Thomas "Tip" O'Neill (D-Massachusetts) sponsored an Easter junket that ranked as one of the grandest tours of Europe and the Middle East ever. Just the cost of flying the Air Force jet overseas and back was $50,076, while comforts on the ground cost over $20,000. Aboard were over a dozen members of Congress, most of whom brought their wives and some staffers. Aboard as State Department escort officer was Tip O'Neill's daughter.

Congressmen begin their junket by filing an itinerary with the State Department, whose job it becomes to escort and assist the congressional delegation, or "codel" in diplomatic parlance. The appropriate committee chairman authorizes the trip (or the Hill leadership may authorize it), which allows the State Department to provide each member of Congress seventy-five dollars per day in living expenses while abroad. The embassy also picks up the tab for travel within the foreign country. Embassies are alerted by cable that a congressional delegation is due to visit, and hotel, car rental and other arrangements are made in advance. An ex-CIA agent attached to the American embassy in Frankfurt, Germany, recalled his duties in advance of a visit by congressmen.

"I had to stock up their hotel rooms with booze, a case of everything from the [military] Class Six store," he said. "It was standard operating procedure. Unless they wired ahead requesting special brands—and some did—I just bought regular brands. Then I had to keep the bar stocked during their stay. When I began I was told that when I visited their rooms I 'didn't see anything.' Sure I saw German girls in their rooms—that could be taken care of. When they would leave I would make sure their gifts were sent after them in diplomatic pouches, which meant there was no custom inspection, no duty to pay."

A retired State Department employee who used to be in charge of escorting congressional delegations on tours of Vietnam said, "I always gave a delegation an option: Are you here on a junket or do you want to know what's going on here? When I did the same kind of work in Vienna a representative came up to me and said, 'Get me a woman.' I said, 'I'm not a pimp.' But the majority of congressmen were decent and did have definite interests. You would get a percentage whose only interest was to eat well, drink well and sleep well with a broad.

"I remember one representative from California," said the ex-State Department employee, "who had an Army lieutenant colonel as an escort. We got the telegram authorizing counterpart funds [money in the local currency kept by the embassy]. I withdrew what I thought was enough to cover room and board for the one day he was staying in Saigon, a hundred and fifty dollars. I met him at the airport, took him to his hotel, got a receipt for the cash and said here's my phone number, call me if you need anything. The next morning, Sunday, he called to say he needed more money, said he was broke and needed two hundred dollars. Well, I called the manager of the Hotel Caravelle and asked, in French, if the congressman had paid his bill. No, said the manager, he hadn't. So I asked what in the hell he did. 'That man is a mongrel,' said the hotel manager, who was a friend of mine. 'He went to the rooftop bar the night before and drunkenly ordered drinks for everyone on his bill.' "

Actually it was the taxpayer's bill. The State Department employee, not wanting to be party to embarrassing his country any further, convinced the embassy's disbursement officer to open an embassy safe and withdraw another two hundred dollars. The staffer found the congressman drinking Bloody Marys while he waited for his money at a swank sidewalk cafe.

In 1976 *The Washington Post* made a request under the Freedom of Information Act to examine State Department travel and expense records pertaining to congressional delegations. Congress does not have to report its junkets in detail and when Congress passed the Freedom of Information Act, ostensibly to open government to the people, it carefully exempted itself from the Act. Four *Post* national desk reporters culled the various receipts that detailed congressional high living abroad and found, among other things, the following:

—Tip O'Neill's Easter, 1976, spree included a fifteenhundred-dollar reception and a slightly more expensive ceremonial dinner at the newly opened Cairo Sheraton. Stopover points included Israel, Greece and Spain. As *The Post* story grandly recounted, "They gazed upon the Pyramids, communed with the Sphinx, visited the Egyptian Middle Kingdom capital of Thebes and the tomb of King Tutankhamen. They dined and drank on the barge, *Omar Khayyam.*"

—On a 1975 trip to Switzerland, Representative Robert Leggett (D-California) hired a car and driver for four days at a cost of six hundred dollars. Leggett acknowledged that one of those days he and his wife took a two-hundred-fifty-mile sightseeing excursion that cost the taxpayers three hundred dollars.

—Representative Daniel Flood (D-Pennsylvania) and his wife flew first class to London with a military escort in 1975, spent four days each in London, Paris and Rome, and two days in Germany. His car rental bill alone totaled nine hundred dollars. And he returned to the United States via deluxe accommodations aboard the *Queen Elizabeth II.*

—Over the 1975 Christmas holiday Representative James Scheuer (D-New York) visited his daughter, who was studying medieval Latin paleography at the University of London, and submitted a Rolls Royce limousine rental bill of eleven hundred dollars to the London embassy. Scheuer told *The Washington Post* he had paid his own airfare and drawn no per diem and that between family get-togethers he had visited health officials and facilities in the London area.

—The Speaker of the House is not required to report in detail his expenditures or the expenditures of members of his travel group. In the summer of 1975 then-Speaker Carl Albert led a planeload of congressmen, staff and families to

Copenhagen, Russia, Yugoslavia and Barcelona. The only expenditure on record at the State Department is nineteen thousand dollars for one week in Yugoslavia, including nearly five thousand dollars for tour buses, guides and other amenities in Dubrovnik, the Miami Beach of Yugoslavia.

The list of congressional freebies is almost endlesss: free delivery of ice to a member's office upon demand; private dining rooms in the Capitol; two thousand wall calendars, five hundred copies of *Our Flag*, one thousand copies of *Our American Government*, and other federal pamphlets congressmen send to constituents each year with warm cover letters. There are free wall maps, scenic photographs from the National Park Service and reproductions of paintings hanging in the National Gallery of Art, a free wooden trunk for each year of service in Congress. Just about the only fringe benefit that pays its own way is the House beauty parlor. The restaurants don't break even, and there's no profit from the stationery store with its fine selection of discount gifts such as attaché cases and Capitol Hill glasses, plates and plaques. But the House beauty parlor, in its humble way, earns for the government a tidy six thousand dollars every year.

If it is difficult to learn of the existence and value of benefits congressmen grant themselves, it is doubly difficult to measure the benefits he receives from people seeking his favor. One freshman congressman boasted there were so many lunches and dinners to which a member of Congress is invited that he saved money by never eating at home or paying for a meal. The popular notion in Washington holds that any congressman who can be bought by a special interest group with a lunch can be bought by the opposition that evening with a dinner, a generalization which should offer scant comfort to the public.

In 1930 H. L. Mencken wrote of legislators, "If the right pressure could be applied to them they would cheerfully be in favor of polygamy, astrology or cannibalism." It was one of the hopes of the shapers of the campaign reform laws that followed Watergate that public disclosure of campaign contributions would at least let the public know who was paying how much to influence which legislators.

As this book is being written, however, two *Washington Post* investigative reporters, Scott Armstrong and Maxine Cheshire, have begun detailing cash gifts to congressmen from friends of the South Korean government. One mechanism used for hiding the money is the use of an "office account," a fund that is exempt from any public disclosure requirements. Armstrong and Cheshire learned, for example, that House Majority Whip John McFall (D-California) received at least four thousand dollars from South Korean businessman Tongsun Park, a wealthy party-giving bachelor who carved a niche for himself in Washington's social life with his charm and cash. McFall at first denied he had received any money from Park, then—after he was safely reelected in early November of 1976—admitted having received three thousand dollars in hundred-dollar bills from Park. Three weeks later he acknowledged receiving another thousand dollars. All the funds, delivered to his office in envelopes, were deposited in an office account, McFall said, for use as interest-free loans to his staff and himself. At least fifty other past and present congressmen were suspected by federal investigators of receiving part of the loot Park was said to have handed out (between five hundred thousand and one million dollars each year since 1970) in an effort to ensure the friendship of American legislators toward the South Korean dictatorship of President Park Chung Hee.

McFall said he had assumed Park's gifts were not legal, although the federal law that prohibits foreign nationals from making political donations had not yet been passed. So McFall put the money in his office account along with several thousand dollars collected from eight Washington lobbyists from the airline industry, the California wine industry and other interests. It is impossible to tell, of course, if money removed from the office account and used for political purposes is the *same* money donated by an interest group or foreign national. Use in campaigns of money from the former must be reported; accepting campaign funds from the latter is illegal.

At the bottom line of Capitol Hill's fringe benefits and funny-money games is a danger greater than the frivolous use of public funds. It is the danger of pride and power. In the early 1970s former presidential press secretary George Reedy wrote that the American Presidency was becoming imperial in its nature, its trappings giving it the air of a European monarchy. The White House and its occupants were becoming distant from the people of the United States. A fawning staff whose job it was to ensure the President suffered as little discomfort in life as possible was in danger of isolating and pampering a chief executive who might forget his power came from the people, not the heavens. The scandals of Watergate only strengthened Reedy's thesis.

Since Reedy's book, *Twilight of the Presidency,* Congress has quietly followed in the footsteps of the executive branch. One retiring congressman tells of arriving in Congress nearly ten years ago and having a staffer approach him to see if he needed his shoes polished. The congressman was appalled. He retired in 1976, partly, he said, because *he* had reached the point where he would walk into a room and begin looking around to see who would shine his shoes.

To serve in a member of Congress' office is to experience what it is like to have a corps of well-educated, well-paid people working toward a common goal: the glorification of The Man. The Man's interests are the interests of everyone in the office. After all, if The Man does not get reelected, his staff is out of work. The Man's time must not be wasted, everything must click on schedule. Little distinction is drawn between The Man's professional and personal lives. If his car breaks down, an aide will take it to the repair shop. The aide's time is much less valuable than The Man's. If the particular congressman or senator is well-known, he may often write magazine articles or books on the great issues of the day; most are ghosted by staffers, though it is The Man's name that appears as a by-line. In 1970 Rudy Maxa worked for several months as a college intern in the office of Senator Charles Mathias, a liberal Republican from Maryland. Mathias, a decent, gentle, unassuming man, was nonetheless heir to the flattery and pampering that surrounds most of his colleagues. Regardless of how much Americans may cling to the notion that their leaders serve at the pleasure of the people and are part of the people, congressional staffs usually work hard to convince those same legislators that they are somehow apart from the electorate. Reedy's observations would apply well to the legislative branch in the late 1970s. The kind of arrogance that once permitted former Representative Bella Abzug (D-New York) to summon a staffer to her home at midnight because her toilet had become clogged is in danger of having greater repercussions.

One man who should know about such things, former Nixon aide John Ehrlichman, said "Washington is pretty unreal. I share some of the responsibility for it. I took all my meals in the White House mess—it's Navy subsidized. I had a limousine, a sauna. But it's got to change. It cuts you off from the real world when you don't ride a bus to work or go to a lunch counter for a sandwich."

To some in Washington it is a measure of status to be accorded convenient courtesies, and it's not always just the officeholder who receives the royal treatment. The former secretary to Representative Phillip Burton (D-California) filed a claim with the Labor Department in 1976 for disability payments and included proof that she had been chauffeur to the Congressman for years. She also claimed she drove Mrs. Burton around Washington on shopping errands and social visits.

Some of the perquisites follow a congressman when he leaves office. The Capitol physician will mail him medication free. An ex-congressman is still permitted to visit on the floor of the House. "Since I will continue to be active in the Congressional Prayer Breakfast group, in the House gym,

Member's dining room and the House floor, I will maintain contact with my good friends who affect legislation," wrote ex-Representative Roger Zion of Indiana in a letter meant to solicit clients for his job as a lobbyist. Congress is also generous at retirement and death. A congressman is vested in the Hill pension plan after five years of service. If a congressman is elected at age thirty and retires at age fifty, at age sixty he begins receiving a pension equal to 50 percent of his average pay in his last three years. In Congress' earlier years, when there was no pension plan, the widow or survivors of a member who died in office would be the recipients of a special bill that would pay them one year of the late congressman's salary. That has become a tradition even though Congress now provides generous health, pension and insurance plans to its members. (Thus when Representative Jerry Litton died in a plane crash with his wife and children in 1976, a sum equal to his year's salary went to his parents.)

British sage Adam Smith offered some advice in his classic book, *The Wealth of Nations,* that would serve Congress well in its present season of dishonor: "It is the highest impertinence and presumption, therefore, in kings and ministers, to pretend to watch over the economy of private people and to restrain their expense. They are themselves always, and without exception, the greatest spendthrifts in the society. Let them look well after their own expense, and they may safely trust private people with theirs. If their own extravagance does not ruin the state, that of their subjects never will."

CHAPTER

THREE

THE HONORABLE WAYNE L. HAYS

WAYNE LEVERE HAYS came to Congress in 1948 and spent
nearly three decades breaking the rules in a small society
where, as former House Speaker Sam Rayburn once advised,
"to get along, you've got to go along." Hays did it differently.
He blustered, scratched, wheedled, threatened and clawed his
way to congressional influence. Instead of seeking a position
on a highly visible committee such as Appropriations or
Ways and Means, Hays settled for an assignment on the
unglamorous House Administration Committee and waited
until the inevitability of the seniority system made him the
committee's chairman. Then he grabbed authority, built a
fiefdom and cowed the House.

Hays's career was proof that the road to power in Congress
need not be marked by obsequiousness; if you are shrewd
enough, Hays demonstrated, the mean tactics of a bully will
serve you well in that branch of government known for the
exaggerated flattery and courtesies that its members bestow
on each other in public. In Wayne Hays's Congress there was
always a shortage of "distinguished colleagues." Instead there
were ambitious young congressmen like Michigan Democrat
Don Riegle, whom Hays once called a "potato head," and
Don Fraser (D-Minnesota), whom Hays labeled "mushhead."
Or senior members like former House Banking and Currency Committee Chairman Wright Patman (D-Texas), to
whom Hays once said on the House floor, "You are com-

pletely senile or you do not know the truth when you see it."

Bombastic, rude, vicious—the collection of pejorative adjectives House members used to describe Wayne Hays could fill a thesaurus. He was vainglorious, preaching sermons on frugality to his colleagues. He was charming, hosting art shows in the House, sporting silk handkerchiefs, Italian loafers and a toupee. He was petty, once refusing to sign the pay voucher of a staffer who worked for Representative Fraser because he had "meddled with my subcommittee" by soliciting witnesses to testify for a bill Hays opposed. He had tiny, pale eyes and big jowls that joined his neck with just a trace of a crease. He looked like a prosperous Midwest insurance salesman but talked like a dockworker, his small straight mouth barely opening to rasp a curse or mock an opponent. Off the floor of the House, one writer observed, "He converses in a tone of voice that most resembles the static of a far radio station." On the floor he clamored and cawed, once whooping, "That was a great speech, I'd be interested in knowing who wrote it for you," after a colleague argued against his position.

There is some evidence that Hays's mocking remarks, like those of most bullies, were largely bluff. During the height of protests against America's involvement in Vietnam, a group of liberal congressmen scheduled an evening session of the House to debate the war. It was timed to coincide with the massive antiwar moratorium in the fall of 1969. Hays was due to depart that day on a European junket, but he took the floor in the morning to announce that he might postpone his journey because he understood a group of "self-appointed emissaries from Hanoi" intended to debate the war that evening. Representative Andrew Jacobs, Jr., (D-Indiana), the first speaker scheduled that night, took a seat near Hays on the floor and said, "I understand that you think my friends and I are emissaries from Hanoi. I thought I'd remind you I have a ten percent disability from the Marine Corps in Korea. And you don't."

Hays, who had been a freshman congressman along with

Jacobs' father in 1948, replied, "Your old man got into these far-out issues and that's why he didn't get reelected in 1950."

Jacobs got angry. "You better goddamn well leave my father out of this, Hays!" he said, and Hays gave a small "awww" and walked away to catch his plane to Europe.

A year later Hays and Jacobs clashed again. In the summer of 1970 Jacobs was seated at a luncheon table with Hays, then-Senator John Tunney (D-California) and eight other men. Someone asked Tunney if anyone had ever made the mistake of not recognizing his father (the prizefighter) and challenging him to a fight. Well, yes, said Tunney. Once a football player did, but when he got out of hospital several days later he recognized his error. Not to be outdone, Hays told the story of a truckdriver who once approached him angrily. Hays said he picked up his tire iron and said, "You son of a bitch, if you come any closer . . ." The trucker, Hays told his lunchmates, backed down.

Later that afternoon Jacobs was in a dour mood as he watched the House pass a Richard Nixon version of a District of Columbia crime bill Jacobs had tried to modify. He listened as Hays insulted liberal Representative Allard Lowenstein (D-New York), whose district had just been gerrymandered out of existence. "You know," Jacobs heard Hays say to Lowenstein in a low hiss, "you can always get a gang in the streets to throw bricks but you [liberals] aren't going to run this place."

Lowenstein did not respond so Hays kept up his attack. He told Lowenstein (who did not need anyone to point out the handwriting on the wall) that he wasn't going to be in the next Congress. Something snapped in Jacobs' mind. Lowenstein, everyone knew, was a political corpse and here was a smug, sarcastic Hays rubbing it in, thought Jacobs, as he turned to face Hays.

"How do you presume to accuse another member of this body of committing a civil crime?" Jacobs asked evenly, referring to Hays's mention of brick-throwing.

In a matter of moments Jacobs and Hays were standing up, engaged in a shouting match that interrupted the floor pro- ceedings and caught the attention of the visitors' gallery. Hays said Jacobs had never won an argument since he had been in the House; Jacobs said he'd never heard Hays make one. Finally Hays challenged, "Well, what are you going to do about it, Jacobs?"

"I'll tell you, you silly son of a bitch," Jacobs shouted. "I'll meet you in the gymnasium in fifteen minutes and on your way down, go by your car and pick up that tire tool and I'll spot you that!"

"Awwww," said Hays as he stalked off the floor. Shortly thereafter he apologized privately to Lowenstein, a gesture that amazed the New York Democrat. Twenty minutes later Hays approached Jacobs in the hallway and said, "You know, Jacobs, Lowenstein and I can settle our differences without you butting in."

"Do you want to settle your differences amicably with me, Hays?" Jacobs asked in the sternest voice he could manage.

Hays looked nonplussed and asked Jacobs what he meant. Jacobs repeated his question.

"Well, yeah," said Hays quietly.

Jacobs stuck out his hand and said, "Then put 'er there."

And Wayne Hays, the meanest man in the House of Representatives, shook Jacobs' hand.

On another occasion, when Iowa Democrat John Culver was a member of the House, he received some press attention when he fell asleep in a taxi taking him home after an evening out. The cabdriver could not wake Culver and finally drove to a local police precinct for help. As an officer shook him, the burly Culver woke up swinging. When Culver was finally subdued, everyone apologized, but the newspapers had fun with the story the next day. So did Wayne Hays, who went around the Hill making cracks about Culver. When Culver heard about Hays's comments, he walked into Hays's office to ask Hays if there "was anything about me that might be bothering you."

"Why, no, not at all," Hays is said to have replied, backing a bit toward a wall. "What makes you ask?"

Culver moved toward Hays and said, "I don't know, Wayne, I just thought maybe something about me displeased you. And if it did, I wanted to know and I'd do something about it."

"No, no, John, everything's fine."

"Well, that's good, Wayne. Because if there is anything about me that's bothering you, I want you to tell me so that I'll know, o.k.?"

"Sure, John, sure."

It was Hays's contrast with other members of the House, the bad boy in him, that earned him his reputation. Where others feared to tread, Hays charged ahead, attacking such popular figures as Common Cause founder John Gardner ("a common crook," Hays said) and Ralph Nader and his volunteers ("a bunch of Jew-boys led by an A-rab"). He combined his surliness with a penchant for work. He answered his constituents' letters promptly and studied the rules of the House so well that he could use a parliamentary point to stall or rush legislation he opposed. At various times in his career he had higher ambitions, coveting the position of Speaker of the House, majority leader, governor of Ohio and—once—President of the United States. In the end it was that hunger for power, that sense of invincibility which can consume the Washington mighty, that triggered his abrupt descent in the House and left him no choice but to return to the calm, green quiet of his three hundred-acre farm near his birthplace.

Hays's roots were in the coal-rich soil of southeastern Ohio's Belmont County, a poor, hilly district Hays would eventually represent in Congress for twenty-eight years. He was born May 13, 1911, the oldest of four children and the son of a proprietor of a small grocery and feed store in tiny Bannock, Ohio. Hays later said it was in the fourth grade that he had the vision of becoming a senator and, after that,

President of the United States. His dream was fueled by his uncle, John D. Hays, who was a state senator in Ohio from 1915 until 1921 and whom young Hays remembered as a man who "always looked very distinguished and people were always consulting him about things."

Hays's grandfather was a horse trader and as a boy Hays developed a fondness for horses that followed him through life. He swam in Wheeling Creek on the edge of Bannock and attended a two-room frame school where he completed eight grades in seven years. During his high school years he worked in his father's store, delivered the local newspaper and, on school vacations, caddied at the local country club. His parents were reportedly frugal, a trait Hays was fond of impressing on fellow House members during his congressional years, though his personal behavior bordered on the lavish. In high school Hays's favorite subject was history. His hobby was debate and his high school debate team won a state championship. While attending Ohio State University he worked on the campaign of an economics professor who ran for Congress. Later Hays worked for Roosevelt after he defeated Hoover in 1932. In 1933 he graduated with a bachelor's degree in political science and studied law at Duke University until lack of funds forced him to take a job teaching history in a Flushing, Ohio, high school. Four years of teaching was enough for Hays. "The way I feel is that a teacher should teach the way he wants to," Hays said in a 1956 interview. "He shouldn't have overeager parents or an overeager board of education dictating every lesson plan for him."

When he left teaching, Hays began his political career, first as a three-term mayor of Flushing, Ohio, (1939-1945), a board of education member and, in 1941, a state senator.* For two years he held all three positions until the day after Pearl

* Hays insisted he only lasted one term in the Ohio state senate because mining and labor interest groups opposed his anti-stripmining stance. Hays said an Ohio Coal Association lobbyist said, "Well, buster, you won't be in the next session," and he wasn't.

Harbor when he volunteered for the Army. Nine months later he received a medical discharge. During four years, from 1945 to 1949, as a Belmont County commissioner Hays finished building a grass-roots network of political support that paid off in 1948 when he was elected to Congress.

From the start Hays was no amiable or gracious politician. After his first reelection to the House, Hays called his defeated opponent to rub some salt in his wounds: "I thought you'd like to know that this was the first election in which I carried the county where you spoke——before it had always gone Republican." At another time Hays told writer Marshall Frady how he dealt with an opponent who tried to score campaign points by bragging about his eleven children. "It began to get tiresome," Hays told Frady for a 1973 *Playboy* article. "Finally, one night, the two of us appeared together to talk to a gathering of Polish miners, a right rough bunch of fellows, and he brought the damn thing up again. So when he was finished, I stood up and said, 'Well, you know, I got a champion bull sired fifty calves, but it's never occurred to me to run him for Congress.' Those Poles started whooping and banging on the tables—they all had about three beers in them by that time—and hollered, 'Go get 'em, Hays! Go after 'im!' Yessir, that gentleman found out a little bit what politics is all about that evening, believe me."

In 1953 Representative Carroll Reece (R-Tennessee) headed an investigation of America's tax-exempt foundations, a pursuit that did not enjoy the support of the nation's liberal community. It also did not enjoy the support of Wayne Hays, who had voted against the formation of the Reece committee but who nonetheless was appointed by Minority Leader Sam Rayburn to serve under Reece. While some may think Hays's caustic nature grew with his takeover of the House Administration Committee in 1971, his performance on the Reece committee eighteen years earlier demonstrated Hays's vintage cantankerousness.

To begin with, the Reece committee needed funds, no small matter considering the money had to come from the

House Administration Committee where Wayne Hays was then a junior member. (Not only was he a junior congressman, his party, the Democrats, was the minority party in the House.) Hays informed Reece—a senior member of the majority party—that he could thwart any funding proposal unless Reece granted him certain demands, including the firing of two persons Reece had hired to aid the investigation. Reece gave in, even though his commission's general counsel would later write that Hays was a "relatively unimportant member of the House, who has attained no eminence." The Reece committee failed to understand that Hays did not rely on eminence to get his way—he simply snorted and threatened. Reece's counsel said Reece did not want to let his budding investigation degenerate into a personality contest. Reece seemed to abide by a Chinese proverb that says, "The wise man is like water, the softest thing which yet breaks the hardest thing." Unfortunately for Reece, the Chinese never met Wayne Hays, who continually disrupted the testimony of witnesses by "heckling" them, according to one account. A sample exchange between Hays and an expert on the operation of educational foundations went like this:

HAYS: Do you believe in astrology?
WITNESS: No, sir; not I.
HAYS: Could you give me any reason why there are so many peculiar people drawn to southern California?
WITNESS: I don't live in southern California, and I wouldn't know.
HAYS: You know, it is a funny thing, but every time we get an extremist letter in my office—and it is either on the left or the right—I don't have to look at the postmark. It either comes from southern California or Houston, Texas. I just wonder if there is some reason for it.

During the same witness' testimony Hays remarked publicly, "I will tell you, if we bring any more [witnesses] down here like some we have now, I am in favor of the committee hiring a staff psychiatrist." Then he "took a walk," leaving the chairman no choice but to close the hearings that day for lack of a quorum.

The next day Hays engaged Reece in some verbal sparring, at one point telling the chairman, "You can pass all the motions you want, but I will interrupt whenever I feel like it. How do you like that? So you might as well save your breath, Jesse." At another point, as Reece banged his gavel in an attempt to rule Hays out of order, Hays said, "Go ahead and hammer. I will keep right on talking when you get through." Later Reece said he refused to be disturbed by Hays's insults, to which Hays responded, "I know. You are pretty hard to disturb. I thought they had more guts in Tennessee." During the three-hour testimony of one witness, Hays interrupted 246 times. In the end the committee's general counsel blamed the premature ending of the hearings on Hays's outbursts and his badgering of witnesses.

Hays did not mellow with the passage of time. More than a decade later, as chairman of a foreign affairs subcommittee, Hays commented on the suicide of a Foreign Service officer who had been "selected out"—the State Department's phrase for "fired"—and soon thereafter killed himself. "I'm sick and tired of being told about this man's suicide," Hays announced. "All of us had it bad during the Depression, but we didn't go out and shoot ourselves." The man's widow was seated in the hearing room.

How did Hays, an ex-schoolteacher and county politician, manage to cultivate such a wintry personality? His early political years were spent in a tough part of Ohio where his constituents were coalworkers, farmers and steelworkers. The largest city in the Eighteenth Congressional District of Ohio is Steubenville, a place Ohio writer John Baskin once described as "an entire town on the wrong side of the tracks. It was the dirtiest city in the United States in 1970. In Steubenville, grass turns blue, cattle lose their teeth and houses turn black overnight. Its red light district is said to be the biggest east of the Mississippi . . . its exports are steel and football players."

Hays had a hard audience to please and he did it with lines like the one he leveled against his opponent who hoped mention of his eleven children would win him votes. Hays received his basic training on his high school debate team and honed his scrappy political skills in the American Legion meeting halls, the union rooms and high school gyms of his nine-county congressional district. He was as plainspoken as his constituency, a street-wise politician who knew if he kept the votes of his district he could get away with any manner of rascality in Washington.

Hays also confided to writer Marshall Frady, "You probably wouldn't ever guess it—I've always hidden it real well—but I have a considerable inferiority complex. Yeah, I used to be so bashful, I'd walk over to the other side of the street just to keep from talking to some important or older person, which is one of the reasons I got into public debate in high school, to try and overcome that."

His was hardly a startling admission. Hays's reluctance to challenge anyone who called his bluff was complemented with a streak of meanness toward the little people in Congress: the elevator operators whose seats he ordered removed, the beauty parlor and barbershop employees whose tips he eliminated, the restaurant employee he berated when he brought Hays a paper napkin instead of a cloth one, the House page he fired after the page wrote a letter to a Washington newspaper critical of a congressional income tax rebate program.

Representative Edward Koch (D-New York) said, "Sure he's sadistic. After he knocks them to the floor, he kicks them."

Representative Andy Jacobs (D-Indiana) said, "One thing you can say about Wayne Hays: He never kicks a man when he's up."

Representative William Frenzel (R-Minnesota) said, "There are few guys up here who aren't gentlemen—Wayne is one of them."

John Gilligan, former governor of Ohio and a former House colleague of Hays, once compared Hays to a "football player who's the best, not because he has talent, but because he hits everything in sight—dummies, people, anything. He strikes out so often and in so many directions that you begin to think, 'My God, my children aren't even safe. . . .' "

Hays reveled in his image. "Up here," he once said, "mealy-mouthed guys finish last." He tended to sulk when he wasn't on the offensive and he used his fierce reputation to his advantage. When he ran for majority leader of the House in 1970 he asked colleagues, "What would you rather have—a happy Wayne Hays as majority leader or an unhappy Wayne Hays as chairman of the Administration committee?"*

His wit was as genuine as it was slashing. When Richard Nixon was trying to pin the label "do-nothing Congress" on the legislators, Hays walked onto the House floor carrying a wire-service report of the President's activities that day and read the complete schedule aloud: At 10 A.M. the President was to meet with an old high school friend and at 3:30 P.M. he was to leave for Key Biscayne. "Now," said a sober-faced Hays, "the President is going to have to slow down. No man can stand that pace."

Lyndon Johnson once called Hays at home at 2 A.M. When Johnson asked if he was disturbing him, Hays replied: "Why, no, Mr. President, I was just sitting here hoping you'd call."

During the 1972 presidential campaign Hays attended a party of influential Republicans and said if *he* were the Democrats' presidential candidate, he'd choose George Wallace as his vice president. You must be kidding, one Republican guest said. "Well," replied Hays, "Nixon ran with Agnew, didn't he?" The room fell silent. "If Wallace was my vice president," Hays continued, "I'd read him the Constitution where it says the duty of the vice president is

* Hays said he decided to run for the House leadership because "last summer when Hale Boggs was drinking and making a horse's ass of himself, he asked me to talk him up. I drew a blank. People didn't want him. They didn't want Udall and his bunch of clowns. I figured what the hell, it was wide open." At a gathering of the five candidates for the majority leader slot, Hays hissed, "Listen, you bastards, I'll bet any one of you a hundred bucks I don't finish last." Everyone laughed but no one took the bet; he finished fourth in the race won by Representative Hale Boggs (D-Louisiana).

to preside over the Senate and I'd tell him to get the hell over there and start presiding."

During the start of the Korean War Hays had a drink at Washington's Mayflower Hotel with the Air Force Chief of Staff, Hoyt Vandenberg, and listened as the general predicted the skirmish would last about six weeks. "General," Hays later recalled saying, "you'd give me a lot more confidence about that if you were over there in Korea leading the troops, instead of in here leaning on the edge of this bar telling me about it."

Hays was as blunt with pen in hand as he was in person. To a man in New York who wrote him concerning campaign financing, quoting a Common Cause official, Hays replied: "Mr.—— can give any set of alleged facts that he wants to. . . . I do not care to get into a spraying contest with a skunk like him."

Though he had established his reputation as curmudgeon of the House long before, 1971 was the year Hays acceded to the chairmanship of the House Administration Committee. The position had been considered so unimportant that Representative Omar Burleson (D-Texas) quit the chairmanship to take a back seat on the Ways and Means Committee in 1968. After the next chairman, Representative Sam Friedel (D-Maryland), lost the 1970 election, Hays assumed the chairmanship and went quickly to work turning the sleepy housekeeping committee into a power base. His major clout came from the Administration committee's power to fund all other House committees, except Appropriations. But little things mean a lot, and Hays made his presence felt as he began personally approving such routine congressional perquisites as parking assignments, office space, travel vouchers and the salaries of and rules governing the House barbers, hairdressers, elevator operators and other staff.

In July, 1971, the House granted Hays's committee the authority to set representatives' benefits and allowances without bringing the matter up for a floor vote, a handy decision that removed from the representatives the responsibility of voting for conspicuous benefits. Hays was set to act as the House "lightning rod," taking all public criticism for increased travel, telephone and staff allowances. The role fit Hays perfectly, and one House liberal admitted happily that most members of the House were delighted with Hays's new power and role. "He talks back to the lobbies, Common Cause and Ralph Nader, who screech every time we get a new allowance, and call our sessions 'vacations,'" the congressman said off-the-record. "It's like having your own hit man."

Hays began holding his meetings in secret more frequently than any other House committee chairmen, including those whose committees dealt with sensitive military or diplomatic matters. Reporters who approached committee staffers encountered sealed lips; Hays was the boss and any misstatement could cost an individual his job. Hays tightened up the House restaurant operations, hiring Pinkerton men to nab a cashier who was stealing nearly one hundred dollars a day. He raised menu prices and eliminated tipping for barbers and hairdressers. In 1974 he increased many allowances for his colleagues, giving them more money to rent offices in their districts, more money for stationery, telephone, travel and telegraph expenses.

Hays increased the size of his committee staff, primarily by beginning the formation of a computerized information retrieval system, a complex project that worried some representatives who wondered how much power would accrue to Hays when the system became operational. Hays tried to raise the price for copying pages of campaign contribution reports from ten cents to one dollar until a court injunction stopped him. He halted the practice of publishing in the *Congressional Record* the costs of junkets by members of Congress. Instead Hays ordered such information to be kept by the individual committees whose members traveled, which made it more difficult to examine the documents.

During his years in Congress Hays never feared he would

lose his seat to a challenger on his home turf; he handily defeated all hopefuls by wide margins. But he faced his loss of power in the House in January of 1975, when the large freshman class of 1974 began toppling entrenched committee chairmen.

The Democratic Caucus (composed of all House Democrats) met, its ranks swelled by seventy-five freshmen, and quickly toppled three veteran committee chairmen in one week. Hays looked like he was next to go. Both *The Washington Post* and *The New York Times* editorialized for his defeat.

But Hays drew strength from several sources. He was the chairman of the Democratic Congressional Campaign Committee—he would be deciding which Democrats would receive fat campaign checks from the party for their next reelection bid. And he had struck an alliance with an on-the-make liberal, Representative Phillip Burton (D-California), who had received Hays's crucial support a month earlier in his successful bid to become chairman of the Democratic Caucus. Burton and Hays couldn't have been farther apart on most major issues, but they both were fluent in the language of power. Hays had helped Burton become Caucus chairman. Now Hays desperately needed the liberal endorsement Burton could provide that could defeat the effort to replace him as head of the Administration committee. He got the endorsement, and Burton was credited with having saved Hays's seat in a 161 to 111 vote.

It was an expensive favor for Burton that would come back to haunt him in December, 1976, when he lunged for the brass ring of House Majority Leader. He lost by one vote to Representative James Wright (D-Texas), and some political observers pointed to Burton's earlier deal-making with Hays (who had by now resigned in disgrace) as the reason for his razor-thin margin of defeat.

Hays surveyed his duchy from behind a Napoleonic desk in a posh suite he had redecorated for himself in 1972. (Nice things like that were always happening for Hays; the room in which his wedding reception was held in 1976 was freshly painted just days before the affair.) Hays said he didn't keep track of the costs of the redecoration of his suite, but assured Americans they could be "proud" of the change. Antiques, chandeliers, original art, Oriental rugs and Federal-period furniture ornamented Hays's Rayburn Building offices.

Some of the accouterments—similar things also decorated his Ohio farmhouse—were purchased by Hays during his overseas junkets, the frequency of which earned him the sobriquet "Marco Polo of the House" from former Ohio Senator Stephen Young. Hays's travel was, again, a demonstration of his remarkable ability to derive the most from obscure posts. He was chairman of the House International Operations Subcommittee, which gave him authority over the section of the State Department that built and maintained U.S. embassies. Hays made sure one of his friends became head of State's Foreign Building Office in 1965. The man, Orlan C. Ralston, once managed a modest department store in Flushing, Ohio, but he and Hays soon began seeing the world at the taxpayers' expense as they inspected American buildings abroad, paying particular attention to the facilities in Hays's favorite European capital, London.

Hays was also permitted extensive travel thanks to his position for sixteen years as chairman of the U.S. North Atlantic Assembly delegation. Hays's trips on behalf of the Assembly, an unofficial organization of West European parliaments, were paid for from an annual twenty-five-thousand-dollar congressional appropriation. Hays never felt compelled to publicly itemize his expenditures though federal law required it.

His positions on the International Operations subcommittee, the House Administration Committee, the Democratic Congressional Campaign Committee and the U.S. North Atlantic Assembly delegation, gave Hays a wide range of power and privilege. When Elizabeth Ray's revelations placed him in the center of a major scandal, Hays's activities in those four areas would come under public scrutiny. But until then Hays was known to relatively few people outside Washington. He was part of the invisible power clique in the House of Representatives. His career rarely caught the eye of the general public or the press, who knew nothing of, say, Hays's International Operations subcommittee's power to dispense construction contracts.

No one much cared about the money spent to finance Hays's North Atlantic parliamentarian activities, even though reporters Walter Pincus and Don Oberdorfer wrote in *Life* magazine in 1960 that Hays had used funds from that account to finance seventy-two round trips to Flushing. That same article also reported that Hays had used House funds to fly a young woman from Denver to Washington over a weekend because, Hays said, she had unique translating talents.

Hays was undaunted. In 1963 he took two guests, a friend from Flushing and the headwaiter of the House restaurant, to the NATO conference in Paris. In 1967, when he was heading the House investigation into Adam Clayton Powell's travels, Hays interrupted the hearings to attend another NATO conference in Paris. The *Wall Street Journal* commented on Hays's behavior: "Hays took his 26-year-old secretary to Bermuda for an informal meeting with British parliamentarians; he chose the same young lady to join another Hays-headed delegation for 20 days in Europe. Then, having spent $6,589, enough to make him congressional travel champ, Mr. Hays came home to head a House subcommittee that investigated and denounced Adam Clayton Powell's female-accompanied private pleasure jaunts at taxpayer expense."

Hays's taste for attractive young women began to be a topic of gossip in Washington. He traveled to the Dominican Republic in January, 1976, to receive a divorce from his wife of thirty-eight years. (He was accompanied by his crony at the State Department, Ralston, who—as he wrote on his travel voucher—used public money to "accompany congressional delegation to inspect government-owned property in connection with the federal building program.") Hays and his first wife, Martha Judkins, had been separated since 1970; for the eight years preceding her divorce, Mrs. Hays lived in Ohio, where the Hayses' adopted daughter, Geeta, also resided. The family had not been close for years, and Hays clumsily blamed it on the demands of his job in a 1974 interview with reporter Myra MacPherson.

"When you're in Congress you really have no time to yourself," Hays told MacPherson, who was writing a book, *The Power Lovers,* about the effects of politics on families. "You have no chance to take the family on vacation. I was able to take Geeta on vacation only once, really. She was three years old. If I'm absent from here I feel uncomfortable, guilty."

Asked why he didn't take his family on some of his European junkets, Hays said, "Ohhh, that usually gets written up in the papers. My wife didn't want to get exposed to that business about taxpayers picking up the cost. They said I took the House waiter over once. I paid his way out of my own pocket. The only thing he ever got from the taxpayers was a seat on the plane."

But Hays's fondness for women was reflected in his offices, which were filled with striking females. And he seemed to enjoy his reputation around Washington as a Romeo. Writer Marshall Frady, in his 1973 *Playboy* profile of Hays, described the following scene that occurred while he was interviewing Hays in the congressman's Washington office:

He suddenly lowered his voice to a conspiratorial croak, "I want you to come with me for a second, I'm gonna show you something that'll knock your eyes out." Tilting his head into the doorway of one of his committee's rear offices, he summoned forth, with a fragile wheeze and a single languid wave of one long age-freckled hand, an extravagantly opulent young female. Dismissing her back to her desk after a short exchange of pleasantries, he then inquired, "Now, what do you think of that? Any of the other fellows around here got anything you've seen that can beat that?"

Frady wrote that the congressman sometimes introduced himself as "Wayne Hays, D.D.—Doctor of Divan." Hays said his ambition was "to be 91 years old and shot at by a jealous husband." When Frady visited Hays's district office in Flushing, Hays described his secretary—the woman he would marry three years later—as "a real sweet person, and the goddamndest *longest*-legged gal, you oughtta see her sometime, in, uh, a bathing suit."

While Hays and his first wife were married, Martha lived in a home in Flushing, whereas Hays liked to spend nights at his Belmont County farmhouse. He returned to his district most weekends, making the five-hour drive from Washington in his car. Angus cattle and Tennessee walking horses shared the acreage with a red brick Victorian home marked by, writer Frady said, "expensively-ornamented emptiness." Hays had a 4 percent interest in a local bank and had invested wisely in real estate, so wisely some local residents charged he used his influence to acquire land at bargain prices for resale to corporations at huge profits.

His land, it seemed, was Hays's pride, his roots. Representative Morris Udall (D-Arizona) recalled a trip to Hays's home district. "I saw a side of him I'd never appreciated in Washington. A very fierce sense of pride in his district and its people and a very real love of the land."

In Washington Hays was on the prowl for victims and opportunities. He was never a legislative genius; the only major bill to bear his name was the Fulbright-Hays Act which he sponsored in the House in 1961. It irked him that the measure, which encouraged international cultural exchange programs, was commonly referred to only in the context of "a *Fulbright* scholar." (His other pet peeve: He hated it when people misspelled his name, Hay*es*.) He supported the war in Vietnam but opposed aid to the dictatorship of Greece. He had a mixed voting record, though he generally voted with the Democratic majority in his later terms. He supported anti-stripmining legislation but worked to weaken public financing of campaigns and bills that called for public disclosure of campaign contributions.

In short, Wayne Hays was a shy schoolteacher from the Ohio hills, an unexceptional legislator who stayed in the House long enough to gain notoriety for his brutal wit, his grab for power, his love of luxury and, finally, his appetite for women.

His twenty-eight pleasant years in the House of Representatives came to an abrupt end when the prophecy of another House member came true.

"One of these days," said a colleague of Hays who wished to remain anonymous in 1974, "old Wayne's going to violate one amenity too many and find out he's run out of grace all of a sudden. Then they'll converge on him, and when they're done, all he'll have left of his empire is the handle stub of his gavel."

4

CHAPTER
FOUR

THE GUMSHOE CHASE

SHE CALLED from a phone booth.

It was a name from the past by then, not uttered for months, not really thought of, almost forgotten but not yet forgiven for so many no-shows at lunch the year before.

"Liz!" said Marion Clark, "I thought you were in California."

"No, I'm back," she said, "I've been back for a couple months. I just haven't called anyone because it's been so terrible and I've been so depressed and they've got me in this room with no one to talk to and it's really horrible. Horrible!"

"God! You poor thing. What happened? I mean why are you back? I thought you said you were in acting school and you loved Los Angeles and everything was great."

"No, it was awful. I had to come back. Listen, can we have lunch?"

Oh boy, thought Clark, here we go again. She couldn't face it. Not today.

"Sure, I'd love to have lunch anytime," she said. "Want to go Friday?"

"No, I meant today," Liz said. Now the vocal chords were stretching tight and the whine was starting that Clark had winced at so many times when Ray had called after missing yet another lunch with woeful tales of doctor's appointments or car breakdowns, or suitcases to pack, phones to get re-

72

connected after late bills, any number of catastrophic reasons.

"I can't today," Clark said, "I've got a lunch." She wasn't dressed for Sans Souci. And she didn't want to hang around the maitre d' again starving.

"We have to go today," Liz said.

"I'd really love to but I can't get out of this lunch. It's business. How about tomorrow?"

"Listen," Liz Ray said, "Hays just had me escorted out of his office by the cops. I'm very upset and I'm going to a psychiatrist this afternoon and I don't know if I'll still want to talk to you tomorrow."

"Hays what?"

"He had me dragged out of the Capitol by his police. I'm in a phone booth across the street right now and I'm scared."

Now she was crying, great hiccuping sobs. "I'm really scared," she got out again, "I . . . don't know . . . what to do. What should I do?"

"I'll meet you in half an hour," Clark said. "Anywhere you want."

"I don't know where to go. Not around here; somebody'll see us." And then the phone booth door opened and Clark could hear Liz stalling someone who was waiting outside, someone nasty.

"Why don't you get out of there," Clark said. "Go home. I'll meet you there; just tell me where you live." Liz was crying again now. She couldn't talk, or wasn't going to.

"Liz! It'll all be all right. Just get in a cab and get out of there. You want me to come and get you?"

"I'll meet you at Stouffers," she said. "You know the Stouffers in Crystal City?"

"No, but I'll find out. Don't worry about it. Meet you there at twelve-thirty."

"Oh God!" she said, "I shouldn't do this. You don't know Hays. If he found out . . . if someone sees us . . ."

"Just go inside and wait in the ladies' room if you want, and I'll come in and get you. I'll look around first for Hays or anyone who looks like they're hanging around."

"I have to go," she said. The phone booth door had opened again and Clark could hear traffic and voices.

"Take care. Don't worry. See you in half an hour," Clark said, and Liz hung up.

"It may be nothing," Clark told Maxa. "She may not even show. She's real nervous. She was crying. But I got the idea that she didn't just want to talk, she had a story to tell."

"Does she know I'm coming?" Maxa asked.

"No, I couldn't bring it up. She sounded like she was too scared to see me even. What I was thinking is that you can wait outside or something and I'll go in and tell her you're with me but that you don't have to come in. I'll tell her we should have you with us because you know all about the law and you're smart and you'll know what to do, you'll know how to handle this."

Maxa waited outside of Stouffers for fifteen minutes. This was no doubt a waste of time, he thought. So what if Liz Ray was sleeping with Hays? Was that anything he could print in his column? And why would he want to? That was their business.

"It's o.k.," Clark said, reeling out the building entrance. "She's a nervous wreck though." Maxa rolled his eyes. He wasn't ready for this.

The two women had already done what they would do dozens of times in the next months: gone into the ladies' room and talked to each other, looking in the mirror while Liz brushed her hair. Liz's sentences were all jumbled up and she couldn't stop them anywhere. She was hyperventilating. She said no to the Maxa idea at once, jumping, and looking at the door like she wanted to bolt. "Well, all right," she said next, "but can you hurry, go get him, I don't want to be here alone."

Maxa and Clark had hoped to get her drinking to calm her down. No luck. She ordered iced tea. She ordered eggs Benedict and didn't eat them. She was convinced the waiter was a plant. She was convinced the men four tables over

were Hays's cronies. She talked so low at times the two reporters couldn't hear her, but what they pieced together
from the flood of broken sentences was that she had been
working for Hays for about two years, now at an annual
salary of fourteen thousand dollars, for serving as his mistress.

Maxa perked up. "But you work in the office too, don't
you?" he asked. "I mean, you do secretarial stuff or something, right?"

"Are you kidding?" said Liz. "I can't even type."

Now *this*, thought Maxa, may be a story.

"You mean he pays you fourteen thousand a year and
you don't have to do anything?" Clark asked.

"Well," said Liz tossing her head back and taking a big
breath, "I perform some duties."

"After five, huh," Clarke said. She was thinking about
what that must be like and wondering if Liz was in love
with Hays or just in it for the job. She was staring into this
huge mass of Hawaiian turkey salad she couldn't face eating
and it dawned on her that Hays wasn't paying Liz. The taxpayers were. *She* herself was paying Liz Ray. But Maxa was
way ahead now. He wanted Liz to tell him dates of employment, he wanted pay records, he wanted to know if she ever
did any work. Did she answer phones? Did she file?

No, said Liz, she didn't know how. "He's got me on
something called the Oversight committee," she said. "But
I call it the Out-of-Sight committee. I don't even go down
there most days. Sometimes I do so I can see friends of mine
and cruise around the House restaurant. After Woodward
[Bob Woodward of *The Post*] was snooping around this
year, Hays asked me to start showing up, so I'd go in for a
couple of hours and, you know, I'd make my personal phone
calls and leave."

"Great job," said Clark.

It wasn't so great though, she said. Hays was mean. She
had been seeing a psychiatrist ever since she started working
there. She didn't have anyone else to confide in. The women

at work resented her and Hays tried to keep her under wraps. He took her to cheap restaurants. He acted like he was ashamed of her. He was incredibly demanding and jealous. She couldn't have a relationship with anyone else because she was "on twenty-four-hour call." Plus, Hays had a big, bad, erratic temper. Liz was paranoid. She told the reporters men had died mysteriously. She said that Hays had once said to her that troublemakers were easy to get rid of.

"Is he sadistic?" Clark asked.

"Let's just say he's kinky," Liz replied.

"Are you in love with him?"

"Are you kidding? When I first got back from California and he was being almost nice to me, I thought he was sweet and I liked him. But I've never loved him. We've never had a relationship. He treats me like a thing, not a person. I mean, if I had an asthma attack or I felt sick, he wouldn't care; he'd just want me to finish up with him."

Maxa and Clark had thought Liz Ray must have come to them because she was heartbroken, ragingly jealous, over Hays's impending marriage to someone else. They figured Liz had her eye on the Mrs. Hays title, with all the little fringes, like the expansive, rolling farm in Ohio, the trips abroad, the clothing allowance, the social whirl in Washington circles. Even if it was a meal at a fancy restaurant, nothing more, they sensed the woman who had grown up poor would go for life with Wayne L. Hays, mean or not.

"I don't care if he's marrying Pat Peak," Liz said. "He says the only thing that's going to change when he marries Pat Peak is her name. We're going to be just the same."

"Who's Pat Peak?" Clark wanted to know. So far in the *Washington Star*'s gossip column, all that had been mentioned was a rumor that Hays was planning to get married again.

"She's his secretary in his home office in Ohio," Liz said. "She's young and blond too. And now Hays has her sister working for him on two payrolls. Nobody knows that. It's unbelievable."

Maxa had gulped down an order of eggs Benedict and had filled a whole notebook by now. "What payrolls?" he wanted to know. He could check that later.

"She's on House Administration and some foreign affairs committee for a total of twenty-five thousand dollars a year," Liz told him.*

There were others on two payrolls. Liz couldn't remember all the details though, and she was bored discussing the subject. It was so common.

"I don't understand why now, all of a sudden, you called and you want to tell us all these things," said Clark.

"I've had it," Liz said. "I just can't go on anymore. You don't know how I feel. You don't know what I've gone through. And now I'm scared. Hays is mean and he's powerful.

"Today when he did that, had me taken out of his office— and those cops were his cops and they were *right there*—I got really frightened. You don't know Hays. He can do anything. I could disappear and they'd say I'd left town and who'd know. I mean . . ." And now her voice was up several octaves and she was eyeing the men at the next table and then she shot her fork into the dead cold eggs Benedict and pushed part of the eggs to the edge of the plate.

"He's a mean bastard," she said. "Excuse me, but he is. That's the only way I know how to say it."

The scene in Hays's antique-filled office that morning had been, according to Liz, as follows:

She had gone to confront him about why "when every single other person on his staff, colored secretaries and everybody," had been invited to his wedding reception, she had not been asked to attend. "That really hurt me," she said. "I'm good enough to go to bed with him and be his mistress but I'm not good enough to be invited to his wedding reception." The reception was going to be very prestigious and

* Paula Peak, Pat Peak's sister, Maxa discovered by checking the House payroll, was not working on House Administration and International Affairs committees simultaneously.

grand. Henry Kissinger and Tip O'Neill and other VIPs were going to be there. And Hays had had the House maintenance crew repainting a special room in the House to hold it in, at taxpayers' expense of course, she pointed out.

So she had walked into Hays's office, after calling him first, and demanded to know why she wasn't desired at his deluxe reception. "I was upset," she said, "but I wasn't causing a scene, and all of a sudden he shouts to Nina Wilson—she knows all about Hays and me; she's his office manager—he says to Nina, 'Get her out of here,' just like that. And then, like they were just waiting, you know, to grab me, these two cops take me by the arms."

At 2 P.M. Liz Ray became very nervous. She had to make her doctor's appointment. She had told the two reporters that her lawyer had suggested a long time ago that if she ever got really frightened Hays was going to do something nasty, she should tell someone who worked for a newspaper because it was good insurance. Now she wasn't sure what to do. She didn't know whether she wanted any part of this story to appear in print. If it was printed, she didn't want her name used. She wanted to talk to her lawyer again, and then she would call. Meanwhile, though, she feared a number of bogeymen. Hays, she said, would never call her again after this morning.

"You're wrong," said Maxa. "He'll call. He wants to keep you happy so you won't cause a scene right before his marriage. He knows you're a keg of dynamite right now, and if I know Hays, he's too smart to let you go off. My guess is he'll call you and try to smooth things over."

"What should I do?" Liz asked in a whine.

"Well," Maxa said, "if you want us to, if he calls and he wants to see you, we could watch over you to see if you're all right."

"Would you really do that?" she said. "That would be good, because sometimes he takes me for drives just off by Arlington Cemetery."

"Well," said Maxa, "we should do that anyway, since we can't print something about this just because you told us it was true. Hays could say you were lying. But if we had our own proof that he's seeing you . . ."

She agreed. Maxa also wanted proof that she did no work. That would be more difficult. It would all hang on whether anyone in her office was willing to vouch for her absence, her inability to type and a number of other things. But right now the two reporters could at least find out if Wayne Hays, the most powerful man in the House of Representatives, was spending his evenings out of sight with the blond from Oversight.

They could find out. If they were lucky.

Ben Bradlee was talking to Shelby Coffey in Coffey's magazine office when Rudy Maxa and Marion Clark returned. They gave him and Bradlee a quick rundown of the fourteen-thousand-dollar deal.

"Will she go on the record?" Bradlee wanted to know.

"She might, she's thinking about going on the record," Clark said.

Then Maxa and Clark told Bradlee they might follow her and Hays on their next date, so the reporters wouldn't just be taking her word for it. It was hard to prove someone was a mistress, much less a mistress who got paid for it with tax money.

"She said we could do it," Clark said. "She's scared he might hurt her and she wouldn't mind us being around."

"Well, let me know," Bradlee said. "You two ever trailed anybody before?"

"No, but I've read a lot about it," Maxa said.

"I've read every book Raymond Chandler ever wrote," Clark added.

"You kids be careful," Bradlee said. "Let me know."

At 5 P.M. Liz phoned. "Hays just called. He wants to see me tonight. He said he was sorry and everything and that he didn't want me around because Pat Peak was on her way in from the airport to visit him in his office. Jeeze, how was I supposed to know?"

Liz didn't know yet what time they were meeting, she said, so she'd call as soon as Hays phoned her again. He had to see what time he could get out of the office.

Maxa and Clark sat in Clark's office plotting and trying to stay calm. They had seen detective movies. They had read detective novels. Maxa had just done a story about private eyes in Washington. But this was the real thing. They decided to take two cars. If one of them was spotted, the other could take up the trail. They would take books to read in the car while they were waiting. Clark called a friend to borrow a car. Maxa called his wife. He wouldn't be home for dinner.

At six, Liz called back. Her apartment at 7 P.M. Hays would be in his black congressional car or in a "sort of red" car of indeterminate make and model. Some kind of little Chevy. No, Ford. Anyway, it would have Ohio plates. He was going to take her to dinner, probably at the Key Bridge Marriott top-floor restaurant, "that cheap Marriott again." She had to run. "He'll take me right back to my apartment," she said, "and then come up. He should be gone by nine. He watches the digital clock in my bedroom and he always leaves by nine. Wait 'til he leaves and then you can come in. I have some more things to tell you."

Maxa called Liz Ray's apartment house and asked directions. It was located in the quagmire of Pentagon access roads and Arlington freeways, where one wrong turn could put you on a one-way highway to Richmond.

They bolted out of the office, grabbed Maxa's car from the parking lot, sped to Marion Clark's house where she threw on a dress for dinner and took a three-minute instruction course from the friend who was lending her his 1973 blue Datsun station wagon. She followed Maxa through the late rush-hour traffic. They were both fast drivers. If Maxa went through an amber light, Clark went through the red. They cut off cars. They dashed across five lanes of the Richmond freeway, almost U-turning, when they discovered their exit to Army-Navy Drive on the right. They made it to number 1300 just as the colored fountain lights came on. It was getting dark and it was 7:05 P.M., April 6, 1976.

Maxa pulled off to the right and parked six slots down from the entrance. Clark headed left and found a space about fifteen cars down. Maxa could see the circular drive. Clark couldn't unless she got out of the car, but she could see anyone who pulled into the long driveway.

They waited. Clark got out her spectacles, cleaned them, lit up a cigarette, found some chewing gum and thought about how scared she was. She fantasized what it would be like when Hays spotted Maxa and she had to take over. Hays would drive down this long, lonely lane in the woods by Arlington Cemetery. She would creep, very very slowly, behind him, lights off. And then big men in dark shirts and white ties and suits with shoulder bulges in them would jump out from everywhere!

Maxa jumped in the car. "They say waiting is the hardest part," he said. "All the books I've read and all the private eyes I talked to said the same thing. Waiting's the hardest part. You think they're never going to show up. But . . . they *always* do.

"Just thought I'd tell you that," he said, and jumped out.

They waited. Clark had brought pictures of Hays she had obtained from the *Post* library. She studied them now because she'd never seen the powerful Wayne Hays. She wouldn't know him in a Chinese laundry. He had a baby face, she thought now, with little eyes, mean little eyes. She could see him, the way he must have looked, when he said, "Get her out of here." Not nice. No. And he was huge.

They waited.

Maxa wondered if they'd missed them. It was 7:25 P.M. Not many cars pulled up to 1300 Army-Navy Drive. It was very quiet. He looked around. Colored fountains stuck in the middle of a large patch of grass. First they were orange, then red, then green. Orange. Red. Green. A man was walking his dog on the grass. Across the highway concrete viaducts and access ramps twisted into the setting sun. Suddenly the whole place seemed sinister, Maxa thought.

They waited.

Liz Ray walked quickly out of the entrance and looked both ways. Maxa waved to her and she rushed over. "Hays is on his way," she said, "but I wanted to tell you something. I talked to my lawyer this afternoon and he says it's o.k. to tell you. I'm writing a book."

"On Hays?" Maxa asked.

"I gotta go. Hays might come any second. Tell you after."

Clark decided they must have left. She couldn't stand not knowing if she and Maxa were just sitting there picking their toes while by now Liz and Hays were having dessert in some restaurant. She got out of the Datsun and walked over to the lobby. The plan was that she would go into the lobby and have the desk call Liz's apartment. If Liz answered, Clark would just tell the desk clerk to tell her Marion was here and that she'd wait outside. That couldn't do much harm.

But when Clark got halfway to the lobby she spotted Liz coming from the direction of Maxa's car. They met in front of the lobby. "Hays is on his way," Liz said. "I just told Rudy and now I'll tell you. I'm really excited. I'm writing a book."

"That's great," Clark said, trying to sound like it was. But she had heard about Liz's book before, that night on the train. Everyone had a book dream. "Do you have a publisher?" Clark asked out of flattery.

"Dell," Liz said.

"Who's going to write it?" Clark asked, remembering the Maas idea and how Liz didn't think she could write it herself.

"It's written. It's at the publishers. It's finished."

My God, thought Clark, this can't be true. But she didn't have time to go slack-jawed. "Here comes Hays!" Liz said, gripping Clark's arm. "Quick, keep walking."

Liz went one way, toward the black car, so Clark walked the other, which happened to be away from her own borrowed car. The only route back where Hays wouldn't see her was around the entrance building. The minute she turned the corner she ran, but by the time she reached the Datsun, Hays was gone, Liz was gone and Maxa was no longer there.

Maxa had swung out behind Hays's car, a car Liz hadn't told them about. This one was black but had Ohio plates. Hays drove so slowly Maxa felt as if he would have to put the Volvo into neutral to stay fifty feet behind. When Hays came to the first stop sign, he waited so long at it Maxa had no choice. He had to pull up alongside of Hays. He was convinced Hays had spotted him and that the congressman realized he was being followed. He was so sure Hays knew that when Hays turned left, Maxa turned right, just to throw him off. Now he'd lost them. He headed for the Marriott, hoping Liz had been right about that.

Clark not only didn't know where anybody had gone, she didn't have the vaguest idea where she was in relation to the Key Bridge Marriott. She knew which way it was as the crow flies, but that was about the extent of it. She headed off and in no time at all was totally lost in the neon wilderness of Arlington. Streets were dead-ending, and all her hunches were too. Worse than that, her bright lights were on and she had no idea how to turn them off. She'd tried everything that came to mind, and now the window wipers were on and the hood latch undone, the panel lights off and the heat on. It was ridiculous.

Now she didn't even want to find Hays. She knew he'd seen her with Liz. Plus, any sly trailing techniques were out of the question now. Nowhere in any Raymond Chandler book did you trail people with your bright lights shining.

Maxa cruised the Marriott's front parking lot, up and down, row after row, looking for the black car with Ohio plates. He went to the back parking lot and did the same. Nothing. He went back to the front and drove more slowly, checking every car darker than yellow. Still no Ohio. Every other state in the Union—the parking lot was jammed. The cherry blossoms brought them like locusts. He drove around back again and discovered an entrance to yet another parking lot under the building. First level, there it was.

Maxa took the elevator up to the restaurant. Hays and Ray were there but Clark wasn't. He took the elevator back down. Where the hell was Clark?

By sheer luck Marion Clark had stumbled on a road she knew, and now she was finally at the Marriott. She grabbed the Datsun handbook out of the glove compartment. Good dinner reading, she thought. Read all about how to dim Datsun bright lights. She was really going to shape up now. She put on her raincoat so Hays wouldn't see her dress again, and she pinned her hair up and put on her glasses. Next time, she decided, she would bring a hat.

A waitress ushered the two reporters to one of the cherished window seats where you can dine looking out over the grand marble monuments of Washington along the Potomac River. They didn't want a window seat now, because Wayne Hays and Liz Ray were sitting a tier above and fourteen tables away. Maxa said he could see Ray's blond hair. He would keep an eye on her.

"What happened to you?" Maxa asked.

"I got lost, what else?" Clark replied. "And I can't get the dumb bright lights off in that car either. I almost killed myself trying."

"You idiot," Maxa said. "The switch is right on the turn signal."

"How am I supposed to know?" She gave the Datsun handbook a heave to the windowsill. "Did you have any trouble?"

"I lost them too," he said. "Hays is the slowest driver I've ever seen."

"Jesus Christ," Clark said. "This is like two dumb blonds chasing another dumb blond."

They ordered steak. "What're they doing now?" Clark

asked and Maxa said they were just back from the salad bar, sitting down.

Wayne Hays may well be one of the slowest drivers this side of Sun City, but he ate at high speed. It was during Maxa and Clark's second bite of steak that Maxa discovered he had been watching the wrong blond.

"They're gone!" he said.

Maxa ran into the kitchen, American Express card in hand, chasing the waiter. Clark ran for the elevator.

This time Clark got the bright lights off and only got slightly lost, but even so, by the time she wheeled into 1300 Army-Navy Drive, Maxa's Volvo was already parked. And empty.

Maxa had even beat Hays to Liz's building, and when he parked he had jumped out, nearly bumping into Hays's car. But this night Hays wasn't staying.

"You know why he told me he wasn't coming up?" Liz said to Maxa. "This pimple on my lip. He said, 'That pimple really turns me off.' "

She was angry and hurt again, and starving. "I told Hays tonight. No more cheap restaurants. He eats so fast, I almost choked to death tonight eating so fast. And when he's done, that's it. No coffee. I can't even finish my food if he's finished."

They went up to Liz's apartment together then, and for Maxa the tension was over.

For Clark it was just revving up. She assumed Hays was in the boudoir and Maxa was lurking in the hall, ear to the wall.

She knew she couldn't go through the lobby because security was strict and she couldn't be announced. So she zipped around to a side entrance and tried the door. It was open. In her notebook she had the apartment number written down: 628.

No one was in the corridor when she reached the sixth floor. She crept down the hall expecting Hays to bolt out the door. This was nasty business, she thought. At 628 she heard music coming through the door. Then she heard Maxa.

The three of them sat talking of Liz's book. Yvonne Dunleavy had written it, the same woman who'd ghost-written *The Happy Hooker,* and it was now in draft form.

The phone rang.

"That'll be Hays," Liz said. "He always calls when he gets home."

"Can we listen in?" Maxa asked. Yes, they could, on the bathroom extension. Liz raced to the bedroom, Maxa and Clark positioned themselves at the bathroom phone. "One, two, three, pick up," Maxa said, and the two reporters put their heads together sharing one receiver.

"Thought I couldn't resist those tits of yours, huh?" said Congressman Hays.

"Well, you did," Liz said.

"Damn right I did. You thought you were going to get me upstairs again and fuck me."

"In what way?"

"Physically."

"Well, you always have before."

"To tell you the truth you turn me off the way you've been acting lately."

"You mean seeing Shelly?"

"You seeing that guy again? I thought I told you I didn't like that guy."

Then Hays told her he thought he ought to "be good for at least one week" before he got married and Liz asked, "What about after?"

"If you behave yourself. We'll see."

"Well, what about my job?"

"Well, if you come in a little."

"Do I still have to screw you?"

"Well, that never mattered."

"Oh? I thought it did."

"I hired you back 'cause I felt sorry for you. You got back from California flat on your ass, just like I said you would."

"That's right."

"And I felt sorry for you."

Hays said he had to go. He was tired.

"I want you to start coming in two hours a day," he said. "If any of those reporters—that Woodward is after me and if he ever found out about you . . ."

"Well, I can't tomorrow," Liz said.

"Why can't you tomorrow? You going to that damn doctor again?"

"Yes, I'm going to the doctor."

They exchanged grumpy good-byes.

This was not a relationship between lovers. That much seemed clear. But then it wasn't a typical congressman-to-staffer relationship either. Hays had asked Liz Ray to "start coming in *two* hours a day." He had admitted a sexual relationship existed. And he had made it clear he was hiding her from the press.

Wayne Hays had said enough for one night. There would be other nights, thought Maxa and Clark. But this was good. In fact, in its peculiar way, astounding. And depressing too. It also was no longer a gossip item.

The next day when the two reporters saw Bradlee, he wanted to know all about it.

"You trailed them?" he asked. They recounted the story. Then they told him they had listened on the phone when Hays called.

"Did she know you were listening?" he asked. He seemed concerned.

"She said we could," Clark said.

"What'd he say on the phone?"

"I'm too embarrassed to tell you," Marion Clark replied.

"He started out—he opened the conversation with, 'Thought I couldn't resist those tits, huh?' " Maxa said.

"And it went downhill from there," Clark added.

They told Bradlee the rest and he said he thought they were onto something and to keep it up and to talk to Woodward. Woodward had a file a foot thick on Hays. He had been working on the congressman ever since he had finished with Watergate.

Woodward told Maxa and Clark that Hays was very smart, that he could cover up so fast you'd think you had only dreamt those things had happened. He was surrounded by loyal people who were scared of his power. Woodward said he could never get anyone to go on the record.

"Did Liz Ray say she'd go on the record?" Woodward asked.

"She's seriously thinking about it," Clark said.

"If Liz Ray goes on the record," Woodward said, "that's a breakthrough. That's a good story. Let me know what happens."

Maxa and Clark had learned enough listening to the off-hours Wayne Hays the night before to suspect Liz Ray was telling the truth. But they had to be sure.

Maxa quietly obtained her payroll records and those of Tresevant Hane, the only other member of the House Administration Oversight Subcommittee.

Ray had told the two reporters that Hays had swapped favors with Mendel Davis, a Democratic congressman from South Carolina, so that she would be put on Davis' payroll when she returned in July, 1975—as Hays said on the phone, "flat on her ass"—from the fling in California. Ray told them that Tres Hane had been Davis' administrative aide at one time and a good friend and that Hane, who had lost out in politics in South Carolina, needed a job. "Davis said he'd put me on his payroll if Hays would put Hane on his," Ray said.

The payroll records showed both Ray and Hane began work on the same day in August: Ray with Davis at twelve thousand dollars; Hane with Hays at twenty-five thousand. So far Ray's story was still checking out.

Ray had told them that a few months later, when she had begged Hays for a raise, he had transferred her to his payroll on House Administration so he could comply. He had created the Oversight subcommittee to put her in, with Tres Hane, and upped the annual ante to fourteen thousand dollars. Payroll showed the move and raise.

Ray said she had no idea what the Oversight committee was supposed to do. She didn't have the slightest notion what Tres Hane was doing since she had never met him. All she knew was that she had been put in a large, luxuriously appointed office in the Longworth building with Paul Panzarella, a young man who was living with Wayne Hays's niece Susan. "Paul comes in less than I do," she said. "He's a nice guy and I think he thought he was really going to have a job, you know. I mean he's smart; he graduated from Yale, I think. Anyway, he's bored to death and he's been looking for another job." When they were in the office together, Ray said, he had been teaching her to play backgammon.

"Hays used to blow his stack when he'd call me in the office and Paul answered the phone," Ray told the reporters. "He always called him 'that guy' and he'd say, 'Get rid of that guy, would you?' Or he'd call me and say, 'Is that guy hanging around?' One day he was really furious and he said, 'I want that guy out of there, whoever he is,' and I said, 'It's Paul Panzarella.' And Hays said, 'Never heard of 'im; who's he work for?' And I said, 'He works for *you!*' "

Maxa and Clark put Paul Panzarella's name on a growing list of people they would call when the time was right: when it would be too late for Hays to change records and shuffle people before the story hit the paper and for the characters in this payroll drama to be warned in advance.

It might prove tricky. Woodward told them a tale of Hays's ability to act in such emergencies. Woodward had once obtained the records of the House restaurant's outstanding bills, which showed what Woodward's sources had promised: that apparently Hays exchanged favors with a large number of Democratic representatives whose support he needed by letting them eat without paying in the House restaurant. The ledger showed long-standing bills, many over three years overdue.

Woodward had then confronted Hays with this information in his congressional office one afternoon, and by the next morning Hays's staff was able to produce the ledger showing almost all of the bills paid.

"He must have had them working all night," Woodward said, "I don't know how they got all the money or who paid or if Hays threw in some of his own money or what, but the whole thing was paid up to date."

Maxa called Dell publishers in New York. Yes, there was a book, due for publication in late August. They wanted to know why Maxa was interested. He said he had heard a rumor and that he didn't know what he was going to write about it, maybe nothing. The Dell people said the book was still in "very rough form, and not ready for any publicity."

Ray called in the afternoon. "He wants me out of town," she wailed. "He said Nina's going to get me a ticket to California and that I better get on that plane and get out of here for his wedding reception. I don't want to go, I told him. Why should I have to go?" She thought of cashing the ticket and hiding out so Hays would think she had gone; she thought of crashing the wedding reception; then she thought about her paycheck. She wanted to stay on the payroll as long as possible before her book publicity tour would begin in the summer.

And then, right before Hays's splendid reception with the powerhouse guest list, Liz Ray did indeed disappear. Some money had been given her for a plane ticket to California. Ray used part of it to pay her overdue rent and the rest to travel to New York for the long weekend. Hays would later call it blackmail, saying he had been forced to pay her rent in exchange for her silence.

Liz Ray would figuratively disappear off and on for the

next six weeks. One day she would answer the phone and bark, "No comment!" before slamming down the receiver; the next day she would be issuing invitations to lunch, to her apartment or to follow her and Hays; and the day after that she would insist she could only communicate through her lawyers.

By the end of April Hays and his new bride had returned from their honeymoon and Maxa and Clark wanted to see if he still intended to visit the boudoir of the other blond in his life. If that proved true, they could wind up the story, do the last-minute phone blitz and get it into print. But Ray didn't see it that way. She desperately wanted to collect one last paycheck, and to do that she had to stay on the payroll until the end of May.

She stalled. It was clear Dell was unhappy too. They wanted publicity but not this kind and not four months before Ray's book, *The Washington Fringe Benefit,* was available. "My lawyers say I can't talk to you anymore," she said late in April, so Maxa called her Washington lawyer for the first time. Monroe Mizel, an old newspaperman himself, told Maxa he didn't care if Ray talked or not, it was Dell that was keeping the lid on.

Clark called Dell and got Ray's publicist, Sarah Gallick, on the phone. The reporter explained that *The Washington Post* was not in the business of selling books and that this was a hard news story that had to be printed. She explained that if the story broke it would very possibly trigger a grand jury investigation, a House ethics investigation and very possibly start a reaction that would last in the news until *The Washington Fringe Benefit* hit the stands. She told Sarah Gallick that by verifying Liz Ray's relationship with Hays in the pages of *The Washington Post,* they would, in a sense, be easing Dell's libel lawyer's problems over using actual names in the book. Clark also pointed out that once before a Washington call girl had written a book that used no real names, and even though her publishers had spent a fortune touring her around the country and advertising the book, it had not sold. No one knew who the author was, no one cared and no one believed her story.

Liz Ray was going to lose her job anyway, Clark told Gallick, the minute Hays found out about the book. Liz Ray was also frightened that Hays might do her harm. But what could Hays do, and get away with, if a newspaper printed her story along with her fears, before he knew about the book?

Sarah Gallick saw the light. "I'll get back to you," she told Clark.

But Liz got back to her first, all sweetness and talk. The embargo had been shelved; the chase was on. Hays had visited her once since the honeymoon, she said, and now he had gone back to Ohio for a long weekend, as was his habit, from Thursday afternoon to Monday night.

For the next three weeks the two reporters trailed Hays and Ray in Maxa's Volvo. "If you hear me screaming from the bedroom," Ray said, "don't rush in. It's all part of the act."

"If you really want help call our names," Clark said. "We'll pound on the walls or scream for help ourselves."

Once, Clark thought of hiding in Ray's bedroom closet and she told Bradlee about it after one of her nights at the colored fountains. Bradlee rolled his eyes and laughed and then he gave her a sharp look and said, "Don't get smart, Clark. What're you going to do? Rush out?"

What would she do? Clark thought. Exactly. Could she stand, smothering in a closet, listening to . . . God knew what. Every time Ray was expecting Hays a satin comforter would appear in the corner of her normally antiseptically neat bedroom, bunched up and covering a pile of . . . something. They didn't know what and didn't ask.

One night when the two reporters were positioned at their normal guard posts outside Ray's apartment door, Ray popped out into the hall to say Hays had just called and said he was too tired to pay another visit. They came in and she said he had been gruff on the phone. "He really frightens me when he talks like that," she said.

And then she told them about what Hays had said to her about Fanne Foxe. "We were eating up in the Marriott," she said, "and this was right after the Fanne Fox-Wilbur Mills thing—and Hays looks out the window down to the Potomac River and he says to me, 'If any broad ever did to me what Fanne Foxe did, she'd be down there.' 'What d'you mean, down there?' I said, and Hays said, 'Down there. Six feet under.' I said, 'You couldn't do that and get away with it,' and he laughed and he said, 'Oh yes I could. It's easy.'

"Then he told me about how all you do is you put some money in an envelope and he knew men you could give it to, and if they liked the money, they took the envelope and then you gave them a slip of paper with the person's name on it, and that was it. 'You never have to even speak to them,' Hays said.

"The next day, I went to my lawyer and I had an affidavit written out right then and I wrote down the whole conversation and it's all in my safety-deposit box."

She begged two things of the reporters. One, that they wouldn't mention her book; two, that they would print Hays's "Fanne Foxe threat."

"I don't want you to quote me either," she told Maxa in a phone conversation a week before the story would appear. "Can't you just say you found out from somebody else?" No, they couldn't.

Clark visited Ray's Longworth office and took her to lunch in the hope she would permit the reporters to quote her. Next door, in a slightly larger office, Bella Abzug's staff of about twenty worked feverishly. Liz's office had no title on the door, not even a number, and inside all was quiet. Two desks, neither of them with any sign of use, were beached next to each other on a thick rug. Along one wall was a soft leather couch, shoe-polish black. Covering the wall above Ray's desk were framed photographs, inscribed to her "with love" from various men: astronaut John Swigert; Paul Anka;

Glen Campbell and lesser known show-biz types. Below sat a red IBM Selectric typewriter with a smoked Plexiglas dust shield covered with dust. (A month later a staffer on the House Administration Committee told friends he inherited Ray's red IBM Selectric typewriter. But he could not figure out why the machine did not work. It wasn't until he asked a secretary for help that he discovered the ribbon cartridge was in the machine upside down.) Paul Panzarella's desktop was totally bare; Ray's had the backgammon board and a copy of *Fear of Flying* between a dictionary and the bookends.

Clark opened Panzarella's desk drawer: empty. She and Maxa had made routine calls to this office to see if anyone ever answered the phone. No one ever did, unless Liz had prearranged that she would be there so they could contact her.

Clark and Ray went to where Ray's 1975 chocolate-colored Corvette was parked in coveted space usually reserved for congressmen and their administrative aides, in the House underground lot. The lot was another of Hays's domains where he could grant favors and take them away with one phone call.

They drove to the Watergate restaurant and over lunch Clark decided she was going to drop Bob Woodward's name because she knew how impressed Liz had been when she had seen Robert Redford playing Woodward in *All the President's Men*. Ray had spoken of it often. "Woodward says there's no story here unless you go on the record," Clark began.

"You told him about me?" she asked, excited.

"Sure," Clark said. "He thinks it's a great story."

"Wow!" Liz Ray exclaimed.

Clark explained to her in simple-worded detail the difference between a story that quoted someone and one that named anonymous sources. She said that even if they quoted Liz, she could still tell Hays anything she wanted. She could go to him and say they had come to her and they knew everything, that she had been scared and remembered what had happened in Watergate and so she decided she had to tell the truth. "Just don't tell us about it," said Clark, "because if anyone asks we'll tell the truth."

Then Clark told her that she thought Ray was going to lose her job whether or not she was quoted and that she thought Ray should start looking for a job if she needed money to tide her over before her book came out.

"Can I stay at your or Rudy's house?" she wanted to know. "I don't want Hays to find me when the story comes out. You know I'm scared."

"I don't blame you," Clark said. "We'll see what we can do."

"When are you going to write it? When's it going to come out? Oh, God! When Hays reads this! He thinks I'm such a dumb little blond he can push around. If he hadn't been so damn mean none of this would have ever happened."

"I think he's going to be very surprised," said Clark as flatly as she could.

"On the record," Clark said to Maxa. "No problem."

"Liz said Hays is going out of town to London to pick up the Magna Charta next Sunday," Maxa said. "Let's try to get it in before that."

They wanted to tail Hays and Ray one more time. On Tuesday, May 18, five days before Hays was to leave, they followed them to another dinner at the Key Bridge Marriott. This time Hays took Liz to the coffee shop on the main floor. He had already eaten at a dinner for Hubert Humphrey, so he ordered iced tea and ice cream. Ray had a BLT. The last cheap dinner, she thought. This time the two reporters were within easy hearing distance. Hays was telling Ray about his trip to London and about his talk with Humphrey. He said he was going to run for the Presidency as a favorite-son candidate from Ohio and that eventually he was going to run for governor of Ohio.

"Hays brags a lot," Ray had told Clark. "He's always talking about flying on Air Force One and about how he's such a good friend of Kissinger's and about how when he goes to Europe he has all this security protection and stuff. That's all he ever does is tell me how important and powerful he is."

Abruptly Hays paid the check and they got up to leave. Maxa and Clark had learned to ask for the check when they ordered their food, so they had already paid for their half-consumed London broils.

They were striding toward Maxa's car when, from behind, two bright headlights caught them in their glare. "Keep walking; don't go toward the car," Maxa said, slipping his arm around Clark's shoulder. "Hays is right behind us in his car. Try to act like we're out on a date."

Liz told them later that Hays had turned to her in the car and quipped, "There're two kids who're gonna get it tonight."

"Jeeze," said Liz, "I thought, if you only *knew* who was gonna get it!"

FIVE

DEADLINE FOR PAGE ONE

FRIDAY AFTERNOON, MAY 21, 1976, Maxa and Clark started writing.

"For nearly two years," the story began, "Rep. Wayne L. Hays (D-Ohio), powerful chairman of the House Administration Committee, has kept a woman on his staff who says she is paid $14,000 a year in public money to serve as his mistress.

" 'I can't type, I can't file, I can't even answer the phone,' says Elizabeth Ray, 27, . . ."

It looked bizarre coming out of the typewriter. It was going to look even more bizarre in print, especially if they ran the publicity shot Liz had had taken of herself in Hollywood with so much cleavage showing. They read over the first two paragraphs. "Just another lazy Sunday feature story," Clark said.

The story would have to be read by lawyers; it would have to have a denial from Hays, some corroboration from Ray's co-workers about her not showing up for work and, they hoped, maybe even a quote from someone who could and would vouch that she couldn't type.

Hays, who had gone to Ohio that morning, was scheduled to make a speech at a dinner in Columbus that night. The reporters would need to reach him before they left work if they hoped to have the story make Saturday's deadline for Sunday morning's edition.

Clark and Maxa jotted down their list of names to call.

They would wait until 5 p.m., when Hays's office in Washington was closed, and try to reach his staffers at home during the evening. Maxa would call Doug Frost, Hays's House Administration Committee staff director, while Clark called Paul Panzarella and Ray's old boss, the one who had introduced her to Hays in the first place, Ken Gray. Now a lobbyist, Gray had been at the time a Democratic congressman from Illinois. Maxa would call Tres Hane of the Oversight subcommittee and Representative Mendel Davis, while Clark phoned Nina Wilson, Hays's House Administration office manager. Then they would call Hays.

Maxa started tracking Hays's home number in Ohio. Flushing, Ohio, information would only give out his office number so Maxa called the office to ask Hays's home number. No dice. Maxa thought of calling an old Ohio University friend who worked on the campus newspaper to see if he knew anyone who had Hays's home number.

"He has it changed so often," said Maxa's friend, "nobody here has a good one for him. Let me call some people I know and see if I can get you anything." Maxa hadn't told him why he wanted it, just that he needed the number that afternoon.

Clark called Flushing information and asked for the listing for the best florist in town. They gave her the name and number of nearby Cadis Florist. She dialed Hays's Ohio office.

"Hello!" she said. "This is Alice White over at Cadis Florist and Congressman Hays called in an order of red roses this morning and I hung up before I checked to see and we're all out. Do you know if yellow would be all right, or is he there for me to ask?"

"Cadis's here?" asked the voice at Hays's office.

"Yes," Clark said. She was going to get caught, she thought, but it was worth a chance.

"Well," said the voice, "I'm afraid I don't know anything about it and Congressman Hays isn't here right now."

"Oh dear," Clark said. "Do you think I could catch him at home. He wanted them delivered this afternoon."

"I just called over there," said the voice, "and no one is there except the maid."

"Oh dear," Clark said, "do you want to give me his number at the farm and I'll try to reach him there later? He sounded like these flowers were pretty important."

"Hold on," the voice said.

Clark held. Was this actually going to work?

"Mrs. White?" said the voice.

"Yes."

"Did you say these flowers were ordered *by* Congressman Hays or *for* him?"

"By him."

"Well, Mrs. Hays just called and I have her on the line now and she says she doesn't know anything about any flowers."

"Oh, no!" Clark said. "I think he wanted them to be a surprise. They're for Mrs. Hays."

"All I can do is try to reach the congressman," said the voice, "but he's giving a speech and then he's going to get right in the car and drive back to the farm tonight from Columbus. I'll tell Mrs. Hays something or other."

"Oh please," Clark said, "tell her it was a mistake."

"What's your number over there?" the voice asked and Clark gave it to her, almost forgetting, and starting to give her the area code first.

So much for that ploy. The receiver was wet with the sweat from her hands. She was already a nervous wreck and the night had just started. It was going to get much worse.

By now Maxa had three Ohio University friends who were now in the fringes of state politics working on finding Hays's number.

Then Liz called frantically from a pay booth somewhere. What was happening? Was it going to run? Could she stay at one of their houses? Yes, she could stay at Clark's house

Yes, her dog too. Did she by any chance know Hays's phone number in Ohio?

"He wouldn't ever give it to me," she said, "because he was so afraid I'd call him at home." The only person she could think of who might have it would be Nina Wilson. "I've gotta go! I've gotta get out of here!" she said. "I'll call you tonight. You gonna be there? I'll call you from dinner. Oh *jeeeze*, I can't believe this is happening!"

Clark called a lawyer she knew in the State Department who had said his closest friend worked in the mayor's office in Cleveland and was buddy-buddy with Hays. He said he'd call him and ask for the number, pretending it was State Department business. He was sure this guy would have it.

Maxa phoned a very good source of his on the Hill who was also trying to help.

Clark called David Kennerly at the White House, Ford's photographer. Clark had just had dinner with him. She thought surely the White House would have Hays's home number in case of an emergency. She told Kennerly, "We need Hays's home number for a story someone is doing. Does the switchboard have it?"

"Let me check," he said. "Hold on."

When Kennerly came back he said the White House operators had the number but they would not divulge it, so if Clark wanted to call Hays, she would have to do it through the White House switchboard. "I could call him through the switchboard for you if you want," Kennerly said. "What's it about?"

"No, you don't want to do that," Clark replied. "It's not a nice story."

"Yeah," Kennerly said, "I guess we better not get involved. It's an election year after all." *

Potomac magazine's secretary, Debbie Fleming, inter-

---

* In August of 1974, when he was Gerald Ford's White House photographer, David Hume Kennerly had two rolls of black and white film developed in the White House photography lab. They were nude pictures of a woman he had met through the dentist they shared. Her name was Elizabeth Ray, and when she became the blond known around the world, Kennerly hastened to

rupted. "Liz is holding on eighty-five and she says it's urgent."

"Marion? I'm in a phone booth. I just broke into Hays's office. I mean, I didn't break in, I had the guard let me in, and I got Hays's number from Nina's address book. There are two numbers." One was Hays's Ohio office, but the other was a new one: 484-0100.

Meanwhile one of Maxa's sources had provided him with three numbers, all of them different from the one Ray had found. Two of them had been disconnected and one didn't answer. Clark tried the 484-0100 number and the phone went absolutely dead. Maxa tried a half-dozen times and the same thing happened. No connection whatsoever.

Maxa made his first call to a co-worker of Ray's, Doug Frost, the House Administration Committee staff director, who should have known the staff if anyone did. Frost said he knew Ray but he didn't see her often because her office was in the House annex. Maxa told him, no, her office was in Longworth. He wasn't sure where she worked, Frost admitted then. "I'd have to be very honest with you," he said, "I'd have to go back and look at the staff roster. I assume she still works as a receptionist and a file clerk. I assume but I'm not sure."

"We understand she can't type," Maxa said. And then Frost became flustered.

"That's a terribly unfair characterization," he said. "I mean that's terribly unfair and that's a very loaded question and I'm going to—now that I see—I'm going to try and get the congressman."

Clark was on the phone to Ken Gray at his Arlington home. "I'm calling you about Liz Ray," she said.

---

tell the press he was a bachelor and had only dated Ray once.

About six weeks after the Hays-Ray story broke, Kennerly was enjoying a dinner with a date at Washington's posh French restaurant, La Bagatelle, when a waiter handed him a note. "See me before you leave," the message read. It was signed with the initials E.R. Kennerly looked slowly around the dark restaurant, afraid that his eyes might meet Elizabeth Ray's. Instead he spotted White House aide Donald Rumsfeld across the room, dining with his wife, a mischievous smile on his face.

"Liz-a-beth Ray," Gray laughed. "That name always invokes a laugh . . . no, all kidding aside, she's a sweet girl. What can I do for you?"

"What did she do for you when she worked for you for a year?"

"She was a receptionist. She was very good at greeting people."

"Did she ever go out with, at your request, constituents of yours or private business friends of yours?"

"Not that I know of. I never knew what my employees did after they left work."

"Did she ever entertain for you on your houseboat?"

"No! She may have been on the boat one or two times when we had office parties."

"Do you know if she can type?"

"She can *now*. She did some filing for me."

"Did you introduce her to Congressman Hays?"

"I may have. It's very possible. I introduce a lot of people to other people."

"What are you doing now in private business?"

"I'd rather not say."

Maxa was on the phone with Tres Hane, having reached him at home. "Really," Hane laughed, "really, I don't work with her. I truly just don't know what she does. I just don't feel really qualified to comment on her. I guess her office is in Longworth or the Capitol. I wouldn't even speculate on whether she does work."

"Has she worked with you on the subcommittee?" Maxa asked.

"No."

"Would you know if she were doing any work related to the subcommittee?"

"Most likely, yes, I would."

Matters were looking up, thought Maxa. The only other person on the Oversight subcommittee doesn't even know Liz Ray really exists, and the House Administration Committee staff director doesn't know where she works or on what.

Clark wanted to find out whether Panzarella actually lived with Wayne Hays's niece. She called information and got the listing for Paul Panzarella. Then, when he answered, she asked "Is this Susan Hays's apartment?"

"Yes," said the man who answered, "would you like to speak to her?"

That answered that question, she thought.

"Actually," she said, "I was looking for Paul Panzarella."

"This is Paul Panzarella," he said.

"Paul, I'm sorry to bother you at home like this but I'm calling from *The Washington Post*. My name is Marion Clark and we're doing a story on Liz Ray and we understand you work in the same office with her."

"Yes I do, but what's this about?"

"It's a story about her and about good jobs on the Hill. She tells us that she doesn't have to come in much to the office."

"I'm not talking about this at home," said Panzarella. "You call me at the office on Monday and I'd be glad to talk to you."

"Monday will be too late. I just need to ask you one more question."

"I refuse to talk about it. I refuse to talk about anything. I have no comment," he said and slammed down the phone.

Chalk up one more thing Liz was right about, thought Clark. No, two more things. Panzarella did live with Hays's niece, number one. Number two, he *was* smart. Caught on right away.

It was time to move fast. The pipeline must be wide open by now. Maxa got Congressman Mendel Davis through his legislative assistant. "Liz worked for me for about a month," Davis said. "She went over to the House Administration Committee because they wanted her and she knew more people over there."

Could she type?

"She wasn't any three-hundred-words-a-minute typist, no," Davis said, "but she could address envelopes. She did a lot of filing for us. We file four copies of every letter that goes out of here. That's a lot of filing."

Sure is, thought Maxa, and a lot of paper costs too.

Clark and Maxa were surer of their story now than they had been since the beginning. Now they needed Hays.

Maxa called Nina Wilson, Hays's office manager, at home. Her niece answered the phone and Maxa was gruff. "Tell her *The Washington Post* is doing a story that involves her and we need to talk to her tonight," he told the young voice. Wilson had never forgiven *The Post* for a series of stories it had done on personnel agencies, a series Wilson thought had closed down her (now ex) husband's agency. She believed it had been malicious and had destroyed her husband. Life had never been the same since. Now she had a child to support and she was alone.

The two reporters tried the various Hays numbers again and still no answer. The one number Ray had given them still went dead like something out of the twilight zone.

Clark called the *Post* operators and asked them if they could check that number with the Steubenville, Ohio, operators. She also asked them to get Hays's number from one of the local operators by saying it was a press emergency. It was close to midnight now and Hays must be home.

The *Post* operators tried getting Hays's phone number and were told there was no listed number; in fact, there was no listing at all for Wayne Hays in or around Steubenville. No, there was no number for anything like Redgate Farm either. No, there wasn't even a number for his Ohio office. It was an unpublished number, the *Post* operators told Marion Clark, and she said, "That's ridiculous. His office is listed. We both got it this afternoon with no problem."

"You know what I think," said one of the *Post* operators, "I think Wayne Hays has the Ohio phone company in his pocket, that's what I think. I've talked to small town operators before—I was a small town operator for a long time —and operators just don't function like these girls were functioning. I know you can check numbers and they said it was impossible to check that number you gave me. They're lying or I'm Santa Claus."

At midnight, Clark called Nina Wilson. No answer.

Maxa, frustrated beyond belief by now, decided to call Paul Panzarella. He had already awakened Doug Frost twice, pumping him for more details, telling him what Tres Hane had said about Liz Ray not doing any work on the subcommittee, but basically trying to annoy him enough to get him to get Hays to call Maxa.

"I'm gonna call Panzarella back," said Maxa, "and I'm gonna say, 'Paul! We've got a banner headline across all eight columns tomorrow morning that says: PAUL PANZARELLA DOES NO WORK. Now, are you going to talk to us or not?' "

No one answered at Susan Hays's apartment. Just as well, they thought. They were getting irrational. The humor was getting black.

Clark tried Nina Wilson's number again and this time she answered. "Who is that . . . that Mr. Max?" she stuttered. "He frightened my niece to death. My niece was crying hysterically when I got home."

"Oh I'm so sorry," Clark said, "oh, that's awful. It's Rudy Maxa and he's really a nice person but he's been under a lot of pressure tonight and he's very tired and I'm sure he didn't mean to frighten anyone. It's just that we have to talk to you about a story *The Post* is going to run tomorrow."

The two women spoke for two hours. Clark explained that it was a sad story and that sometimes these things happened but that they couldn't ignore what had been brought to their attention. They had to print a story if it was true. Not to do so would be dishonest, manipulation of the press. It would even be corrupt.

"I'm afraid of newspapers," Nina Wilson said. She told Clark about her husband and about the child she was supporting and the members of her family she was taking care of too. She wailed at one point that she herself had turned into a nun since the marriage broke up. She was clean, for God's sake.

At one point, Maxa broke in on the line. "Listen, Miss Wilson," he said. "You're part of this story too and you better talk. So stop bullshitting around!"

"Marion," Wilson said, "can't you get him off the phone? We were having such a nice conversation before that rude, nasty Mr. Max interrupted us."

It was turning into a bad cop-good cop routine. But Clark didn't know if she was conning Wilson or if Wilson had been conning her. At last, after two and a half hours of what seemed more like group therapy than a business call, Clark pressed home.

"Listen," she said. "There's only one hope that we can stop this story. If we can talk to Wayne Hays before tomorrow noon and if he can defend himself in such a way that we can't print the story, then we may be able to persuade the editors not to run it."

"I don't know if I even have his new phone number," said Wilson.

"Is it four-eight-four-O-one-hundred?" asked Clark.

"I don't think so," said Wilson, "but I will try my hardest to get the congressman to call you."

It was now 2:30 A.M. Maxa and Clark were tired and upset and had a feeling of hopelessness. The story would not run Sunday after all. And then Hays would be in London, and by the time he came back he would have had Liz Ray fired and every trace of her working habits erased. More than that, Clark now believed every single thing Liz Ray had said about Hays's being mean and powerful and knowing how to take care of people quietly. He could have her and Maxa deep-sixed along with Ray.

She was frightened too, and where was Liz? During her last call at around 11 P.M. Ray had said she was spending the night with someone—"just a friend"—in a hotel somewhere.

The two reporters typed up a list of questions for Hays,

just on the wild chance that he would call them during the night. Nina Wilson had asked Clark for her home number. They threw in some questions to which they already knew the answers so they could check his veracity. One was, "Have you seen Liz Ray since your marriage to Pat Peak?" Another was, "Have you ever been out to dinner with Liz Ray?" And another was, "Have you ever been in her apartment?" In all, there were fourteen questions. The last question was the clincher. "Isn't it true, Congressman Hays, that Elizabeth Ray is employed by you as a mistress?" They decided that, however remote the possibility, if Hays actually called, he might hang up fast. Whomever he called, should have question number fourteen ready to zing to the top of the list.

"Chances are," Maxa said, "we'll make it no farther than question three."

They staggered home. Clark dropped into bed and had nightmares.

At first she thought it was part of the nightmare. The phone was ringing and she couldn't answer it. Then she was awake and the phone *was* ringing. She looked at the clock. It was six.

"This is Congressman Hays," said the familiar voice. The voice was crisp and alert, loud and waiting.

"Oh, Congressman Hays," Clark heard herself saying, "thank you so much for calling me."

What was she going to say now? Wake up, brain, she thought, where in God's name is the list?

"You're up early," she said.

"Well, you know, the pups get me up so I get up."

"I know what you mean," Clark said. "My dog gets me up too. Would you mind holding on for one second? I just want to get a light on."

She put the receiver on the bed. Don't hang up. Don't hang up. Don't hang up. Please. She ran downstairs, grabbed the list from the kitchen table and picked up the kitchen phone.

"I'm sorry all this has happened," she said. And then she

more or less read off the precede she and Maxa had written three hours earlier. "We're doing a story on an employee of yours. There are some serious charges involved. We have a list of questions and we'd like you to have a chance to comment on them."

There was silence at the other end of the line.

"What is Elizabeth Ray's job?" Clark asked.

"She does work on the subcommittee," Hays said. "I've talked candidly to her about coming into work . . ."

That led right into question number two. Clearly Hays had been briefed and was on his guard.

"How often *does* she come into work?" Clark asked.

"I don't know," said the man who had asked Liz Ray to please come in for two hours a day. "She misses a lot because of her doctor. But she seems to be getting better lately."

"Have you had dinner with her since your honeymoon with the new Mrs. Hays?" Here we go, thought Clark, get number fourteen ready to go.

"No, I haven't," he said.

The next question looked dumb now. Maybe it was the clear light of dawn. It said, "We understand she rarely comes into work and when she does it's only for a few hours." Sounded like a repeat. Clark skipped it and went to number five.

"Have you ever told her to start coming into work at least two hours a day?"

"I've told her to come in at nine and stay until five, like everyone else on the staff," he boomed. Wayne Hays was a slow boiler but the water was getting hot now.

"Our sources say she can't type or file and doesn't know how to answer the phone properly."

"That's hogwash."

"Have you ever been to her apartment?"

"One night I was, months ago. Her aunt called me up and she said she was threatening to commit suicide. So I went over there."

"You didn't go in her apartment on the nights of May fourth and May tenth this spring?"

"No."

"When did she return to your staff from Mendel Davis' staff?"

"She's still on Davis' committee as far as I know," Hays said with some hesitation.

Well, Clark thought, maybe Congressman Hays wasn't as clever as everyone thought. He should know that the payroll records would show Ray had returned to his staff.

"Did you give her a promotion a few months ago?" Clark asked.

"No."

"Then why did she get a raise?"

"I felt sorry for her," Hays said. "She was deeply in debt. She told me the credit bureau was after her, the landlord was after her. She said she was going to take typing classes and try to improve herself, so I gave her a raise."

No, Hays wasn't being very clever. Not even alert. He admitted he gave Elizabeth Ray a raise, but he had said she was on Mendel Davis' payroll. And he gave her a raise because he felt sorry for her, he said, adding that typing class motive as a slow afterthought.

"Have you ever been out to dinner with Elizabeth Ray?" Clark asked.

"No," said Hays.

Now there, thought Clark, is an innocent enough question. Lots of bosses take employees out to dinner, for any number of guiltless reasons. Yet Hays had lied.

"Have you ever said anything to her like 'If anyone ever did to me what Fanne Foxe did to Wilbur Mills, she'd be six feet under'?"

"That's all a figment of her imagination," Hays said. "Liz gets it in her head that people are trying to kill her. Everything she says is ninety-nine percent fiction."

He elaborated, telling Clark that Ray was "a very dis

turbed girl," who "was raped by her stepfather when she was twelve years old," and who was seeing a psychiatrist. Hays told Clark Ray's psychiatrist's name and said that he had talked to him about Ray. (Later Liz Ray's psychiatrist would deny ever having discussed his patient's case with Hays, and her aunt would deny ever having called Hays to tell him anything.)

"I'm not the only guy she talks about," Hays said then. "She treats lots of other guys the same way. As far as I'm concerned all she has going for her is her body. And even that isn't so great."

Hays was getting chatty now. "You know," he said, "I'm a firm believer in not saying insulting things about a fellow congressman and this is nothing I'd ever want to be quoted on, but this morning when my wife Pat heard about this thing, when I told her, the first thing she said was 'Well, you should have known better than to hire someone from Ken Gray's staff.' And I hate to say it, but my wife's right. Gray had the kind of girls working for him—well, let's just say they aren't the kind of girls I'd like to be associated with."

"I think I know what you mean," Clark said. And then she thanked him for being so patient, apologized again for bothering him and said she had to ask him one more question:

"Isn't it true, Congressman," she asked, "that Elizabeth Ray is employed by you as a mistress?"

"Hell's fire!" Hays shouted, "I'm a very happily married man."

"O.K.," Clark said, thinking that was a pretty oblique denial and wondering if Pat Peak was, at that moment, sitting by his side. "I'll talk to Bradlee about all this and tell him what you've told me about Elizabeth Ray, and I'll let you know what he says about the story."

"I don't think Ben Bradlee likes me," Hays said.

Clark remembered there had been a gossip item in *New Times* magazine that month saying that when Bob Woodward had interviewed Hays he had asked him when he was going to marry Pat Peak, and Hays had quipped, "When Bradlee makes an honest woman out of Quinn."

"You mean," she asked Hays, "because of what you said about him and Sally Quinn?"

"You know," Hays said, "I never said that. I wish I had. Someone told me that's what I should have said, and I guess that's how it got misinterpreted. I didn't even know who Miss Quinn was at the time."

"Well, it doesn't matter," Clark said. "Mr. Bradlee took it in good humor. In fact when I told him about this story he said the first thing you were going to say was 'What's the difference between what I'm doing and what Bradlee's doing?' "

Now Hays was laughing. He had been remarkably good-natured on the phone. Hanging up definitely wasn't his style. Clark thought he was a superb actor. The charm must go on, despite these incredible questions about his most personal life, despite the accusations that surely he must realize could jeopardize his career. Not to mention his new marriage. My God, thought Clark, what is Pat Peak going to do when she reads this story in the paper? The honeymoon will be over.

The reporter and the congressman hung up the phone as the Washington sun hit pale against Clark's kitchen windows. It was almost 7 A.M. She would need to retype the story completely, putting in Hays's responses and pitting them against all the other quotes they had obtained the night before. Bradlee was leaving for his country house at 9:30 A.M. and he wanted to see the story before then, with the denials from Hays.

The phone rang fifteen minutes later. It was Hays again. "I just found out Paul Panzarella is living with my niece," he said. "That shocks me to my bone marrow."

Clark kept typing. It was getting late. The phone rang at 8:30 A.M. Hays again. Had Clark talked to Bradlee? "I knew that girl was trouble with a capital T when I hired her back after she came back from California," he said.

At ten to nine the phone rang once more. This time it was

Liz Ray. She was in a phone booth and she wanted Clark to come for her. She was nervous. She could not talk without taking deep breaths between every other word. Was the story going to run? What did Hays say?

"He said, 'Hell's Fire! I'm a very happily married man,' " Clark told her.

"Ohhh Jeeeze!" said Liz.

She wanted to come over immediately. She hadn't slept all night. She was frightened and lost. She didn't even know where she was, just at some Holiday Inn downtown. Clark told her to call Maxa because she was on her way to Bradlee's house.

She finished typing and called Bradlee at 9:15 A.M. "Bring it over," he said, "right now. Get your jogging shoes on and jog down." They lived about a mile from each other.

Sally Quinn made Clark a cup of coffee while Bradlee read the story. "It's terrific," he said. He read it again. He wanted a line added at the end that said, "Hays leaves today for London on a congressional trip to bring back the Magna Charta." He also wanted the word "screw" changed to "s——." He called Chris Little, the *Post* lawyer, and asked him to read it immediately. He sent over a copy. He called the *Post* editor in charge of Sunday's page makeup and told him he had a story for the front page. He wanted three pictures. One photo Clark and Maxa had assigned to Matt Lewis, *Potomac* magazine's photographer. It showed Ray in her Longworth Building office. Another had been given to them by Liz. In it she was wearing a low-cut dress and was posing a la Marilyn Monroe on a white rug; the third was a head shot of Congressman Hays taken from *The Post* picture library.

Maxa left Ray with his wife, Kathy, and their month-old daughter, Sarah, and joined Clark at *The Post.*

Bradlee had wanted to list the names of all the men whose pictures were inscribed to Liz Ray in her office, because the photographs showed up in Matt Lewis' picture of Ray in her office. The desk editors thought the men should not be named. They also thought Ray's allegation that Hays had threatened her should be deleted. They also thought three pictures were a lot of photos for one story on the front page. They called Bradlee at his farm in Virginia. Maxa and Clark got on the phone with Bradlee and two editors. He relented on the list of names.

"What about this threat?" asked one of the editors.

"I have no problem with that," Bradlee said.

"Do you think three pictures are too many for the story?" asked another editor.

"Got any better art for tomorrow?" Bradlee asked.

"Frankly, no," the editor said.

"One more thing, fella," Bradlee said, "I want it above the fold."

Maxa and Clark left to ferry Liz Ray to her apartment so that she could pick up her clothes and her dog.

Maxa said, "Liz kept asking me this morning, do you think Marion went to Bradlee's house and Bradlee said, 'Go with it,' like he said in the movie?"

"You know what he did say," Clark told Maxa. "As I was going out the door he said, '*This* is going to cause a beeeg stink.' "

CHAPTER SIX

MISS ELIZABETH RAY

Liz Ray looked at her fingers. "I can't wear this nail polish," she moaned, and then she looked around and everything—but *everything*—was all wrong. She didn't look good. Great pools of deep purple rippled beneath her eyes. All night she'd been confused—panic-stricken really. What in Jesus' name had she done? That was just a fantasy last night, one big laugh down there in *The Washington Post* pressroom, wearing those silly earplugs and tiptoeing down greasy catwalk after greasy catwalk to find the giant press printing page one. She remembered a foolish-looking pressman, wearing one of those folded newspaper hats, scooping up a damp copy of the front page for her. He pointed at her picture and then he pointed at her. She had giggled and nodded and squealed YESSS. Lord, it was noisy down there. Marion had screamed something at her. She couldn't hear herself 'or Marion yell. She just remembered seeing these identical pictures of herself rolling a jillion miles an hour off the press. Thousands of them. It was UNREAL. It was so unreal that it must all be . . . somebody else's life.

But now it was Sunday morning, like some New Year's Day horror scene when you didn't know how you'd gotten home, or if, or with whom or why. She didn't know where she was now. Marion's house, somewhere in Washington. She always kept her doors locked on the Corvette when she had to drive through Washington. The place wasn't safe. Everyone got raped by big black men.

And then this morning, just as a sick sun struck her lying there in bed, she'd heard someone walk up to the house. Someone coming to get them. No. Just someone delivering the morning paper. She heard it WHAP against the front door. Just the Sunday *Post*. Oh God! This was really happening. This *had* happened already. The river of no return, millions of copies WHAPPING against doors. Hays . . . oh, God, no . . . Hays. Her stomach—now her heart.

Get to the phone; call her shrink; call her lawyer; call her aunt; call her mother; call Shelly, the guy she'd gone out with in New York; call Duke.

Call God.

It wasn't even 10 A.M. and already the networks were phoning. CBS wanted her on coast-to-coast television in an hour. She had to have some pink nail polish. She couldn't go on television looking like a siren in chipped red nail polish. And she needed some Vaseline Intensive Care Lotion. Plus some Valiums. She had to wash her hair. Oh no! No plug in the bathroom for her electric rollers. And she didn't have a blouse to wear under the beige linen suit she'd brought . . . just in case . . . because yesterday Sally Quinn—*the* Sally Quinn—had said to Marion, "You tell Liz Ray to wash her hair because they're going to want her on television *tomorrow*." Well, she had planned to wear the nice linen suit without a blouse because it had always looked sexy that way with some cleavage showing, but this was Sunday morning and all of a sudden she didn't want to look sexy. She wanted to look like she'd just left a shiny fifty-cent piece in the collection basket at Mass like a good Catholic girl, all squeaky clean and plenty pretty. The American Beauty Rose. Fresh. Breathtakingly fresh, and honest.

She could call Hays. She could tell him they *made* her do it. They threatened her. They knew everything. She could cry.

ABC was on the phone. NBC was in the front hall. A team of CBS cameramen was in the living room setting up lights Two UPI men were emerging from a basement rental unit in Marion Clark's house where they had stumbled by mistake. In the den, Liz Ray's new dog, Maurius, a toy poodle, was making puddles and small brown piles on what would never again be a white nine-by-twelve rug. Marion's boyfriend had been dispatched to bring back nail polish remover, "any kind of pink nail polish," Vaseline Intensive Care Lotion, Valiums (if he could talk the neighborhood pharmacist into it) and dog food. Liz had locked herself in the bathroom. They could wait. They could all wait. She wasn't going on TV from sea to shining sea not looking right. She didn't know what she was going to say on TV but, by God, she knew how she was going to look. Perfect.

Marion was knocking on the bathroom door now. It had been forty-five minutes since she'd seen Liz Ray, ghastly white with her hair yanked up in a knot, take one final, shaking plunge into the bathroom. "I brought you some English muffins and orange juice," Marion said through the locked door. "You should eat something. And don't worry about this TV thing. Everyone down there seems very nice."

Everyone down there was losing patience fast. They were grumpy, tired of being polite. They'd been called out of bed for this assignment. A lot of them had hangovers.

"You think this skirt's too long?" Liz asked, pulling open the door. She stood in front of the full-length mirror: pressed linen suit, gold necklaces and earrings and bracelets and rings, beige tinted stockings matching beige sling-back shoes, newborn blue eyes without circles and all agleam, pink-polished nails, hair that looked like Vidal Sassoon had worked all night on it, and a face that could have sold Camay to grandmothers. She looked like the kind of young American beauty a college man would give a year's allowance and his fraternity pin for.

A metamorphosis. A bathroom triumph. Most women stand in front of bathroom medicine cabinet mirrors for fifteen minutes and come away looking almost *exactly* the same. Liz Ray couldn't do a number of things well—type, cook, balance a checkbook, carry on any kind of witty conversation

—but she had mastered completely the fine art of "getting ready to go out." Freshening up, as women used to say, excusing themselves to spread on more lip gloss. It was more than habit for Liz though. It had become, slowly and more mechanically with each passing year since age thirteen, an occupation. Getting ready for men. Getting sexy, getting clean from long hours in the bubble bath, getting just right from eyebrow to toenail, until, as Little Richard used to say after so much time had gone by in front of the backstage mirror, "O.K., that's it. I can't *look* any better than this!"

Liz Ray can't really remember back far enough to what it felt like before the days of her life turned into just pre-nights, expanses of hours before anything of real account sprang to life with the street lights. First there were boys, a little older than she, keeping her out late in parked cars. You know the scene—dirt roads, steamy windows, state troopers—and she got to believing them about her body. This was in the Fifties when the same lines used in Midwest drive-ins worked down in the Marshall, North Carolina, countryside where Liz grew up. They went something like this: "What's the matter? Are you ashamed of your body? Let me feel it then. Let me touch your breasts. Oh, your breasts. Soo pretty, soo beautiful." This tactic usually worked, and in the morning there'd be some boasting going on in the boys' locker room.

There were some added complexities in Liz's youth, however, and if you wanted to be entirely simpleminded about her whole life—which you could say is basically a long string of clichés—you could argue over whether the whole secret of why Liz Ray turned out the way she has is (1) because her father, or stepfather (Liz isn't sure) tried to rape her when she was thirteen, or did rape her (depending on whom you want to believe, since Liz tells it both ways, Hays tells it one way, her aunt tells it another, her mother yet another, the newspapers down there don't know, and so forth); or (?) because Liz Ray was blessed or cursed (again depending on how you look at it) with the kind of body that was too much for any red-blooded youth to handle in the Fifties. She swept into puberty—fresh from this rape or near-rape—with suddenly enormous breasts and the rest of the *Playboy* centerfold figure to match. Another curse—or blessing—was that she had naturally blond hair, so light that with a splash of Blond Minx rinse it switched on to neon platinum with no dark roots giving even that secret away.

So, when out-of-breath young men whispered to Liz through the steam and damp wool of sweater-to-sweater backseat mashes that her breasts were . . . incredible and her body was a shrine, she checked it out for herself in the mirror the next morning and, yes, she got to thinking they were right. "Everybody I went out with from the time I was fourteen years old," she says, "kept saying the same thing to me. 'You have a beautiful body. You should be in *Playboy*.' It started making sense to me and I got to thinking, well, why not? Other girls were in *Playboy* and they didn't even have as nice bodies as I did. So why shouldn't I be in *Playboy*?" (It took her twenty years to get in and, of course, like so many of these monumental fantasies, once reached, they lose a little something. "I hate my picture," she said, and slammed shut the magazine.)

And then—you know the story——there was the reality of those deadly boring days at a small-town school in the southern heat. Those classic Tennessee Williams afternoons when the whole outside was rotting like hot compost and you couldn't move and even the air coming through your bedroom window smelled like sex. You couldn't wait. What else—name one thing else—came close to being any kind of excitement?

And then—you know the story again—some girls had strict parents, some didn't. Liz's mother, whom she heard from mainly through rumor, was "wild." Beautiful in a sultry sort of way and loose in the old-fashioned way. It was never clear, Liz says, who her father was exactly, but he was not married to her mother. He may have been the man, Liz thinks, who died in a car crash when she was in her teens.

At any rate, Liz and her mother were even on one score back when Liz was blossoming into womanhood in Chevy convertibles. The mother didn't know where the daughter was, and the daughter didn't know where the mother was.

A Dumb Blond. In the Fifties it was even fashionable. But somewhere along the way a good number of Fifties Dumb Blonds splintered off. They let their hair grow out and started trying to contribute to mixed-company conversations. It wasn't easy cranking open locked chambers, sticking your neck out as it were, talking to men as if you—of all the gall —thought you could compete in the brain department. You got dirty looks and love pats that said "Cool it, Honey," like some Barbie Doll who wasn't being cute as advertised.

There's a theory battered around by culture watchers that everyone stops picking up new fads at some point in his or her life. A fall season comes when you don't run out and buy a midiskirt, for instance. You just stick with the old knee-length A-line, and you stop learning the L.A. Hustle because from now on you don't really care. When you have occasion to dance, the Lindy, or the Frug, the Twist, the Bump, the Jerk—whatever—will do just fine. And so you see professors still wearing button-down shirts and Weejuns or suspenders and felt hats regardless of style; and forty-five-year-old rich women picking up their children from school in kilts and penny loafers. Liz just stayed with the Fifties' fad, paying no mind to the Sixties' no-makeup, free-love woman, or the Seventies' liberated, Me-Decade female. The clothes changed but the sweater girl heart lingered on.

Still the Dumb Blond Syndrome looms. "I never got out of it," she says now. "I'm so used to men thinking I'm dumb that I play along."

And like so many pretends, after years it isn't quite pretend anymore. "You know everything there is to know about Liz," said Duke Zeibert, her one-time constant escort, "great body, empty head."

Of course, the head is not empty. The head is filled with oversized ambitions, the kind F. Scott Fitzgerald wrote that the girls had who went to Hollywood "with one good dress and a bottle of Peroxide." And filled, too, with those evenings Fitzgerald wrote about, the 3 A.M.'s of the dark night of the soul, when midnight's glamour cracks to smithereens.

All her life Liz Ray has wanted to be a calendar girl, bubbling and beautiful, fun and sexy and sought after, that's all. Plus rich—a few minks, steak dinners, fast cars—and famous. It would have helped if the Good Lord had given her some kind of talent along with the great body, but she has managed, mostly through being sexy, to eke out at least a flashy life-style. "My Gawd," her mother stammered to the press about her very rare visit to see her little girl all grown up in Washington, "she was living in a penthouse!" Only a lower floor really of a high-rise, but nonetheless classy considering Liz's mother is still doing her own dusting in a trailer out there in the fields of North Carolina.

This is not to mention the dark chocolate Corvette and a few fun furs, plus hundreds of hangers draped with a whole history of temptress outfits, from micro-skirts to daytime suede pantsuits and nighttime decolleté satins. Even her toy poodle is part of the flash—more accessory than pet. And the license plates on her car, which were lifted one night last summer for souvenirs, were special ordered to read "LIZ II." Until Liz sounded the gong on Wayne Hays, her apartment looked as if she'd dialed Hollywood direct and furnished it out of stage props. Red, totally red, from Vincent Price Blood Castle heavy mock-velvet drapes to crimson, crushed velvetine, stuffed furniture. In each corner, dusty white fake ferns spread like cobwebs out of imitation wormwood buckets. Stained-glass red lamps, spongy thick carpet that flowed like Moses' Red Sea into the boudoir. Here the same props switched to baby-blue and white. A surreal, powdery blue fake fern wept over a king-sized, antique-white Mediterranean bed. The carpet, same spongy thickness, was white; the princess phone, baby-blue.

The red drapes and the fake ferns disappeared about a month after the Hays story broke, the same week Liz started going to catechism, though this was a passing fancy. Marion arrived at her apartment one day to find sunlight pouring through dusty windows on to dozens of new plants, bought in bulk—another phone call, different props. "I'm going to auction off my bed," Liz said. "How much do you think I can get for it? The bed Wayne Hays slept in. Plus the shower head Hays made me put in, and the digital clock. It's bad memories. I'm changing my image." Squinting against the foreign sun, she looked at the new jungle hanging everywhere. "I hope they don't die," she said, and knew it was hopeless.

She also knew by then that the fame she'd sent away for had come back the wrong size. It didn't fit, wasn't wearing well, and she was having a horrible time trying to alter it into the America's Sweetheart variety. She had wanted Hollywood, big bucks, the silver screen. Instead she had been dealt notoriety and sleazy tabloid reporters. Where were the big movie producers? Gone, every one, like so many good times. Gone with the drapes.

Now her life had gotten dirty around the edges. She could have been a quiet cliché, not a reminder to a whole nation that the one-night stand was alive and dangerous. It was aberrant behavior almost, this whistle-blowing on her boss. It should have been cut from the script, X-ed out because it didn't fit the character. Good-time girls who wanted to be Mistress USA didn't lose their tempers in public and shoot down numero uno sugar daddies in front of their friends. She'd done it now, something irrevocable. Something that made her die more than all the small deaths combined of all the loveless mornings since she'd left the South.

It had been higgledy-piggledy, the trek up—the Chevy love nests giving way to one long romance with a nobody who's still down South and still nobody. After that the relationships got shorter by the week, then by the night, until each existed only to promise something better. Sleeping with a car salesman was introduction to sleeping with the owner of the lot. She competed in the Miss Asheville beauty contest, spending her nights sleeping with any judge she could, her days behind a candy counter at a downtown Asheville dime store. "I was still better than my mother," she once said; and when she lost the beauty contest, she proved it. She did what her mother never had the broad vision to do. She got out of town on a Greyhound bus, young and alone. She ended up in Florida and ostensibly she was attending stewardess school; but it was the same old story, filled with nights of glory, until eventually, in 1966, she looked up the big Asheville car lot owner at his Washington branch and suitcased it into the Nation's capital.

She had her letter of introduction—not exactly Dickensesque—nevertheless sufficient to land her, Oliver Twist manner, in with thieves. The introduction came from the fancy car lot owner, who told a restaurant owner friend of his that Liz was "easy" and poor. It was a mess. The restaurant wasn't much of a restaurant. It was Capitol Hill call girl headquarters thinly veiled by a hamburger front. The first friend Liz made was a nice lady who turned out to be a pseudo–call girl who was really a CIA agent. "I got out of there," said Liz, "as soon as I figured it out."

Bettering herself once more, she moved into wider restaurant circles in the netherworld of suburban, Mafia-tainted nightlife, where all the women seemed to drive fast 'vettes and the men had something going in the back room or out of phone booths that brought them easy-come-easy-go cash. The money had a nice way of easy-going to Liz and her friends, and our heroine would have been comfortably happy had it not been for this nagging stardom fantasy she had from mooning eternally over Marilyn Monroe—of whom too many people had told her she reminded them—plus the sad fact that she went and fell in love with the worst man in the bunch.

He owned an Italian restaurant in Arlington, was a feisty man, hot-tempered, long on passion, but short on loyalty to Liz. She stuck it out for two years, sometimes threatening suicide, sometimes causing enormous scenes in public, and

She had a face that looked like trouble, Marion Clark thought when she first met Elizabeth Ray on a train in the fall of 1974. In 1975 Ray went to Hollywood to become a star and posed for Tom Kelly, the man who had taken the publicity photos of her idol, Marilyn Monroe.

(PHOTOGRAPH BY TOM KELLY)

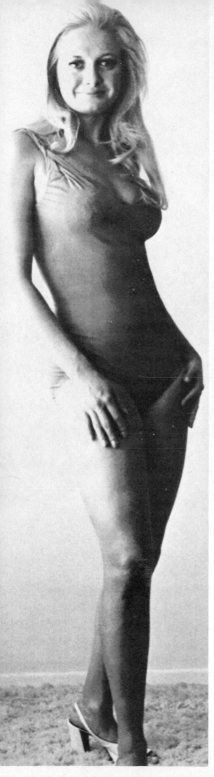

Elizabeth Ray's Capitol Hill office was bare except for a backgammon board, a couple of paperback books and autographed photos from public figures she had met. When Clark and Maxa visited her office, the desk drawers were empty and a layer of dust covered Ray's IBM Selectric typewriter. Sometimes she brought her high-strung poodle, Maurius, to Capitol Hill for company.

(MATTHEW LEWIS—*The Washington Post*)

Before and during the Hays-Ray scandal, restaurant owner Duke Zeibert was one of Elizabeth Ray's most faithful companions. "When you get to be my age," Zeibert told Marion Clark, "you don't need sex appeal anymore. You know why? Because you have all you need. You have *checks-appeal*."

(HARRY NALTCHAYAN—*The Washington Post*)

◄

For several years Elizabeth Ray tried to become famous by plying the beauty contest circuit. She never won big, though she posed in this photograph as Miss Virginia during the 1973 Miss International USA pageant held in New Orleans.

(WIDE WORLD PHOTOS)

For several days after her story appeared on the front page of *The Washington Post,* Elizabeth Ray obligingly posed for photographers with mementos of her years on Capitol Hill. "Me! A poor little girl from the South! Sleeping with congressmen and senators," she marveled as the press began covering her every move.

(ED STREEKY—CAMERA 5)

(Bottom far left) Even as a young congressman, Wayne Levere Hays (shown here in a 1955 photo) was no Mr. Nice Guy. After his first re-election to the House, Hays called his defeated opponent to rub salt in his wounds: "I thought you'd like to know that this was the first election in which I carried the county where you spoke—before it had always gone Republican."

(WIDE WORLD PHOTOS)

(Bottom left) He looked like a prosperous Midwest insurance agent, but Wayne Hays talked like a dockworker, labeling fellow House members "potato head," "mushhead," and "senile" on the floor of Congress. No one missed the irony when Hays's indiscretions drove him from office and brought about the tightening of House rules governing hiring and fringe benefits.

(JAMES K. W. ATHERTON
—*The Washington Post*)

Shortly after her husband was elected to Congress in 1948, Wayne Hays's first wife, Martha Judkins, posed for a portrait. Hays traveled to the Dominican Republic in January of 1976 to receive a divorce.

(HARRIS & EWING)

As the Hays-Ray scandal unfolded, the new Mrs. Hays, the former Patricia Peak, continually threatened to leave her husband, according to close associates. Two months after the *Post* story, Representative and Mrs. Hays attended a State Department reception in one of their few public appearances together.

(LINDA WHEELER
—*The Washington Post*)

"Waiting," Maxa said to Clark when they prepared to follow Wayne Hays, "is always the hardest part." From a parking space under a wing of Elizabeth Ray's apartment building, the reporters had a clear view of the entrance at which Hays would pick up his employee for dinner dates.

(PHOTOGRAPH BY
BETSY K. FRAMPTON)

Several days after she accused Rep. John Young (D-Texas) of paying her nearly $26,000 a year because she slept with him, a weary and distraught Colleen Gardner met with the press to say that she and Elizabeth Ray were not the only play-for-pay women the taxpayers were supporting.

(LARRY MORRIS
—*The Washington Post*)

(*Bottom*) Rep. John Young (D-Texas) blustered when *The New York Times* reported Colleen Gardner's allegation that he paid her handsomely for sexual reasons, but he never denied he had slept with women on his staff. "When a man is holding public office, the greatest thing they can say about him is that he's a man of the people," Young said. "Then when they find out he is, that's when the trouble starts."

(JAMES K. W. ATHERTON
—*The Washington Post*)

Before the press learned of the questionable lobbying techniques of South Korean agents in Washington, the now-House Speaker Tip O'Neill (D-Massachusetts) and his daughter were the honored guests at a 1974 birthday dinner given by Tongsun Park. A South Korean millionaire, Park left the United States as the public began reading reports of his generosity to congressmen. In March of 1977 the IRS attached his assets, including two mansions, in Washington.

(HARRY NALTCHAYAN
—*The Washington Post*)

A major figure in what Washington was beginning to call "Koreagate," Suzi Thomson found reporters asking questions about her job in former House Speaker Carl Albert's office and her parties for congressmen. Rep. Robert Leggett (D-California) admitted he began having an affair with Thomson in 1973. And in 1976 Leggett became the target of a Justice Department probe of congressional influence-peddling by South Korean agents and Tongsun Park in Washington.

(LARRY MORRIS—*The Washington Post*)

As a college student attending a conference in Washington in 1968, Bette Jane Ackerman (shown here in a Boston University yearbook photo) had an affair with then-Rep. Donald Riegle (D-Michigan). In 1976 their old affair became news when excerpts from tape recordings Ackerman had kept of her romantic conversations with Riegle found their way to the *Detroit News*. A Library of Congress researcher and close friend of Suzi Thomson and Tongsun Park, Ackerman said she meant Riegle no harm; in fact, some observers said the lurid exposé created a sympathy backlash that helped Riegle win his close Senate race in 1976.

routinely crying herself to sleep. One night she found another woman's Corvette outside the restaurant owner's house and went berserk. She took her car key and scraped it around the entire car, mercilessly gouging the new paint. She attacked the aerial, the rear view mirror, and was pounding at the sides when the Arlington police stepped in. Things had gotten out of hand. "I'd never had that before," Liz said. "I was so in love with him and he just kept treating me like dirt."

She was working odd jobs, some odder than others: car rental clerk, telephone operator, bunny-suited waitress, hostess, receptionist, airlines counter girl, limousine driver. One night the restaurant owner called his pal Ken Gray, a congressman from Illinois, and begged him to get Liz off his back. He was going crazy, he told Gray. Gray met Liz at the Watergate restaurant, where she was hostessing the bar. He hired her right away as a clerk in his House office.

This was hot July in Washington, 1972, and Gray's notorious houseboat, where he entertained for practical reasons—like getting votes and more tangible rewards—was at full throttle on the Potomac. Liz changed her name, her aspirations and her modus operandi. She had already changed her nose and her age—for five years now she had not gotten any older. She had been born Betty Lou Ray on May 14, 1943. "I changed my name to Elizabeth," she says, "because it sounded like a nice name, a name a pretty girl would have." Congress was a great place to be.

She used to keep her southern slum background under wraps. It wasn't until after the Hays story broke that she realized it could be a great excuse for not quite behaving herself. "Me! A poor little girl from the South! Sleeping with congressmen and senators," she took to saying to *Time* and *Newsweek* reporters. It seemed to sanctify things; it fit the cliché. How could the poor child know any better? Ah, yes, magazine articles would say, trying to wrench some sociological meaning from the Liz Ray story, some lesson for us all. Liz Ray was a victim, like so many small-town girls, seduced by power. It could happen to anyone.

In Congress her calendar-girl dreams were coming true. Even stodgy places have room for comic relief and here she was received like one perpetual wad of sexual Silly Putty. She table-hopped at the House restaurant. She flirted with anyone under the age of seventy and flattered egos that needed to be reminded that underneath the gray suit and sheaves of Title-114 briefs a normal, lusty heart beat, longing to be aroused. Jokes had it, the day after the first Hays-Ray story ran, that "four busloads of dumb blonds were seen leaving Capitol Hill today," but, truth be known, there was a shortage of cheesecake. Plus, Liz had played the role longer and more faithfully than most. She had it down to a perfection, from tossing her head when she talked so her brilliantly clean hair flipped to and fro, to laying rubber on the House parking lot ramp while driving the Corvette. "We miss you!" Congressman John Brademas said to Liz at a party months after Hays had lost his House Administration chairmanship in 1976. "She was a mascot," the House assistant sergeant at arms told Marion Clark. "She brightened up the place. They ought to erect a statue to her."

The more attention she reaped the more she craved, and as her self-image grew she took to calling senators and congressmen she hadn't yet met to introduce herself . . . as if they *ought* to know her. Toward the end of her stay, partitioned off from the mainstream in the Longworth Building, her flirtatious propensities curtailed by Hays, Liz took to calling a number of congressmen, like Barry Goldwater, Jr., frequently, just to chat them up . . . to pass the time. She was usually tolerated, sometimes welcomed.

In the beginning, Congressman Gray used to tell her what kinds of things to wear to nighttime social functions, says Liz, and then he finally came down to asking for the same dress over and over again. It was white satin, floor-length, with a mandarin collar on top of a two-inch-slit that plummeted to her belly button. From floor to thigh on each side were matching slits. It was very tight.

She remembers the night "things first got bad with Gray," a few months into the job. She'd put on the white dress and gone to the Sheraton for a Big Brothers dinner to which Gray had invited some home-state businessmen. "He used to tell me to flirt with these old guys," says Liz, "just make them feel good, you know, so they'd have a good time. I got so I didn't mind it. Gray'd make these jokes about my breasts when he introduced me. He'd say 'Elizabeth has a chest cold, poor thing. Look how it's all swollen up.'" So she'd spent a few hours sitting on laps and taking the corny come-ons good-naturedly, and she was almost having a good time when Gray came up to her.

"'Get your coat on,' he said, 'You're leaving.' I said, 'I'm having a good time, I don't want to leave yet,' and he yanked my arm and he said, 'I told you you're leaving. Now get your coat on. A friend of mine is waiting for you down at the Quality Inn in Northwest.' I told him I didn't want to go to the Quality Inn down there. It was dangerous, I told him, and he said to me, 'You don't go down there and you don't come in to work tomorrow either . . . or ever.'"

She went to the Quality Inn. Gray's friend was sitting waiting for her at the bar. "He's the one I call Pudgy Contractor in the book," she says now. "He was so horrible. I could have been crushed under a guy like that. He weighed at least three hundred pounds." She says that was the first time she was asked to do more than tease.

It was a small compromise in a way. There were good nights and bad. She had to do these distasteful things to keep the job that was promoting her every day in every way toward more widespread recognition. Last summer, after all the Hays publicity, the impossible finally happened. She got a letter that had been put through the U.S. mail addressed simply: Elizabeth Ray, Virginia. She started to shake.

But not from joy

Around that time last summer she started listening to the radio as much as possible hoping she'd hear "Rhinestone Cowboy" one more time so she could get *all* the words memorized. It was her song, she said, right down to the part about "the train taking the long way." "The train ride we took is even in it," she told Marion one morning in her Arlington apartment last June. She was pulling together a wardrobe to go to London on a book promo tour while dialing her usual list of people on the princess phone—her Washington lawyer, her New York lawyer, Duke, her psychiatrist, her aunt. Marion was flying up to New York with her to catch the London plane because she said she couldn't travel alone. Yvonne Dunleavy, her ghost-writer, would take over from New York to London.

The apartment smelled strongly of ammonia from the relentless "cleaning up after Maurius," which was done by her twenty-four-hour nurse, Helen. The nurse was showing Marion "little nips" the dog had taken out of her arm when the song came on the radio. "This is it! This is it!" Liz shouted whipping up the volume. She loved Glen Campbell more than her Corvette, her mink, cold cash and hot publicity. And now she was singing along, nodding her head . . . "getting cards and letters from people I don't even know, and offers comin' over the phone."

Now she was shouting, gazing out the window. "There's been A LOAD OF COMPROMISING ON THE ROAD TO MY HORIZON, but I'M GONNA BE WHERE THE LIGHTS ARE SHINING ON ME . . ."

Her book, *The Washington Fringe Benefit,* totally ghostwritten, had been on the stands for four days in Washington, churned out faster than grease through Dell Publishing's presses, so fast Liz hadn't even read the book herself. She and Marion stopped by National Airport's quicky bookstand on the way to the Eastern shuttle and bought two copies.

That week in Washington a little game flourished over who could guess the real names of the senators and congressmen mentioned in Liz's book. Who was the "Senator Sincere" with "the famous three initials" Dunleavy had opened the book with in a juicy short chapter that had Liz visiting him for a fast one between the monogrammed sheets? Who was the young, athletic senator she sneaked to see so often in his Georgetown house? And so forth. Senator Otis Battle, of course, was Hays—"the curmudgeon from New England," the mean boss who constantly watched the digital clock during nocturnal sessions Liz called, according to Dunleavy, "Wild West Shows." When Battle tells Liz at the end of the book that he's getting married to his home-office secretary of fifteen years, he quips, "You're being promoted, from Mistress Number Two to Mister Number One!"

Gray appeared in the book twice, once disguised as lobbyist Elan Bright and again as Congressman Billy Bob Blank—both times a Capitol Hill boss who gave Liz's body as a personal public relations gesture to constituents and legislators. In the book Liz, through Dunleavy, talks about a bill that got passed because Blank had her service "Senator Boulder" on his houseboat. "I called it 'The Ray Act' when it got passed," she told Marion on the plane. "You know who Boulder is, don't you? Boulder. Think about it. Boulder, gravel . . . Mike Gravel. He's the guy who helped Gray get his Visitors' Center bill passed. It's my Visitors' Center!" The National Visitor Center, built into what was previously Washington's Union Station, is still being written about as a grand mistake, an idea that ended up costing the taxpayers millions of dollars, a place that now, as Washington columnist Frank Mankiewicz wrote, attracts no visitors. "I went down to see it," said Liz, "and I walked around and *nobody* was there. My center! I was all alone in my center."

In fact, Gravel had very little to do with passing the Visitor Center bill and denies ever having slept with Liz.

Marion asked a man sitting next to them in the plane for a match and he handed her a pack that had "Digital World" printed across the cover. "Ohhh, no! I don't believe it," Liz screamed. "It's me and Hays." She borrowed four more packs, then sold the fellow, a computer salesman, one of the two books they'd bought for twenty-five cents less than they'd paid for it.

The other book she inscribed to Marion:

"Hi Marion,

"This is all your fault. If it were not for you and the *train wreck,* I could be having fun and playing backgammon. But I can't do that now instead I'm on my way to London. Take care, Love ye, Elizabeeth."

She had spelled her own name wrong.

"Everyone wants to know who the other men are," she said; "that's all they care about. Well, I'm not going to get anybody else in trouble. That *National Enquirer*—you wouldn't believe what they did to me. That guy, that John somebody, John South, slept in my lobby for days! He followed me and my girlfriend to Mass. To Mass! They sent flowers, yellow and white ones, and telegrams, and one night they stuck money under my door with this terrible note that said, 'Do you need any ready cash?' I called the police. The Arlington police have the money. You can check it out."

They had finally won though, offering twenty thousand dollars to Liz if she'd consent to an exclusive interview. The deal was they would put her and her dog up in a suite at the Mayflower Hotel for eight days, feed her, walk Maurius, everything. She wouldn't be allowed to talk to anyone else and would be escorted everywhere she went outside the suite.

"First thing they did was sit me down and say, 'O.K., now who else did you sleep with? We want names.' I said I couldn't tell them that. Even if they said a hundred thousand dollars, I'm not going to hurt people. They had one editor there who filled my bathtub, and another one who walked Maurius. Jan Goodwin, the big editor, slept on the couch, and someone slept in with me. They brought in cots. I went out once to Drug Fair to buy some bubble bath and they wouldn't let me go alone. Finally, I called Ahern (Albert Ahern, her new Washington attorney) and said, 'Get me out of here. I don't care what happens. Just come and get me— NOW.' "

She had lasted ten hours, she said.

"The only thing I want to know," said Marion, "and I can't help it, I've got to ask you, is . . . did you really sleep with Hubert Humphrey?"

"Why?" Liz asked.

"Because I can't stand it," Marion said. "I couldn't sleep last night. I had a nightmare that I slept with Hubert Humphrey. Can you believe it? I mean when I start having nightmares that I'm sleeping with Hubert Humphrey something's got to be wrong. I just kept thinking when I was reading your book, No!, she couldn't have. Not Hubey, that little Hubey Humphrey. He couldn't stop talking that long."

"No comment," Liz said and she was giggling now out the window. The plane was dipping over the sprawl of Queens heading for landing and Liz was only hours away from London where, in the next few days, her main talk show appearance would be cut short by a Bugs Bunny cartoon because, as the British press put it, "She was such a bore."

"Let's just say," she said to Marion, "the person you were talking about was . . . personal."

All three networks plus the *Times, Post* and *Daily News* swarmed the La Guardia gate. Why was Liz Ray in New York, they wanted to know. "She's here for a rest," said Seymore Feig, her New York show-biz lawyer, suddenly appearing. "No questions. No comment."

'Twas always thus. The Rhinestone Cowgirl, "riding out on a horse in a star-spangled rodeo," hair perfect, sunglasses intact, didn't like talking to the press unless she could deliver one-liners that fit the coquettish image she'd worked at her whole life. Even back waitressing at small-time places, she'd bend over some lone male diner so he could see her cleavage and coo, "We've got chicken tonight. What'll it be, a breast or a leg?"

This was tough. She could die, she wanted the publicity so much, wanted her name a household word, her every move chronicled like Jackie O. But they asked all the wrong questions. How could she get off a one-liner when some nut from AP was asking her if it were true she'd taken a typing course in high school? Or, if another deadbeat from the *Today* show wanted to know if she was going to provide the Justice Department with the tapes she'd made of all her lovers in bed. They were treating her like . . . a criminal, not a star. Where was their sense of humor? This was supposed to be fun. She only got to say the same thing over and over again. The same dumb line. Sometimes she'd toss her hair back and flutter her eyelids when she said, "I have no comment on that," as if she knew something that could blow the lid off American politics. Other times she pouted, hurt and taken aback, when she said it. But usually she said it straight, looking down at the mike: "No comment." Period.

"I sold a book on the plane," she told Seymore Feig and Yvonne Dunleavy in the limousine on the way into Manhattan from the airport.

"How much did you sell it for?" Dunleavy asked.

"A dollar fifty," Liz said.

"You should have sold it for twenty dollars with the autograph," said Dunleavy. "Auction it off. Make a fortune."

"That's not legal, is it?" asked Liz.

"Of course it's *legal*," Dunleavy snorted, giving her a sideways glance that said "I give up."

The writer marriage had not been made in heaven. Liz heard there were "dirty words, filthy language," in the book, and that all "the good scenes got shortened down so much they weren't anything." Dunleavy claimed she was furious at Dell for editing it badly and she had taken her name off the cover. Now she was more or less being forced to accompany Liz on promo tours, which was definitely a drag. Later, Dunleavy would throw her hands up in complete despair, considering 50 percent of the take on the book was hers by contract, when Liz, having gone into psychic collapse over the prospect that some old nude pictures taken of her by an industrious Washington photographer were being hustled by him to *Hustler* magazine for megabucks, abruptly canceled a promotion tour through the Midwest Dell had set up for her at a cost of thousands. She simply didn't show up at the airport. Dell, infuriated, canceled all promotion on the book. "They wanted me to talk to a bunch of ladies in Osh-Gosh, Wisconsin," Liz said. "Besides, my doctor said I was too upset. I couldn't go or he'd cancel me as a patient."

The limousine was heading for the *National Star* offices downtown, where Feig had set up a photo session for Liz to go with a new deal he'd cut for Liz's book to be excerpted by them for around fifteen thousand dollars, now that the *Enquirer* deal had been blown to kingdom come. After the photo session, it would be right back on the expressway to Kennedy Airport for the London plane.

Liz was telling Dunleavy that she'd come up in the world as an author. "First book you wrote about a hooker, next book you wrote about a stripper, now you've written about a mistress. Next you'll be writing about nuns."

"Yeah," said Dunleavy. "I've heard some things about nuns."

"Well," said Feig, looking more like Uncle Milty than Milton Berle had in years, "I stuck up for you, Liz, on TV this morning. I made you look forty feet tall, I tell you. The media is horrible. They trapped me into it. They had Jack Anderson on remote from Washington asking me questions."

Anderson was no great Liz lover. He'd written as much in more than one recent column, claiming she had come to him with the Hays story two years earlier, a fact Liz hooted at, pointing out that she wasn't even working for Hays then.

"Anderson said to me over this remote on TV," said Feig, " 'You know she's a liar, Feig.' Well, I told him what I thought of him and his so-called reporters. I said, 'Call me Mr. Lawyer, not Feig.' And then I said, 'I can tell you as her New York attorney that this girl could make millions, and I mean millions, if she wanted to condemn people. But she won't do it. She won't capitalize on what she knows.' "

He had once told Marion that Liz Ray was a "saint" and

that this whole thing "was something out of Kafka." She was a "girl who could make a goddam fortune" and yet he couldn't get her to do one even slightly off-color thing, like perform in an X-rated movie. The burlesque houses had all called immediately. "Liz says only R-rated movies, that's all. She'll go nude, but no heavy stuff," Feig had said. He agreed they weren't out to make fast bucks and a quick fade, no sirree.

Liz had already fired her original Washington lawyer, Monroe Mizel, because, among other things, she said, he tried "to make a deal with *Hustler* magazine behind my back for twenty-five thousand dollars." Also, he had prevented her from talking to the press and all those wonderful TV people just when she thought she would be allowed to stand up for herself, right after the story broke. Also, and this was perhaps the sorest point, one night right after the story ran, Liz had phoned Mizel begging for help. She needed a place to stay. The editors at *The Post* had balked at the idea of her moving in with one of their reporters and had ordered Marion Clark to ask her to leave immediately. Mizel had put her up on a couch in the house of Marion Clark's neighborhood pharmacist, a man Mizel had gone to high school with. Liz, frightened out of her mind, had wept all night and cursed Mizel. She had no one to call for help. "I have no friends," she wailed to Marion when she phoned her at 7 A.M. "I'm all alone. I've lost my job. Hays hates me. Everyone hates me. I have to testify now in some court. I don't have any money. I don't know where I am. Lord God, what have I done?" She'd never forgiven Mizel for that. She wanted to sue him.

Later she would complain about Feig, too, threatening at one point to sue him. This was another word Liz learned to say perfectly: sue. She wanted to sue the photographer and his agent who had hawked her nude pictures to *Hustler* and other "even worse" magazines. She wanted to sue *Genesis* because they ran her picture more than once. She wanted to sue *Playboy* because its articles editor, Peter Range, had written a story about Liz she didn't like. She wanted to sue the Watergate because they wouldn't let her rent an apartment there. She wanted to sue the *Washington Star* because they wrote "such terrible things" about her in their gossip column. And she wanted to sue whoever had written a memo about her that someone told her was on the House bulletin board and gave her address. She also wanted to sue Dell, just on general principle. She hadn't been allowed to read the final manuscript, for one thing, she said. If she had, she would have taken out things like where she was supposed to have said, "In Washington the real job is secondary to the blow job." This was not Calendar Girl style at all and it didn't sound right for "a poor little southern girl" to say things that crass.

When she finally got to Heathrow Airport outside London, she wasn't greeted by the kind of fun, scandal-loving British press she'd heard so much about, those dry-witted fellows who could appreciate the humor in all of this. She was met instead by a solemn crew of news people who wanted to know how she felt about Hays just having taken an overdose of sleeping pills. "You don't know how I felt," she told Marion later. "No one would believe me, how upset I was. I cried and cried and cried. Jeez, I felt so sorry for the guy, you know. I felt like I'd done this terrible thing to him. He may have been mean to me, but the poor guy didn't deserve this." She talked to her psychiatrist long-distance from London all through the night.

Liz had begun working for Hays when Gray retired from Congress in 1974. Gray's houseboat was being written about regularly in the papers by then, and rumor had it the Justice Department was looking into the party-girl matter. He took care of Liz, who had been good to him, by virtually handing her over to Wayne Hays. "Hays told me," said Liz, "I'll start you at eleven thousand, and if you can prove to me that you can keep your mouth shut, I'll raise you."

He was possessive, Liz said, not like Gray at all. "He didn't

congressman was out to lunch so now they could call. A lot of times you could hear giggles in the background and you got the feeling the whole office was listening in on the call. They were having more fun than they did telling this same old gossip, worn thin by weeks of use, to yet another confidant over tuna salad in the cafeteria. Now they were telling *The Washington Post* and some day soon, they hoped, a million readers. This was high-stakes gossip, a whole new thrill.

That night at work Marion Clark wrote up a list of sixteen congressmen and their girlfriends, compiled from all the "tips" and rampant rumors she herself had listened to over the phone all day long. The list was incredible. Who knew the reasons for the calls? Jealousy? Outrage over being passed over for a promotion? Revenge for being fired? Civic duty? A prank? At the top of the list, Clark penned in "Fun Couples."

The list grew like an underground *Who's Who,* and now gossip was coming in through the mails. One woman from San Francisco sent a large package special delivery with this message printed in red crayon on the top: "Be the first to print the story that makes Wayne Hays and Liz Ray look like kindergarten! Yours . . . EXCLUSIVE." Inside, she had enclosed publicity shots of herself and a list, beginning with Henry Kissinger, of all the powerful men she'd slept with. Another package came in with a long letter plus photographs about "Powerlust"—pictures of women in leathers holding whips— from an outfit in New York claiming they had taken a poll, nationwide, and found that congressmen, more than any other patrons of prostitutes, were into perverted sex. Some men saying they were homosexuals phoned in to let the press know that congressmen and senators had forced them into sexual acts. And women from every rank lower than GS-14 wrote or called to let *The Washington Post* know that they had been victimized, like Liz Ray, by these men of elected power. In the bombarded atmosphere of *The Post,* it was increasingly more difficult not to believe that *something* aberrant was going on up on Capitol Hill.

What was aberrant was not that bosses were sleeping with secretaries, married men with someone other than their wives. This may not be moral, but it isn't exactly strange behavior, since by now most of us have gotten used to the reality that monogamy is not a perfect institution. The difference here was that so many women felt abused by it and that so much sex—if the stories were true—was being used to further careers. It became clear that some congressmen and senators were not exactly hiring and firing and promoting through fair practice. The typing test had been replaced by the extracurricular physical exam. The chic little dinner party technique for getting a floor member's vote or a constituent's backing had also, on more occasions than imagined, apparently been one-upped by the generous gift of a body in some congressman's employ.

Both strange and logical-sounding tales kept flowing into *The Post*. Marion Clark was assigned by her editor to track down "other women." She started doing what she called "Dialing for Dollies."

She waded through the Congressional Directory, correcting spelling on her "Fun Couples" list and jotting down office phone numbers. What was she going to say? "Hi, this is Marion Clark from *The Washington Post* calling and I was just wondering if you're doing nookie with your boss." Or maybe do it radio style: "Hello there, Marion Clark here, *Washington Post*. We're Dialing for Dollies and *you* could be one of them if you answer our question correctly. Are you typing or tricking?"

She could try calling older women on the staff on the premise that they might be handling—single-handedly—the work overload and would now like to talk, at least off-the-record, about whose work they were doing.

The phone rang. It was a woman identifying herself as Ava Jacobs. She had slept with Hays, she said, because she had to or she couldn't have kept her job with him. "I was just watching him on television," she said, "and when he said Liz Ray was crazy, I thought, oh no mister, obviously you're the mental case. You've been doing this for years. Let the old guy screw around I thought, but not on public funds. So I called you."

Clark and Scott Armstrong, the newspaper's hottest new investigative reporter, drove to Ava Jacobs' apartment in the suburbs. They came back believing her story was legitimate. She wanted to go on the record. She had worked for Hays briefly in 1968 and she was only eighteen at the time. She said Ken Gray, whom she had dated, had introduced her to Hays. "I can't remember doing any work," she told the reporters. "Once I stuffed some envelopes for Hays's campaign."

"You have to get corroboration," Clark's editor said. "Get her coworkers to vouch for the fact that she did no work. And try to find someone who knew she was sleeping with Hays."

By now Clark knew Dialing for Dollies wasn't any fun. Women had hung up on her all over the country. It could take hours just to track down a phone number of someone who could be the answer, someone who might talk about her old boss now that she'd gone home to Biloxi or Santa Fe. As for women still working for a congressman or senator, for the most part they were so frightened they barely admitted to having met their boss at all. Some women, in cracking whispers, promised to call back but didn't. Others were suddenly on leaves of absence. But most were simply "out to lunch" or "gone for the day" no matter what time you called back after the first time they had hung up. Dialing for Dollies was about as much fun as having to call someone to tell him his mother had died.

Maxa said to Clark, "I feel like the whole city is a time bomb ticking away with millions of stories ready to be told."

"I feel," Clark said, "like the whole world has hung up

on me. I want to go back to the magazine where people are glad when you call them."

Ava Jacobs had told Armstrong and Clark that the only woman who knew what was going on between her and Hays was Kathy Lefik, a close friend who had once worked on the Hill. She had lost track of her years ago because Kathy Lefik had married and moved away. At the time Scott Armstrong was working on uncovering syndicate crime in Prince Georges County with possible congressional connections, so Clark took up the dialing duty.

Did Ava Jacobs have any idea where Kathy Lefik's parents lived? "I think it's somewhere in Pennsylvania," she said. "Once I went home to visit them with her. But I don't know where. All I remember is we were in Erie and we got in the car and drove for about an hour. They lived in a little town and I think it was near a dam, because I remember we stopped to look at it right before we got there."

Clark asked Paul McCarthy, *The Post*'s copy aide supervisor who was from Erie, if he knew any small towns an hour's drive from Erie that had a dam. He gave her the name of one but he thought it was more like two hours from Erie. Maybe they drove fast. She called long distance information. No luck. She got a map of Pennsylvania and started calling any town in Northwest Pennsylvania that showed a dam near it. Still no luck.

She called the congressman Kathy Lefik had worked for. Had he kept track of her? No, he had not, but she was a great girl, he said. Did he remember Ava Jacobs? No. But if he could see a picture of her. He met so many people, helped so many women get jobs. Clark told him vaguely why she was trying to get in touch with Kathy Lefik. "If Kathy Lefik tells you something is true, it's true," said the congressman. "And if Ava|what's-her-name is a friend of Kathy's she must be telling the truth too."

Clark had already spent six hours phoning every name that was listed on Hays's staff in the Congressional Directory of 1968. One man, retired and living in Chevy Chase, had taken the opportunity to articulate every vitriolic sentiment he harbored against *The Post* before he slammed down the receiver. Another, working in private business, said he vaguely remembered Ava Jacobs; he thought she'd done some office Xeroxing. But he wasn't sure. One woman, still working on the Hill, said she didn't remember Ava Jacobs and she also told Clark that one of the women she was looking for had died. The other woman Clark asked her about, she said, had married and moved away. At one number Clark called, the tenants said the man she was looking for had retired to somewhere outside of Miami, Florida. After some time with the Florida operator, Clark thought she'd found the man's listing in Del Ray. She called. It was disconnected. Six hours: one dead person; one outraged man; one woman with no recollection; one man with some, but not the right, recollections; one woman who had disappeared; and one man whose phone was disconnected somewhere in Florida. She was giving up temporarily on the coworkers.

Clark started calling anyplace at all in Pennsylvania for a listing for Lefik. Finally, a flash of luck. A Lefik listing outside Philadelphia. A woman answered. It was Kathy Lefik's aunt! Kathy's new name was Powers and she lived right across the Potomac River in Arlington. The aunt didn't know her phone number. Clark called Arlington information. The number was listed!

Such was Dialing for Dollies that just getting the home number of someone who could be the pot of gold at the end of the digital rainbow seemed like victory itself. There was a great rush of satisfaction. You almost didn't want to call the number so you could quit while you were ahead.

It would happen again and again. You would have almost forgotten who you were calling this time when The Voice you'd been chasing for an eternity finally answered.

Kathy Powers was still working for a congressman on the Hill. She remembered Ava Jacobs and, yes, they had been good friends, but, no, she really didn't want to get involved. Her job. Her husband. It was understandable.

There were very few rewards in Dialing for Dollies. Just stories that repeated themselves: scared women who would talk off-the-record about other women; sad tales that sounded all too believable.

Sometimes, though, puzzle pieces came together in odd ways. One day in June the rarest variety of tipster called—someone who left his name and number and a message that went something like this: "has inside information on——." Clark called back.

"Listen," the man said, "I want to tell you that Hays didn't just like white girls; he liked black girls too. I know because my brother's girlfriend is working for Hays right now and my brother's tired of being hassled by her having to sleep with him all the time. He won't call you, but I will." He told Clark the name of the woman. It was the same name Woodward had mentioned months ago. It was the same name another reliable source who worked close to Hays had mentioned to Clark, telling her that Hays had "dragged her in" from a menial job in the suburbs to work for him. It was the same name Liz Ray had mentioned when she said Hays had made her call the woman one night to have a "ménage à trois" and another night to procure her services because Liz was in the hospital and couldn't perform her night duties. It was the same woman mentioned as "a Chinese girl" in detail in Liz Ray's book. It was also the same woman, not named, who would be cited in a *Washington Star* story six months later as very possibly the primary reason Wayne Hays finally decided to resign. She was going to testify. It turned out she didn't have to.

The caller also told Clark about another black woman Woodward had already heard about, from two separate sources, who had been transferred to House Siberia from Hays's staff because she wouldn't, allegedly, perform oral sex on him. She had been summoned to Hays's apartment one afternoon, Woodward's sources had told him, and asked to do the deed but to wash her mouth out with Listerine first.

Clark called both women. The first told her not to bother her. The second told her it was all true but that there was no way she could find another job. It was long over she said. She had left Hays's office right away and now she wanted to leave well enough alone.

There were other tales to check. Tales of two senators who rented an apartment so they could have young clerks over for group sex. Tales of pregnancies aborted with money from the congressmen, and of employee after employee who did virtually no office work. One congressman's secretary, the reporters learned from disparate sources, kept a famous chart in her desk drawer of all the congressmen and senators she'd slept with and their individual performance rating.

Outraged over the man who had made them stand up all day, the House elevator operators called in droves. They wanted to tell *The Post* about all the seamy scenes they'd witnessed over the years, like invisible people, in their elevators. They'd seen the late night comings and goings of numerous office rendezvous. They wanted to talk about all the nights they'd seen his nibs, the mighty Hays, squiring a young lovely out of the Longworth Building. The women operators wanted to talk about Carl Albert's terrible habit of putting his hands on them. "I've been around prostitutes all my life," said one older male operator, "and I'll tell you something. I have never seen more prostitutes than right here in the Longworth Building."

An administrative aide met Marion Clark for a drink several times at Hogates in the cavernous piano lounge to elaborate on scenes he'd witnessed for fifteen years. "The big joke down there now," he said one night, "is to go up to Tip O'Neill and ask him what Linda's duties are. They call her Linda Speaker around the House, or Lindathighs." He told Clark that Suzi Thomson, Carl Albert's ex-friend, now attached to Bob Leggett, was called "the six-million-dollar woman" because she had had her face lifted, her teeth completely redone, her fanny lifted, her thighs narrowed, plastic surgery done on her eyes, and her tummy tucked. In one of the more bizarre moments at *The Post* during this time, Representative Leggett appeared one afternoon wanting to see Ben Bradlee. In Bradlee's glass-walled office overlooking the newsroom, Leggett confessed in a three-hour-long taped interview most, if not all, of his relationship with Suzi Thomson and several members of his staff. *The Post*'s gossip columnist, Maxine Cheshire, had been keeping tabs on him for over a year. "Do you know why he finally talked?" Cheshire asked Clark on the night after the interview. "I showed him a copy of Suzi Thomson's birth certificate. She told him she was thirty-five." She was really forty-six.

The administrative assistant called daily with newly remembered information and new developments. So-and so's secretary had taken a quick leave of absence. This secretary was now showing up at 9 A.M. for work. That congressman had just read Liz Ray's book and was no longer using a particular briefcase he had been described in *The Washington Fringe Benefit* as constantly carrying, and he was now "scuttling around the halls with his hair standing up on end." The old "breakfast club" of a clique of congressional party girls had temporarily been called off. An all-woman baseball team from the Hill had switched their T-shirts, which said "A Woman's Place is in the House—and the Senate," to ones that said "I Can Type."

Ken Gray had anchored his houseboat out in the Atlantic somewhere with its name covered with paint. Tom Zito, a *Post* cultural reporter, had written some front page stories that included among their houseboat tidbits the fact that the taxpayers, not Gray, paid for the boat's electricity. Gray wasn't talking anymore. As the list of women reportedly involved in his night cruises grew longer, *Post* reporters began driving to various women's homes at night, hoping to catch them in an unguarded moment. Zito and Clark knocked on one woman's door only to have her say that they were the fifteenth crew of reporters who had been around to see her.

If she was ever going to talk, she said, she was going to give her story to "the nice man from AP."

Everyone was Dialing for Dollies.

The Post finally ran what it hoped would be the definitive article on "Aphrodite on the Hill," with the information gathered over six weeks by several different reporters. It played inside the "A" section of a Sunday edition and it concluded that sex in Congress wasn't any more or less common than sex in corporate offices.

Any story inside Congress could be matched with the same story in the lives of women tucked in small or large offices all over Washington. The location was interchangeable with New York, San Francisco, Atlanta, or any large city.

It was a very old story. Some women marry in high school or college. Some do not. Some decide to live and work someplace that offers more social and career opportunities than their hometown. Some women move to big cities and end up married. Some do not. Some have affairs with married men or single men or both. Some have affairs with their bosses. It just happens. To some women.

For every dramatic tale there is another that's very simple and commonplace. In Washington there may be more loneliness among women than in other large cities—just an edge more—simply because Washington is a man's town. The ratio of women to men at last count was ten to one. The ratio of single women to single men, of course, is even more dismal. And the jobs for women are predominantly and boringly clerical. It is a bureaucratic place with probably more paper to shuffle than any other city on earth.

There is some vicarious glamour. You can write home that you were there watching Jimmy Carter in person as he walked right by you on Pennsylvania Avenue during his inaugural march. If you were in Los Angeles, you might just as well write home that you'd seen Robert Redford stroll by while you were on the tour bus through Universal Studios.

If you want to generalize more, you could say that a

woman in New York may unwittingly go out with a married man because he stays in town on weeknights and does not advertise the fact that his wife and children live in West-chester County. In Washington a woman dates other women's husbands because, even though she knows they are married, she may well be desperate to go out with anybody. Washington is not a great nightlife town. Even now the bars and restaurants are filled with couples. If you're lucky you may live with four other women in one of Georgetown's quaint, over-priced townhouses, and for nightlife every once in a while the five of you may have a little dinner party. These parties are sometimes more depressing than watching Mary Hartman reruns on television. But once, if you're lucky, you might snag a date with the man you've asked to share your home-cooked beef Stroganoff.

More likely though, if you've settled in Washington, you live in an efficiency in the suburbs where the rent is cheap enough to be covered by your government salary. You get to like simple pleasures: the plants you nurture by your windows, a new record album, a new series of *Upstairs, Downstairs* on TV. You look forward to coming home at night where a certain anonymity covers you like a goosedown comforter, tucked away as you are from those people whom you don't want to find out you . . . don't date.

It's an easy town to live in. The pace is slow, the shopping convenient, the work at most government jobs less than demanding. If you can type, you've got it made.

So you settle in. It's Newton's Law. A body at rest with a comfortable apartment and a secure job tends to stay at rest.

The women who work on Capitol Hill are not, contrary to recent media lore, predominantly from the South. They are not the clichéd poor little southern lasses who don't know any better and are drawn from Squawk Holler Junction to Washington because, as Peter Range wrote in a recent *Playboy* article, "Atlanta is the good time, but Washington is the big time." The women who work for a congressman are more often than not from small towns in his home state. They are drawn from everywhere, looking for a particular genre of excitement which, to their minds, has more substance than the flash of New York or Hollywood. It is excitement couched in the immediacy of being a desk away from those people of power who shape our country, and matter in a real sense.

Ava Jacobs came to Washington from New Jersey looking for excitement. She was determined. She'd been used to excitement at home. She was flashy and sexy and had already been around. She died her naturally dark blond hair jet black, wore it teased and lacquered. She made herself look much older than her eighteen years and, like Liz Ray, she flirted with the Virginia beauty pageant circuit. She went out with all the kinds of men her mother disapproved of. Since Ava's early teens her mother had urged her to find a rich man. Her mother pushed her into beauty pageants. She had moved to Washington with her family, and Ava Jacobs remembers now that "one night I came home in a limousine and my mother flipped. She was so happy." The man who had brought her home was as close to being a stranger as any-one could be with whom you had just made love.

She met Ken Gray, she says, through a friend of hers who was working on the Hill. "I went out with him a few times and then he introduced me to Hays." Hays gave her a job. "I didn't really mind not having much work to do," she said, "because I was going out a lot for long lunch dates with men." Ava Jacobs had reached a level of excitement in Washington that some terribly lonely women with lesser physical endowments would have died to have. At least she was going out. Finally Ava met a man she fell in love with who was outraged over her behavior. She took courses at a secretarial school and then enrolled at Northern Virginia Community College. She married the man and dropped out of sight. She stopped wearing makeup and let her hair grow very long so that now it reaches to her waist in sandy blond splendor. When she looks at old pictures of herself in the tight dresses and teased black hair she can't believe the image she sees. "I got out just in time," she says. "I was one of the lucky ones."

Colleen Gardner, who once worked in Congressman Young's office, described the sex-play atmosphere. "It wasn't all his fault. The women on the staff played up to him like he was a demigod. They did the whole braless thing, the whole sexy number around the office." It had all started to feel so natural for everyone. Ordinary behavior. These things just evolved. It was a clubby kind of place, Congress, and this was just another clubby kind of office. You wrote your own rules. You hired and fired whomever you wanted. Women came and went.

Marion Clark had a good friend who is still working for the House on Capitol Hill. They had been roommates for a while when the two of them first came to Washington from the Midwest. Her friend, who had a fine arts degree, could type 120 words a minute and she landed a better than average job with a congressman from Idaho. She was extremely good-looking and was chased by more married men than any single woman should have to put up with. She didn't go out with any of them and finally, at age thirty, she married a man who had been a Fifties rock 'n' roll star. He moved her to a beautiful house in the Smokies down by Asheville, North Carolina, where she could have taken up her sculpturing again, had children and settled into a kind of purist artistic life. A year later she was back at Congress. She and her husband had reached an impasse. He hated Washington, she couldn't stay away. "I love this town," she told Clark. "I just have to be where things that I think are important are happening. I want to know what's going on. I have to be close to politics. I don't know why." He kept the house in Asheville. They didn't get divorced. "I love him," she said.

Clark's friend rented a little house in the suburbs and got

a job typing up financial briefs for a congressional committee. She missed her husband terribly. He missed her too. But
she stayed.

During a Dialing for Dollies session last summer, Clark
called up her old friend to ask her if she knew any inside
dirt. When her friend got on the phone, Clark could not
bring herself to pose the question. They talked instead about
how her friend had not seen her husband in over a year, and
that she wasn't dating anyone now.

"How are things down there?" Clark finally asked her,
"are they still chasing you around?"

"Yeah," said her friend, "it's still pretty bad. I just keep
telling them I'm married."

Was she still glad she'd come back to The Hill?

"Still glad," her friend said. "I love it."

CHAPTER

EIGHT

THE WIDENING CIRCLE

THE NEWSPAPER BUSINESS in Washington is a ropedancer's game. Reporters at *The Washington Post*, the *Washington Star* and the Washington bureau of *The New York Times* work hard to scoop each other, and all three newspapers are loath to play catch-up on a major story from the competition. The Hays-Ray story, begun with a splash on *The Post's* front page on Sunday, May 23, was not exactly embraced by other newspapers. Monday's *New York Times*, *The Post's* in-house journalism critic would later observe, "treated it as one treats a particularly offensive bit of trash. Grasping it carefully between two fingers, the *Times* dropped [the story] into page 53, the next to last page of the paper." The *Times's* headline was understated: "Hays Defers Trip in Wake of Charges by Woman."

At the *Washington Star* the story made page 3 with the headline "Hays Accuser Plans Paperback Book." Hays's decision not to leave Sunday for London with a congressional delegation picking up a copy of the Magna Charta was mentioned in all news accounts. And the wire services noticed the first crack in the wall of denials Hays had issued Sunday. On network television Hays denied ever having taken Ray to dinner and said he had not seen her "all this week or last week." Later when a reporter pointed out that *The Post* claimed to have witnessed him at dinner with Ray six days before the story was published, Hays modified his denial.

Yes, he told the United Press International, he had bought Ray dinner at the Key Bridge Marriott restaurant a week before, but only after "she called me and said she had no money, was very hungry and was going to commit suicide."

On Sunday a national desk reporter, Morton Mintz, called Maxa from *The Post*. Well-known as one of the most thoughtful and decent reporters in *The Post* newsroom, Mintz was concerned: What, he wanted to know, was going to be in the news pages of *The Post* the next day about the scandal the newspaper had disclosed? No one had really considered a follow-up story.

"We can't just run this incredible story on the front page on Sunday and not have a follow-up on Monday," Mintz said. His desk editors agreed and Mintz tried to call congressmen for their reaction to *The Post*'s story. Representative John Flynt (D-Georgia), chairman of the House Committee on Standards of Official Conduct, also known as the ethics committee, could not be reached for comment. Hays's traveling colleagues, the House leaders who had left for London the afternoon of *The Post* story, could not be disturbed, an embassy spokesman in London said, because they were tired after their transatlantic flight. It was a time for lying low, a time for sniffing the political winds. No one wanted to be the first to call for the head of Wayne Hays on the basis of the first story. After all, Hays was firm in his denials, and to line up with the wrong side in this affair could be a fatal political mistake.

On Monday, May 24, Clark and Maxa were assigned to write "the story behind the story," an explanation of Ray's motives, with special attention to her publishing plans and her future appearance in *Playboy*. It was obvious that Ray's hopes of collecting her last paycheck by keeping news of her book from Hays would be in vain.

"Elizabeth Ray," began Clark and Maxa's article, "decided to tell her story seven weeks ago after Hays ordered Capitol police to escort her out of his office." The story recounted Ray's anger at her exclusion from Hays's wedding reception, her frantic lunch with Clark and Maxa, and her decision to let the reporters listen to her telephone conversations with Hays. The story offered the Hays camp the first details of the extent to which Ray had cooperated with *The Post.*

In Washington, New York and Ohio, the Hays-Ray affair began to grow to scandal proportions and began to take on a life of its own.

The Post's executive editor, Ben Bradlee, called reporters Clark, Maxa, Bob Woodward, Larry Stern, Scott Armstrong, John Goshko and Walter Pincus into his office. Telephone tips about congressional misdeeds were flooding *The Post*'s switchboard. Public interest in Hays and the small empire he had built was growing. "I think the iron is hot," Bradlee said. His hope was to broaden the scope of *The Post*'s coverage beyond Hays to the more fundamental questions of congressional misuse of power, whether they concerned junketing, payroll padding, the seniority system or questionable campaign contributions. It had always been difficult to report interestingly on the congressional power structure. Hit-and-run coverage of selected congressional abuses would not have much impact unless the public was aroused enough to press their legislators for change. The Hays affair, Bradlee said, might just be the handle that could fit the larger story of congressional excesses, much the way Watergate had forced an examination of the role of the executive branch. Working under Stern, the reporters were to begin a wide-ranging examination of Congress. Outside *The Post* other reporters nicknamed Bradlee's *ad hoc* team the "Pussy Posse" and the "Beaver Patrol." In fact, while other journalists began a hot pursuit of sex-for-pay stories, *The Post* was beginning the more mundane task of examining public records and searching out travel vouchers.

In New York, Elizabeth Ray's publisher, Dell, was swamped with calls asking for details about her book. Dell had planned to publish the book in August; the company's promotional literature and time schedule were geared to a late-summer release. When Ray's story broke in *The Post,* her book was in the form of a rough manuscript. For over a year she had worked with ghostwriter Yvonne Dunleavy, and the book was still not complete. Ray said she had wanted to use real names in her book, but Dell feared legal repercussions and had opted for fake names and fictionalized accounts of stories Ray said were fact. The developing scandal did not change the minds of Dell's attorneys.

On Monday, one day after *The Post*'s story, executives of Dell met and decided to push production of Ray's manuscript. Lawyers poured over the pages, suggesting drastic changes. "This book is a novel," Dell attorney Steve Blair told Maxa. "The fact is the characters are not real people. The events may be reminiscent of some of the reports that have been in the newspapers, but the characters are just not real characters. . . . It's very difficult for us as publishers to conduct an independent investigation and we felt under the circumstances it should be presented as a novel."

Ghostwriter Dunleavy was reportedly given only fifteen minutes to read over the revised manuscript. Dell's president approved massive amounts of overtime pay for the staff, and just a few weeks after *The Post* story—and two months ahead of the planned publication date—Dell's printer was working twenty-four hours a day to produce over one million copies of *The Washington Fringe Benefit,* an X-rated, thinly disguised memoir of Elizabeth Ray's life in Washington. It sold quickly, but Ray was not kidding when a newsman asked her what she thought of her book. "I don't know," she replied. "I haven't read it."

In Belmont County, Ohio, Hays's constituents appeared willing to stand by their man when news of the scandal first reached them. "To err is human, to forgive is divine," read the announcement board at the Bannock Methodist Church. The pastor of the church told a *Washington Star* reporter, "I think the people around here believe his relationship with the woman is his own business . . . and are a little bit embarrassed for him." At his first public appearance in his home district after the story appeared, Hays dedicated a war memorial and in an emotional voice said, "This town means a lot to me. I was born here. My mother and father died here. This is where I get my strength. . . . You couldn't get this big a crowd in Times Square to celebrate Memorial Day . . . if you had Saint Peter to make the main speech."

Ohio subscribers to *The Washington Post-Los Angeles Times* News Service, which distributed the Clark-Maxa article early Saturday evening in time for most papers' Sunday editions, varied in their use of the scandal story. The largest newspaper in Ohio, *The Cleveland Plain Dealer,* ran the article on its front page. At the more timid *Toledo Blade* editors passed the wire copy around as if it were a dirty book; a *Blade* reporter said later his editors hungrily read every word but could not bring themselves to print the story, preferring to wait until the following day to run a Hays reaction. The day before *The Post* story appeared, Wayne Hays had huddled with the senior staff of *The Blade* to discuss his plans to run for the governorship of Ohio in 1978.

In Ohio and Washington Hays met with the key members of his staff. His original denial had read in part as follows:

> Let me say that I have never maintained Miss Elizabeth Ray or any other woman on any payroll as a mistress. This totally untrue report has caused much anguish for my bride of six weeks whom I love very deeply.
>
> Miss Ray has been under the care of a psychiatrist, Dr. Albert Messore, and in the past I have spoken with him about Miss Ray. I feel very badly, but she is a very sick young woman.
>
> Further let me emphasize that *The Washington Post* has sought to ruin my congressional career for some time. And in recent months *The Post* has engaged in a personal ven-

detta against me. It is indeed unfortunate to see an irresponsible newspaper team up with an irrational woman to produce such flagrant yellow journalism.

I will be consulting with my attorneys this week to determine the possibility of filing suit against *The Post* for this malicious article. Until then, I feel it proper to withhold any further comment.

Ben Bradlee was asked for a response to Hays's statement. "That's a lot of bullshit," he said. "The facts speak for themselves. Nobody's denied anything." The answer was typical Bradlee, tough and blunt, so much so that even his own newspaper had to put hyphens in "bull----" when it quoted him.

For Wayne Hays, the center would not hold. Sunday, the day of *The Post*'s story, the Justice Department dispatched FBI agents to begin an investigation to determine if Hays had misused public funds. At the recommendation of the Watergate Special Prosecutor's office, Justice had formed a public integrity section charged with investigating and prosecuting corruption in government and politics. In a matter of hours the head of that unit, John Henderson, knew Hays's flat denials were untrue. The resident manager of Elizabeth Ray's apartment building confirmed to FBI agents that Hays was a frequent visitor at Ray's apartment.

Nina Wilson, the office manager of Hays's House Administration Committee, told Hays's press secretary, Carol Clawson, that her marathon phone conversation with Clark had led her to believe *The Post* had followed Hays on some of his dates with Ray. Clawson and Hays knew they were trapped.* Hays's new wife, Pat Peak, was threatening to leave him. By Tuesday Hays knew he had to abandon his original strategy of absolute denials. "In a shaky voice," *New Times* reported,

---

* Some of the detail of what was occurring in the Hays camp is taken from an October 15, 1976, *New Times* article by Robert Shrum, "The Final Days of Wayne Hays." Shrum was friends with Doug Frost, then staff director of the House Administration Committee, and thus enjoyed some entrée to Hays's inner circle.

"he asked Doug Frost to prepare a statement but leave it vague about the period after his marriage: the truth, slightly shaded. Dawson Mathis of Georgia, another of Hays' young Southern protégés on House Administration, the son of a Baptist minister, polished the confession."

Then in an extraordinary moment on the floor of the House, Wayne Hays, the meanest man in Congress, stood before nearly three hundred of his colleagues—some of whom he had savaged on the floor or in committee during his twenty-eight years in Washington—and admitted that he had a "personal relationship" with Elizabeth Ray.

He was humble. "I have been called more names than any member of Congress in my memory," Hays told the hushed chamber. "I have been called arrogant, ruthless, cold-blooded, vicious, temperamental and mean . . . just to mention a few of the ones that are printable. No one has ever said that I am also a human being capable of emotions and of errors. But I am . . . and I have erred."

Hays said he had tried to help Ray during her tour of duty on Capitol Hill. He said when he told her he intended to marry Pat Peak, Ray threatened suicide and blackmail.

"Only time will tell whether Miss Ray will be successful in destroying my career," Hays said at the end of his speech. "I pray to God she will not have destroyed my marriage. I hope that when the time comes to leave this House, which I love, Wayne Hays may be remembered as mean, arrogant, cantankerous and tough, but I hope Wayne Hays will never be thought of as dishonest."

The House received Hays's speech with modest applause. It was the first time in anyone's memory that a congressman had admitted on the House floor that he kept a mistress. Still, if Ray had actually done work for her pay, Hays had violated no law. Two dozen House members and Hays himself asked the House ethics committee to investigate Ray's charges. "Her lies must be laid bare," Hays said, "not only to clear my name, but more importantly to protect the integrity of the United States House of Representatives."

It would turn out that the unreported findings of the House ethics committee proved so damaging that Hays could not afford to stay in Washington and face a public inquiry into his extracurricular sexual activities.

Just as the Ray scandal seemed consigned to the House ethics committee and the Justice Department, another woman went public with her charges that she had been paid over twenty thousand dollars annually for more than two years to sleep with her boss. The woman was Colleen Gardner, blond, well-spoken, attractive. Her boss was Representative John Young, a liberal Texas Democrat who had served in Congress for twenty years.

This story belonged to *The New York Times,* which reported it on June 11, 1976. Curiously, Bob Woodward of *The Post* had known about Gardner. More than a week before the *Times* story he had interviewed her in the red, Mediterranean-design living room of her suburban Virginia apartment. She had been nervous, offering Woodward a beer (he declined; she drank one herself). She made it clear to Woodward that she had had sex with Young but insisted she worked hard in his office, sometimes up to sixty hours a week as Young's liaison with the Joint Atomic Energy Commission.

Each evening United Press International photographs the front page of the next day's *New York Times* and transmits a copy to *The Post.* The wire service does the same to *The Post* for the *Times.* Near midnight on Thursday, June 10, Maxa received a call from *The Post*'s national desk.

"You ever heard of a woman named Colleen Gardner?" a desk editor asked him.

The name sounded familiar, but Maxa had spent the previous two weeks filling pages of notes with women's names and he couldn't be sure. Then he remembered the memo Woodward had written after his interview with Gardner.

"Yeah, Woodward talked to her. She wasn't a story because she claimed she worked hard for her paycheck," Maxa said.

"That's not what the *Times* says tomorrow," the desk editor told him.

Maxa drove to *The Post* newsroom and found Woodward's memo. He skimmed Woodward's description of Gardner and her apartment. "Colleen insists that she does work hard in office," Woodward had written. "Sometimes 60 hours a week; but she has managed to go to school (American U.) full-time at night and accumulate in the last four years all but eight credit hours she needs for a degree."

No one answered the telephone at Gardner's apartment. Maxa drove to the high-rise and asked the reception desk to ring Colleen Gardner. Still no answer. He waited near the desk, engaging the clerk in small talk. It was a long shot, but it was a technique a private detective had once told him about. Sure enough, a few minutes later Gardner rang the front desk. She wanted to know who had been calling her. Before the desk clerk could answer, Maxa asked for the phone.

"Miss Gardner?" he asked.

"Yes?"

The voice was hesitant, apprehensive. God, thought Maxa, is everyone in Washington afraid to answer his phone these days? He identified himself and said he worked with Bob Woodward. He apologized for disturbing her but said *The Post* had just learned of her confession to the *Times,* a confession that did not quite jibe with what she had told Woodward. Would she mind discussing it for a moment? Gardner was flustered. No, she finally said, you'll have to talk to my lawyer tomorrow. Nothing could persuade her to invite Maxa to her apartment. She gave him her lawyer's name and phone number. On the drive back to Washington Maxa felt frustrated, a feeling he told himself resembled what other reporters had experienced in their frantic, unsuccessful attempts to interview Ray. The realization brought little comfort. But why had Colleen Gardner changed her story?

The next day, assigned the unpleasant job of rewriting the

Times story, Maxa called Gardner's attorney, Sol Rosen. Why, he asked Rosen, had she told Bob Woodward the opposite of what she told the *Times?* Rosen spoke to the point.

"Mainly to—how shall we say it—to keep *The Post* off the track," Rosen said. "The true story is in the *Times.* The *Times* was working on it and she felt *The Post* getting it might jeopardize the investigation of the *Times.* Too many cooks spoil the broth."

But that was not the complete story. It turned out Sol Rosen had another client, the pressmen's union that had been on strike at *The Post* for nine months. The bitter labor dispute, marked the night the walkout began by violence to the pressroom and a foreman, had resulted in *The Post's* hiring nonunion labor to man the presses. As Rosen eventually admitted, "I'm not out to help Kay Graham sell newspapers." So he had advised his client, Colleen Gardner, to mislead Woodward. And Rosen didn't drop his grudge immediately; Gardner's next interview was with the *Washington Star.*

Maxa stifled his first impulse to rewrite the *Times* story with heavy emphasis on the contradiction between what Gardner had told that newspaper and what she had told Woodward. Finally, two days after the *Times* story, Rosen called Maxa to say Colleen Gardner would consent to an interview by *The Post.*

Gardner was considerably more articulate than Ray. And she had tapes, hours of recordings of conversations with Young and other members of his office staff. In order to document Young's behavior, Gardner had called him to inform him Bob Woodward had visited her apartment to ask questions about the congressman's employment practices. The congressman, not suspecting Gardner was about to blow the whistle on him in *The New York Times* the next week, said he thought another ex-employee was talking to the press; he told Gardner that if she, his wife and he all stuck to the same story, he would deny everything. He thanked Gardner for suggesting that he could attribute the high salaries he paid sexually cooperative women to his deep concern for women's liberation.

The other woman in the *Times* Gardner-Young story, Melanie Hall, verified to the newspaper that Young had made sexual advances toward her too. She quit Young's staff two months before the *Times* story broke to take a job with a Washington law firm, and she ducked the press for months thereafter. But in a phone conversation Gardner had taped earlier, Hall confessed she could not "live with myself" since Young had forced his attentions on her.

Hall recalled how Young had first hired her.

"He looked at my legs and said, 'I'll offer you ten thousand five hundred and if that's agreeable we'll see you in two weeks,'" Hall told Gardner. "He didn't even ask me my skills."

"Did you have on a short skirt?" Gardner asked.

"I just had on a dress. I had on a plain dress. Isn't that funny?"

Then, during a gathering on a boat, Hall found herself alone with the congressman.

"He just leaped on me," she told Gardner. "And I was so ill after that. I had just started dating [a friend]. And I came home and threw up and cried. I didn't think I'd ever quit crying, I was so repulsed.

"I'm just going to tell him no," Hall resolved to Gardner. "I'm committed to someone else and I can't do it. I can't live with myself. I've had a difficult time dealing with it since I last saw him. . . . I feel angry that it was just expected of me."

Young denied to the press that he paid Gardner and Hall handsome salaries to have sex with him in his office and in suburban motels. But he would not answer the question of whether he had had sex with women on his staff. He told reporters he understood why the public worried about the "moral climate" in Congress but he noted politicians were mortals too.

"When a man is holding public office, the greatest thing they can say about him is that he's a man of the people," Young said. "Then when they find out he is, that's when the trouble starts."

Young spoke bravely about having the House ethics committee investigate the charges against him, but that did not come to pass. The ethics committee only investigates a member of the House if the member officially requests such an investigation, or if another representative presents a sworn complaint, or if a private individual—having been refused by three congressmen—submits a sworn complaint, or if the ethics committee itself chooses to investigate.

The committee made no move to conduct an investigation of Young and, despite his statements to the public, Young never wrote a letter to the ethics committee demanding his name be cleared.

In retrospect, Young managed to avoid a congressional investigation probably because other congressmen took his place in the public spotlight. The many reports of sex and congressmen began to get confusing, and pressure to investigate one House member or another was dissipated by the number of men involved in the summer of scandal.

Representative Charles Vanik (D-Ohio) admitted keeping a former prostitute on the payroll of his district office even though she was unable to work because of an illness. Vanik said he hadn't known of his employee's past and that he had continued paying her out of compassion.

Representative Allan T. Howe (D-Utah) garnered considerable press attention when he solicited two women he thought were prostitutes in Salt Lake City; the women were working for the police.

Washington's Metropolitan Police confirmed a news story that reported another congressman, Joe D. Waggonner (D-Louisiana), had also solicited a decoy streetwalker in Washington. But after the police learned they had snared a congressman, Waggonner was released, a customary practice that stemmed from an interpretation of the first article of the Constitution, which says members of Congress shall "be privileged from arrest during their attendance at the session of their respective houses and in going to and returning from the same." For over one hundred years congressmen have claimed immunity in the District of Columbia from prosecution for a variety of offenses under that general clause. And the local police, who had to go to Congress each year for their operating funds, traditionally did not press the issue. In 1976, after Waggonner denied he had been involved in an incident with an undercover policewoman, the assistant police chief in Washington asked the Justice Department for a ruling on congressional immunity. The decision: In the future congressmen will be subject to the same laws in Washington as any other citizen, with the exception of parking violations; cars with congressional license plates may still ignore parking tickets.

Colleen Gardner and Elizabeth Ray, it turned out, were not strangers to each other. Gardner charged, and Ray confirmed, that the two of them had once entertained Senator Mike Gravel (D-Alaska) and then-Congressman Ken Gray aboard Gray's houseboat in 1972. At the time Ray was a receptionist on Gray's staff. Though Gardner said she did not have sex with either man, she told federal investigators she had witnessed Gravel and Ray making love the evening of August 10, 1972, shortly before Congress passed a bill Gray had sponsored to build a national visitors' center in Washington.

As head of the House Public Buildings and Grounds Subcommittee during his last years in Congress, Gray had pushed hard to convert the decaying train station near the Capitol into a combination visitors' center, train depot and parking garage. Gray promised Congress the railroads would pick up the tab, but it was not to be. The visitors' center, still far from completion as of this writing, is one of Washington's bigger boondoggles and may wind up costing taxpayers over fifty million dollars. In the summer of 1972, as Gray worked to launch the center, his counterpart in the Senate was Gravel, then chairman of the Senate Buildings and Grounds Subcommittee. Gravel's support for the project was crucial and an August 10, 1972, newspaper report described Gravel as "not as enthusiastic as Gray" about the center though he "considered the proposal logical."

At the time of Gravel's alleged rendezvous aboard Gray's houseboat, no legislation for the visitors' center was pending before his subcommittee. But the two men had cochaired a meeting the day before concerning a civic center in Washington. And on Gravel's personal calendar for August 10 was a notation to meet Gray for dinner. Pressed by reporters, Gravel said he didn't recall where he had met Gray for dinner, denied he had ever been aboard Gray's houseboat and said he had never met Elizabeth Ray.

Maxa and Clark reread the notes of their initial interviews with Elizabeth Ray. She had told them that a condition of her employment with Gray was that she have sex with his friends. Sometimes, Ray said, Gray would give her the workday off so she could prepare herself for an evening out. The evenings, she said, were spent aboard Gray's houseboat, docked on the Potomac River, where "two men and two women" were usually present. She refused to reveal the names of legislators she entertained at Gray's behest.

Gray told Clark he "never knew what my employees did after work" and that Ray was only on his houseboat "maybe two times for big office parties." When the Gravel story appeared, Gray acknowledged to the *Washington Star* that Ray, Gardner and Gravel "probably" had been aboard his boat at one time or another, which meant Gravel was the only one of the four persons involved who could not recall having set foot on Gray's boat.

Two weeks after *The Post* published its initial story about Wayne Hays, he began discussing suicide with close associates. In private his new wife continued to waver between leaving him and staying; in public she agreed to appear with him at lunch at the House Members' Dining Room, and once, over Memorial Day weekend, she and Hays walked across their front lawn together for the benefit of newsmen and photographers camped in Belmont County.

In Washington congressmen who had remained neutral during the early days of the scandal began getting mail from their constituents demanding the Congress act against Hays. First, the members removed him from his chairmanship of the Democratic Congressional Campaign Committee. Wayne Hays's name was not the signature Democrats facing reelection needed on the bottom of the checks they were scheduled to receive from their party. On June 3, 1976, after chilly meetings with House Speaker Carl Albert and Majority Leader Tip O'Neill, Hays agreed to give up the campaign committee post.

Hays was down but far from out. He telephoned Hubert Humphrey, and approached Barry Goldwater, Jr., on the House floor. He hinted to both that their names might be dragged into the scandal because "a friend of mine on the *Times*" told him Ray had named them as bedmates to investigators. Humphrey, already known to Capitol Hill reporters for his wandering eye, denied he had had an affair with Ray. Representative Goldwater, who had once put Ray in touch with a friend in Hollywood when she was pursuing her acting career, felt Hays was spreading the rumors in order to take some of the heat off himself.

"I'm not telling you this to make you lose any sleep," Goldwater said a solicitous Hays explained to him.

If Hays was trying to spread the scandal, he should have been cheered when, on the first day of June, the *Chicago Tribune* reported that thirteen congressmen and two senators had been involved sexually with Ray and that she had hours of bedroom tapes to prove it. Ray denied the story with a gallant statement. "Have no fear, gentlemen. I will not do anything to hurt you," she told a network reporter that evening. Other reporters could not confirm the story, though a source gave Maxa the name of the electronics store that had supposedly sold Ray several tape recorders. Two salesclerks remembered Ray's purchases, but Maxa spent four hours going through the store's sales receipts for the previous two years and could find none made out to Ray. When Clark and Maxa asked Ray about the tapes, she said she had bought tape recorders to rehearse lines for her acting classes but that she had never taped lovemaking sessions or phone conversations. As of this writing, no tapes have surfaced.

The diversion provided by the sensational story of secret sex tapes did not make life easier for Hays. Instead, it increased public and congressional pressure to resolve the matter quickly. On June 8 he won his primary election by a 20 percent margin, considerably less than the 60 percent margin he normally enjoyed in primary races.

The next day Hays flew from Washington to Pittsburgh and made the hour's drive to Belmont County. That night he took a severe overdose of sleeping pills; friends assumed it was the suicide attempt he had been considering the week before. The press descended on the hospital in Barnesville, Ohio, for a deathwatch.

In the offices of Congress where Wayne Hays had once ruled with an iron hand, the troops were mostly loyal. Judah Best, the attorney who had handled Spiro Agnew's plea bargaining, had instructed Hays's office and committee staffs not to talk to the press. Best took charge of coordinating Hays's entire defense. All office and House Administration Committee business ceased, the rooms taking on the atmosphere of a bunker. FBI agents, House ethics committee investigators and reporters confronted staffers with lists of questions. Obscene letters arrived in the mail. One Arizona man wrote Nina Wilson, Hays's office manager, to say he had a "gorgeous friend who can't type but she's great in bed—can she get a job?"

When Hays emerged from his coma he called the staff director of the House Administration Committee, Doug Frost, who put Hays on his office's speaker-phone. Several office workers, including some summer interns, were invited into Frost's office. There they heard the tired and feeble voice of Wayne Hays.

"I just wanted to tell you all how sorry I am," Hays said from his hospital bed.

There was an uncomfortable silence.

Then Frost tried to cheer up his boss. "What are you sorry about?" he said bravely. "We just want you to come back." One person in the room said later he was dumbfounded by Hays's dejection, surprised the congressman seemed ready to give up his fight.

In a final attempt to encourage Hays, Frost called for a cheer. With awkward enthusiasm the five people in the office gathered around the speaker-phone and mustered some cheers as they halfheartedly applauded Wayne Hays via long-distance.

Until 1975, the House Committee on Standards of Official Conduct was a sleepy group of congressmen with a staff that spent most of its time offering advisory opinions to House members curious about the propriety of accepting free travel from foreign governments, the use of the franking privilege and related matters. It wasn't until the Adam Clayton Powell case that the House, in 1966, took the first step toward drafting a code of ethics. The next year the House got around to setting up a committee to recommend such a code. In 1968 the House finally adopted a code and granted the ethics committee some investigative and enforcement power.

Then, in 1975, the ethics committee made news when it faced the ticklish question of whether Representative Michael Harrington (D-Massachusetts) had violated House rules by revealing CIA activities in Chile, information he had been privy to as a congressman on the foreign affairs committee. The matter was finally dropped when the ethics committee's new chairman, Representative John Flynt (D-Georgia), told the committee Harrington had received the information during a hearing that was not legally a closed session.

In February, 1976, the House ordered the ethics committee

to investigate the leaking of the Otis Pike committee report on United States intelligence operations. That effort, which cost at least $150,000, culminated inconclusively when Daniel Schorr, the CBS newsman who had given the report to the *Village Voice,* refused to identify his source for the confidential House report.

In July of 1976 the House reprimanded its first member since the Powell affair. He was Representative Robert L. F. Sikes (D-Florida), who was found by the ethics committee to have:

——failed to report ownership of stock in Fairchild Industries as required by a House rule.

—invested in a bank he had been instrumental, while a congressman, in establishing.

—sponsored legislation in 1961 removing restrictions on Florida land parcels in which he had a financial interest.

Despite the unusual reprimand, an unrepentant Sikes was reelected in 1976.

Then, several days after *The Post* story about his relationship with Elizabeth Ray appeared, Wayne Hays became the ethics committee's next customer. At the same time a federal grand jury in Washington began hearing testimony on the case, but it was the ethics committee investigation that would prove to be Hays's undoing.

While Hays tried to keep a grip on his disappearing power base in the House, six ethics committee investigators, hired specifically to investigate Wayne Hays, began interviewing current and former members of Hays's staff. Their assignment was a broad one. By an 11–0 vote, the ethics committee had decided on June 2, 1976, to "proceed immediately with a full investigation *of the Hays matter* in conformity with the request made by 28 members and also Mr. Hays himself."

The committee staff began looking for the answers to two major questions: Had Elizabeth Ray done any work for her congressional salary, and was having sex with Hays a condition of employment in his offices?

The answer to the first question was no. Since her return

to Washington from Hollywood, Elizabeth Ray had not done any work for the salary she was paid by the American tax-payer. In the early days of the investigation, two of Hays's attorneys presented the committee with a handsome notebook. The first section of the notebook consisted of letters Ray had typed at different times during her several jobs on Capitol Hill as well as telephone messages she had taken as a receptionist for Ken Gray. (The former congressman had been displaying the messages to reporters since the first week of the scandal; the letters Ray had typed for him were riddled with typographical errors, sometimes dozens to a page. Not all congressmen remembered Ray the same way Gray did. One East Coast representative told friends that when Ray worked for the House Administration Committee—before she left for Hollywood—staffers would return to find telephone messages that read simply: "A man called.")

The second part of the notebook contained letters written by House Administration Committee staffers attesting to Ray's diligence and office skills, a section given little weight by the investigators since Hays's attorneys had solicited the glowing letters. The only person to share Ray's office was the man who had been living with Hays's niece, Paul Panzarella. He did not help the case of his girlfriend's uncle when he told committee investigators he had not seen Ray do any work.

Several years ago Wayne Hays told a reporter that the subject of sex and politicians was overrated. "In fact," he said, "there's a built-in caution if you're a politician. Too many people watching. You get a girl pregnant, that's a story."

Wayne Hays, according to sources close to the ethics committee investigation, did not follow his own advice. In the course of interviewing women who had worked for Hays, the investigators found that Elizabeth Ray was not the only staffer Hays had taken to bed. Nearly a dozen women told investigators that Hays had propositioned them, taken them to bed or hinted they could improve their position and salary by sleeping with him. Several consented.

Before she left for Hollywood, Ray told investigators, she had arranged at least one three-way evening of sex for Hays with a black woman who worked as a secretary on one of Hays's committee staffs. The trio had first gone to dinner and then returned to Ray's apartment where, as one ethics committee staffer put it, "Hays started in Liz and ended up in the other woman." Within two months of the liaison, the secretary was given a thousand-dollar raise. Although investigators suspected the raise was related to her sexual favors, they expected difficulty proving the connection; unlike the executive branch, the legislative branch of government can grant raises at any time for any reason so there was no sure way to prove Hays's approval of a raise for the woman was anything but arbitrary.

The investigators had routinely questioned the secretary before Ray told them of their three-way evening with Hays. When the committee staff moved to call her back, her attorney balked. Had Hays not resigned, and had the ethics committee begun public hearings, the committee would have subpoenaed her.

Ray, accompanied by her attorney, was questioned for three days, each session lasting several hours. Investigators found her to have "a childlike quality with sort of washed-out looks," and they were initially dubious about the preciseness of her recollection of dates, times and places. She referred to no notes. But to the best of the committee staff's knowledge, they found her to be accurate and truthful.

During the investigation Hays tried repeatedly to talk directly with the committee's chairman, John Flynt. The Georgia Democrat refused to take Hays's calls. Flynt told a friend that when he was a young prosecutor in Georgia, his father, a judge, had told him, "Son, a lot of people are going to come to you and want to make deals. There are only three answers to give them: no, no and no."

At one point in the investigation Hays's lead attorney, Judah Best, asked to address the ethics committee in executive session. He told the congressmen that Hays and his wife were seeing a Pittsburgh psychiatrist and that Hays wouldn't even talk with his own counsel about the affair. Which meant Best could not prepare an adequate defense for his client.

"Nobody would believe Hays was that far gone," a staffer said later, "and the climate of opinion on the committee was that if he was, he shouldn't be in the House of Representatives."

Best invited the committee to send psychiatrists to interview Hays—one staffer, in a display of gallows humor, privately suggested sending Masters and Johnson, the sex researchers—but Best's appeal fell on deaf ears. The committee voted to push forward with a public hearing. The committee's mood did not change when Hays resigned as chairman of the House Administration Committee in mid-June while recovering from the drug overdose he called accidental.

The committee staff had initially worried that it would have difficulty quantifying the word "work." How much work had Ray had to perform for her salary? When the investigators could find no evidence of Ray's doing any work after her return from Hollywood, the problem was solved.

And when the testimony women offered about Hays's sexual habits was assembled, said one person involved in the investigation, "You had to say, 'Oh, boy, Liz Ray was not a one-time thing.' "

Wayne Hays knew what the House ethics committee knew. The committee staff produced for Hays's attorneys a list of prospective witnesses for public hearings. Included on the list were the dozen women who could offer ribald testimony that would make banner headlines that would ruin whatever might be left of Wayne Hays's reputation and wreck his already troubled marriage.

After he had tried every avenue to halt the hearings, after he had contacted his old political ally, Democratic Caucus leader Phil Burton, and after he had implored Carl Albert to intercede on his behalf with the House ethics committee, Hays knew he had to resign. It was the only way to avoid public hearings. Since the ethics committee has no jurisdiction over a former congressman, the investigative process would stop and the files would never be made public.

Under Ohio law a congressional candidate must resign prior to eighty days before an election in order for another candidate of the same party to be named to the ballot. Just hours before that deadline, on August 13, 1976, the Columbiana County Board of Elections received a hand-delivered letter from Wayne Hays informing the board he was withdrawing from the November election. Hays's press secretary, Carol Clawson, said the letter had been typed three days earlier and Hays had carried it in his pocket while he weighed his decision to retire.

Hays's statement to the press said he was quitting Congress with "a heavy heart," but "the current state of my health, coupled with the harassment my family and I have taken from *The Washington Post* have led me to conclude that I should step down at the end of my current term."

Nearly three months after it had begun, the Wayne Hays sex scandal was over.

NINE

POST-WATERGATE WASHINGTON

WATERGATE CHANGED men. Charles Colson once lived by the slogan "If you got 'em by the balls, their hearts and minds will follow." After Watergate he got religion. A couple of the President's best men, Jeb Stuart Magruder and Egil Krogh, repudiated their fascination with power. John Dean confessed to blind ambition.

Watergate also changed Washington. In the stonewallers' wake lingered a Post-Watergate Morality, a new ethic that hinted hard guys would no longer finish first in the nation's capital. No more military jets for grouse-hunting jaunts, no more stashed campaign cash. The promise of clean government could be seen in Senator Sam Ervin's jowls that shook with righteous indignation when John Ehrlichman pleaded ignorance of the meaning of the word "surreptitious." Closed-door government was decried regularly as former White House aids faced sentencing in Washington's District Court; everything would be different from now on, people said.

Congress was riding high in the spring of 1976. The nation seemed more interested in the trial of Patricia Hearst than the two political stories that held the attention of Washington: the Presidential primaries and the style of the new President, Gerald Ford. The only hint of political scandal came under the category of history: Judith Campbell Exner's proposal to write a kiss-and-tell book had generated some newspaper and magazine articles speculating on the roving eye of the late John Kennedy. But on the whole official Washington was filled with a pleasant, self-congratulatory feeling of the new Post-Watergate Morality, a sense of well-being heightened by the release of the movie, *All The President's Men,* and the second Woodward-Bernstein book, *The Final Days,* both of which brought the decline and fall of Richard Nixon back as a popular topic for dinner conversation. High crimes and misdemeanors had been exposed and dealt with.

Spiro Agnew was probably the first politician to articulate the subtle change in Washington rules. "The intricate tangle of criminal charges leveled at me . . . boils down to the accusation that I permitted my fund-raising activities and my contract-dispensing activities to overlap in an unethical and unlawful manner," Agnew confessed in his Good Night, America, speech in the fall of 1973. "Perhaps judged by the new Post-Watergate Morality, I did."

Agnew's implication was, of course, that such "overlapping" would have been the clubby thing to do at an earlier time, a reason for celebrating instead of plea bargaining. Prescient in his downfall, Agnew knew there was something in the air. But beyond apologies and political cocktail conversation, would the Post-Watergate Morality be as brief and bothersome as a Washington pollution alert, merely a time to lie low and let it all pass?

Image, Agnew was fond of saying, superceded reality in "this technological age." And in a town like Washington, with so many ready microphones and television cameras, born-again politicians willing to jawbone morality were plentiful, so plentiful that economist J. Kenneth Galbraith predicted "a drawing of morals until healthy stomachs retch." Galbraith was right; any politician who had avoided complicity in Watergate was quick to wear his colors. The freshman congressional class of 1974 swept into the House of Representatives with vows of reform and virtue. Gerald Ford promised an end to "our long national nightmare" and asked for the nation's prayers. He didn't ask for, but he got, a feisty Congress more anxious than ever to examine critically the

White House's requests, an attitude applauded by editorialists and political scientists lamenting the concentration of power in the executive branch.

The Post-Watergate Morality did not fare too badly according to a survey of official Washington conducted by Maxa and Saul Friedman, *Detroit Free Press* Washington correspondent. The reporters found that little things that may or may not have meant a lot were marking a new era:

—The late Senator Philip Hart (D-Michigan), who had never taken much of anything anyhow, nevertheless sent word to his office staff that boxes of candy from visiting lobbyists were to be refused.

—A senator on the District of Columbia Committee stopped accepting gifts of liquor from a prominent Washington businessman.

—Staffers at the Senate Democratic Policy Committee recalled the good old days when they shared batches of free cheese sent regularly by the Wisconsin dairy industry to Wisconsin's Senator Gaylord Nelson. The good old days ended with Watergate.

—One congressional office staff, emboldened by the new morality, refused for the first time in 1973 to address their boss's personal Christmas card envelopes.

—So many senators and representatives began revealing their financial holdings that in 1973 *Congressional Quarterly* published, for the first time, a fat supplement on their disclosures.

Consider the lot of one well-established interest group in Washington, the milk producers' lobby, which traditionally had been an easy touch for a five-figure lecture fee or contribution until the question of milk price supports became tangled in the morass of Watergate. After the scandal some congressmen actually began *returning* so-called "milk money," and except for a legislator with a constituency heavy with cows, bragging about milk lobby connections was about as shrewd as posing for a campaign photo with G. Gordon Liddy.

"The current atmosphere creates problems," acknowledged one milk lobbyist who preferred to remain unnamed. "The taint of milk has made it more difficult to present our point of view. If we were to attempt to persuade members of Congress to take some price support legislation to the floor, it would be much more difficult now than it would have been before."

For a dairy industry booster to refer to "the taint of milk," the times must have grown tough for special interests groups accustomed to working easily behind the scenes to influence legislation.

Other members of the powerful agribusiness lobby in Washington felt the new boldness that Watergate helped bring on. A Republican congressman, Pete Peyser, from a mostly suburban New York district, asked for and received a seat on the House Agriculture Committee so he could affect bills that had long bothered him but about which he knew too little to debate. Eventually Peyser led what ranked as one of the first Great Peanut Debates. In an action that startled congressmen who had spent their legislative lives watching protective bills for peanut barons sail effortlessly through the House, Peyser brought a plastic, foot-long peanut onto the House floor with an oversized, half-billion-dollar price tag attached. Peyser wanted to halt the Agriculture Department's Commodity Credit Corporation from guaranteeing farmers a certain price for a field of peanut plants. Although the debate lasted only half an hour and Peyser lost the vote 100 to 4, that qualified as both a great debate and a close vote in the annals of the American peanut industry.

"More intellectual honesty," said Peyser's administrative assistant when he was asked if Watergate hadn't given reformers on Capitol Hill a little more running room. "There's more attention to detail now, more daring."

Another Hill staffer agreed that any "technical adjustment bill" for industries such as oil or coal now arrived on the floor of the House and Senate burdened with the stigmatic assumption that somewhere, somehow, some industrial giant would profit hugely from the legislation.

Individuals as well as industries had to reconsider politics as usual. One victim of the Post-Watergate Morality was John "Fat Jack" Buckley, a chunky, amiable private investigator who favored Republican clients. One of his old friends, Representative Lawrence Hogan (R-Maryland) had decided to run for governor of Maryland in 1974, and Buckley volunteered to help by conducting what in Washington is politely termed "opposition research," the pursuit of damaging information about an opponent. When word leaked that Buckley, an ex-FBI agent, intended to gumshoe around the Maryland state capital, the media pounced on the story. A bumper sticker appeared that read, "Fat Jack Is Watching." And a flustered Hogan quickly called off his hunt for evidence of Democratic political shenanigans.

Buckley had picked up his nickname from the company he kept during the 1972 Nixon reelection campaign. When not pursuing his government duties as the chief of the Office of Economic Opportunity's investigators division, Buckley scrunched in the back seat of a Washington taxi to photograph internal documents from the Muskie campaign headquarters. He then delivered his film to a man who stood in front of the old Roger Smith Hotel, a man Buckley knew as Ed Warran. The meetings were brief and uncomfortable affairs. Neither man trusted the other.

The James Bond routine blew up in Buckley's face when Ed Warran, who had dubbed Buckley "Fat Jack," turned out to be Watergate conspirator E. Howard Hunt. Hunt told on Buckley, who in turn revealed his arrangement with a semiretired taxi driver. Buckley had suggested the driver volunteer to run messages for the Muskie camp. The driver did and performed his work faithfully, except for the times he detoured to give Buckley a peek at his cargo.

Blinking into the eye of the television camera that covered the Senate Watergate hearings, Buckley was not contrite about his campaign snooping; rather, he was surprised that so much should be made of it, that Georgia's Senator Herman Talmadge should crankily ask, "Do you not think taking someone else's personal documents and photographing them and delivering them elsewhere is theft?"

"No, sir," Buckley answered, "I do not."

"What do you think it is?" Talmadge asked.

"I am not sure what I think it is," Buckley answered.

"You do not think it is singing in a choir, do you?"

No, Buckley testified, adding that he was just engaging in a little political espionage, some of the old infiltration and penetration, the stuff "that occurs in every major election that happened in this country."

With Buckley's notoriety and with Washington poised on the brink of a new morality, all it took was a hint in 1973 that Buckley intended to help Hogan in his campaign against the corruption and cronyism that had long marked Maryland politics. Buckley, by all accounts, had lifted not a finger before word of his intentions leaked and Hogan scrambled to field the reaction. The congressman admitted to an error in judgment.

"Obviously to avoid evil you have to avoid the appearance of evil and, looking back, the congressman didn't look at Buckley in the context of the Muskie thing," Hogan's press aid said. The incident illustrated one problem with the Post-Watergate Morality. Hogan was in a bind, as his press secretary explained: "We had rumors of wrongdoing but it would be irresponsible to say anything without checking. But if he tried to check, everyone will say that Hogan is unleashing his private eyes. There are areas that may not be illegal but may be unethical or political—certainly proper areas to look into. Since all this publicity of Fat Jack, the congressman has the problem of how to look into these things."

(As it turned out, Hogan and Buckley might have performed a public service. In 1976 the victor in that 1974 gubernatorial race, Marvin Mandel, was indicted by a grand jury in Baltimore on a host of charges involving mail fraud and racketeering.)

Other incidents demonstrated that Washington in the mid-Seventies was becoming more image-conscious in the aftermath of its White House scandals. Campaign veteran Bob Keefe of the Democratic National Committee was priming one of the Dominican Republic's finest, sliding the big cigar in and out of his mouth, moistening the wrapping leaves as he settled his large frame into a seat to hear an attorney lecture on congressional financing in the upcoming 1974 campaigns.

"I want to know," a member of the audience asked the young attorney, "what do you do when a contributor refuses to give you his name and address as required by law?"

"Use a dummy name, John Doe it or something," the attorney replied glibly.

Bob Keefe, his political morality seasoned by stints as Senator Birch Bayh's administrative assistant, staffer for the political arm of the AFL-CIO and as the executive director of the Democratic National Committee, knew all about the John Doe contributors. He postponed lighting his cigar.

"Uh, no, I'm sure you can't dummy it," he interrupted from his seat. "You have to get the real information."

The John Buckley affair and lesser incidents such as Bob Keefe's careful recognition of the new, tougher campaign contributions laws seemed to bode well for Washington. Senator Robert Dole said that since Watergate he no longer felt comfortable hitching a weekend ride to Kansas aboard the private plane of a businessman friend because he felt compelled to report the trip as a campaign contribution. One southern senator said he had stopped requisitioning a military plane when he felt like going home for a hunting trip. Senators Herman Talmadge and Hubert Humphrey were prepared to kill a proposal to repeal antitrust exemptions granted earlier to several dairy cooperatives. Then the morning of the Senate vote, columnist Jack Anderson listed the milk co-op contributions to Democrats, including Talmadge and Humphrey; the two took no position and the measure passed 63-7. It was beginning to look as though politics was becoming a more honorable profession.

The Senate emerged well from Watergate, Sam Ervin's televised hearings having given national display to the rogues of Nixon's White House. Even the House, which suffers from the stigma of being the "lower body," was conceded to have conducted itself with dignity. At least two members of the House Judiciary Committee that had laid the impeachment groundwork, Peter Rodino (D-New Jersey) and Barbara Jordan (D-Texas), earned national reputations for their grace and eloquence. Such honor normally falls on the shoulders of senators, who generally consider themselves cut more from the statesman mold than their more numerous, more parochial colleagues on the House side of Capitol Hill.

No one could have predicted that the scandal that would envelop Wayne Hays—the only powerful committee chairman challenged by the ambitious freshman congressional class of 1974 who had been permitted to retain his seat—would bring such dishonor on Congress so quickly. No one could have known the higher expectations of the Post-Watergate Morality that Congress helped foster would wreak such vengeance that incumbents would be forced on the defensive when they faced the voters in the fall of 1976. It was supposed to have been a time of glory, especially for the large number of first-termers proud of the reforms they had helped effect. Instead, a record number of congressmen retired—eight senators and thirty-one representatives. And for the first time in recent history, many congressmen actually campaigned against Congress as they sought to outdo opponents who were gaining political mileage by making an issue of congressional waste and venality.

Most serious congressional misbehavior—the kind that can get a man indicted—stems from selling influence for hard cash. A Library of Congress survey found of the sixteen members of Congress indicted between 1955 and 1975, a dozen were convicted or pleaded guilty to charges such as tax evasion or accepting kickbacks from businesses or staffers.

Historically the penalties against congressional felons have been light. In 1856 a drunken congressman shot and killed an uppity waiter in a downtown Washington hotel and never served a day for his deed, a state of justice that hasn't changed much. In 1974, Brooklyn Democrat Frank Brasco was convicted of taking a bribe from a local trucking company allegedly controlled by the Mafia in return for steering a post office contract in the firm's direction. His sentence: three months in jail and a ten-thousand-dollar fine. Representative Bertram Podell, another Brooklyn Democrat, pleaded guilty several months later to receiving money for helping win federal permission for an airline to fly more profitable routes. His sentence was six months in jail and a five-thousand-dollar fine. Ex-Representative J. Irving Whalley (R-Pennsylvania) received an eleven-thousand-dollar fine and three years' probation when he pleaded guilty in 1973 to charges of mail fraud stemming from accusations that he forced his staff to kick back part of their salaries to him.

Special favors for friends and moneyed interest groups are temptations almost every senator and representative faces. It is rare that a clear quid pro quo is proven against a congressman, the legislative and regulatory processes being complex ones in which influence can be brought to bear subtly. But under the campaign financing disclosure laws passed in the wake of the Watergate scandal, the public at least has access to contribution records maintained by the Federal Election Commission. On public file, then, is a list of the contributors to the campaigns of all elected federal officials, though learning the identity of some of the "political action" committees maintained by large corporations is not always so easy. Many companies and unions solicit political donations from their executives and members, consolidate that money and donate it to friendly legislators. The theory is that one five-hundred-dollar donation from, say, a bank has more effect (that is, gets more respect from a congressman) than one hundred five-dollar donations from people who happen to work for that same bank. To avoid publicity some groups give themselves vague names. Thus the Tacoma Fund is really the name of the Weyerhaeuser Company's political contribution group. The Good Government Club represents the Southern Arizona Bank and Trust Company, while the Good Government *Committee* is the Wells Fargo Bank's political fund.

(To the everlasting gratitude of Washington's investigative reporters, another journalist, Ed Zuckerman, and his wife, Amelia, spent over a year cross-indexing the names of registered lobbyists, political action groups and registered foreign agents, and in 1975 they issued their own guide called *The Washington Influence Directory*. The volume permits researchers and reporters to scan lists of political contributors or innocuously named political action groups to see if they are affiliated with known interest groups.)

Even in the post-Watergate era senators and representatives who should have known better fell prey to the blandishments of corporations or business friends. Four days after he won reelection to the Senate in 1974, Georgia Democrat Herman Talmadge, a former member of the Ervin Watergate committee, treated his Washington staff to some rest and relaxation at a plush resort owned by a corporate giant who had every reason to curry Talmadge's favor. Though Talmadge's staff refused to identify the corporation to *The Washington Post* in 1976, it was the major timber concern, Union Camp Corporation, which owns thousands of acres of forest land in Georgia and other southern states.* Talmadge is chairman of the Senate Agriculture and Forestry Committee. At the invitation of Union Camp, about one third of Talmadge's office staff was feted at the company's Palmetto Bluff, South Carolina, hunting lodge for a couple of days. Their air fare was paid for from Talmadge's excess

---

* In the summer of 1976, when Maxa pressed Talmadge's administrative assistant, Roger Wade, for the name of the corporation, Wade said it would be impolite because other politicians would nag the company for similar invitations.

campaign funds; Union Camp's hospitality was not recorded as a campaign contribution by Talmadge.

When he was governor of Georgia, Jimmy Carter was also a guest at Union Camp's lodge. When news of Gerald Ford's golfing trips, courtesy of U.S. Steel, made the newspapers during the 1976 presidential campaign, Carter disclosed his vacations at Union Camp's and Brunswick Pulp Paper Company's resorts. Carter said, "It would have been better not to" accept such corporate kindness, and his press secretary said Carter would not do it again in light of different standards imposed since the Watergate scandals and campaign financing disclosures.

It was in this post-Watergate climate, this season of higher expectations, that Wayne Hays and other members of the 94th Congress had the misfortune to achieve prominence.

TEN

POWERSEX

WHEN SHE DRIVES through Washington traffic, she is surrounded by the rock music of the Jefferson Starship, her tape deck pumping stereo sound through four speakers in her Cadillac Seville. She is thrilled with the car, delighted that it is expensive and plush but not too flashy. The personalized license plates with her initials might be a bit showy, but why not? She has hustled herself off the mean streets of Washington, where every twenty-dollar hooker owes her soul to a pusher and a pimp. It took a couple of years, but she made the climb from streetwalker to hotel bar trick and now—her body still lithe, her face only showing the hardness a bit around the eyes—she works by referral only and no one touches a blond hair on her head without putting at least one hundred dollars on the nightstand.

Call her Dolly—the name by which most men know her isn't her real one anyway—and color her rich and classy. She is one of Washington's high-priced call girls who everyone thinks shares the beds of the city's powerful men and therefore knows plenty of Washington's secrets.

She may share those beds occasionally, but she doesn't know any secrets because Dolly doesn't *care* about them. She has no idea how many members of Congress have used her services—she thinks that as a group congressmen are cheapskates—and didn't even know she had met Wilbur Mills until she saw his face splashed across the nation's front pages along with Fanne Foxe's. Then Dolly rummaged through her Christmas cards from the previous year and, sure enough, there was a card from the man she had once entertained, season's greetings from one Wilbur Mills. She decided to save it.

Born to a large family whose father moved around the country during her childhood, Dolly is a cool blond who does not share the illusions of the small-town girls who arrive on Capitol Hill eager to work for low pay and a chance to find high-powered romance. Dolly says she doesn't have time for romance. Besides servicing individual customers, she and another call girl have a specialty act for bachelor parties: For one hundred dollars each they circulate at stag parties, strip, make love to each other and retire to bedrooms to entertain men willing to pay another fifty dollars to fraternize.

"It turns the men on and they get to see the merchandise before they buy," she explains with the casualness of a shopgirl.

Dolly entertains most of her clients in her neat frame townhouse on Capitol Hill—"It's the best location," she says —where her neighbors are oblivious to her profession. She owns a Washington boutique with the woman who is her partner in the lesbian act. The boutique, which Dolly plans to run full-time when she retires from prostitution, doesn't make much money yet; she subsidizes the operation with part of the thousand dollars a week she claims she earns from the calls that come over her home telephone. Washington has more phones per capita than any other city in the United States and, in her own way, Dolly contributes to that statistic: She has three lines into her townhouse so a customer need never suffer a busy signal.

Sex-for-pay is plentiful in Washington. Five blocks from the White House, on Fourteenth Street, hookers walk the sidewalks from ten in the morning until 3 A.M. If you're shy, they'll hop in the passenger seat of your car as you wait for the light to change, an aggressive marketing technique that has led the police to put decoy policewomen on the street in an attempt to reduce the number of male customers who cruise the Thomas Circle area. If front seat sex is distasteful, over one hundred massage parlors cater to a busy trade. With names like Tiffany's Velvet Touch, The Harem, Lady Godiva, The Play Pen and Foxy Lady, the parlors charge from twenty-five dollars for simple masturbation to over one hundred for kinky sex. Major credit cards are accepted, and the 1976 Yellow Pages ad for one of the area's oldest massage parlors, the Tiki-Tiki, sported the official "Welcome Visitors —Bicentennial" emblem.

Not interested in cruising Fourteenth Street or visiting a massage parlor? Doctors may have given it up long ago, but in Washington working women make house calls. The unofficial prince of that industry is Hal O'Brien. From a cramped downtown office overlooking Connecticut Avenue, O'Brien works his telephones in a business that has apparently succeeded in skirting laws against prostitution. A lonely gentleman can phone O'Brien and arrange for a visit from one of his dozen young women, who will lie down nude on her customer's bed.

What happens next Hal O'Brien doesn't want to know, though he supposes "on every assignment, a woman is getting raped." And that's the rub. As O'Brien makes clear in his lengthy phone recitation to a customer, the naked lady on the bed will never solicit sex because that would be illegal. Instead, for sixty-nine dollars she allows herself to be raped for an hour. (The slow rapist must pay an additional one dollar for each minute over the hour.) Then the woman chooses not to report the rape.

The customer presumably tells no one, the woman does likewise and O'Brien, well, he only knows that he sent a woman to a hotel room. As the middleman, he gets sixteen of the sixty-nine dollars as well as free sex once a week from each woman in his stable. The most lucrative of his call girls keeps in touch with O'Brien via a radio telephone in her car.

O'Brien's command post is a cramped office that he keeps at a chilly temperature. He believes cold air kills bacteria so, even as his window air-conditioners run in the winter, he stays dressed in his summer uniform: baggy Bermuda shorts that reveal pasty white legs, a rumpled T-shirt that covers an ample gut, and slippers. He is a self-described loner whose only pleasure is sex. He grew up in New Hampshire, the oldest of six children in a poor family whose father died young. When he entered the sex business in 1959, O'Brien offered himself as a stud for women. Free. He still lists that service in the Yellow Pages under "Insemination, Artificial," though O'Brien stresses there is nothing artificial about it.

If a woman chose O'Brien to father her child and then had a son who resembled O'Brien, the boy would look much like a leprechaun.* Short, pudgy, with sandy hair and a giggle, O'Brien single-handedly runs his sex circus with the help of fifteen telephone lines. When O'Brien's office refrigerator —which isn't grounded—switches on, all the lines ring and blink crazily.

Like Dolly, O'Brien doesn't know if his women have catered to congressmen. He is satisfied that his sixty-nine-dollar price tag prevents "undesirable" men from patronizing his service, and he notices an upsurge in his hotel trade when banking groups or lawyers' associations hold conventions in town. But neither he nor his women ask their clients' names.

Both Dolly and Hal O'Brien operate on the fringes of powersex, a world in which different elements of Washington —public officials, private detectives, lobbyists and call girls— come together for their mutual satisfaction. It is a dark side of the nation's capital where discretion is the key to survival. The people who have been caught in the act of enjoying powersex have been careless or overconfident, too sure of

* A 1965 FBI report described him this way: "O'Brien was sloppy in appearance, arrogant, uncouth, pompous, a fast-talker who attempted to dominate the conversation."

their clout and position to think their after-hours activities would become public. When Bobby Baker became a household name, magazines blossomed with stories about his nightlife and women. When Elizabeth Ray told of her affair with Wayne Hays, it wasn't long before the House ethics committee confronted Hays's lawyer with a list of the congressman's girlfriends. When the spotlight of publicity focused on Wilbur Mills, the glare ruined his career and gave the nation a glimpse of archetypal powersex: an influential congressman spending his nights in an alcoholic haze at Washington striptease houses and B-girl bars.

There are some places in Washington where powersex can almost be seen and touched. The Gaslight Club, a key club featuring women in scanty costumes, is one such place. Founded during the 1950s by a nephew of Dwight Eisenhower, the Gaslight Club is in an unmarked townhouse two blocks from the White House. Its clientele is a rich mixture of private eyes, lobbyists, association executives, politicians and lawyers.

The person who enjoys a monopoly on Washington area beauty pageants, a swarthy man with a pockmarked complexion, dines at the Gaslight Club with some of his pageants' contestants.

The head of a national association is a regular customer, his table usually filled with striking-looking women who smile broadly as he introduces them to close friends whom they will want to get to know better. He has also approached women to encourage them to "turn pro," that is, to sell their sexual services.

A lobbyist arrives every night flanked by young women, none of whom is his wife. One of the few times in 1976 he did bring his wife, special instructions were given to the regular waitresses lest they reveal her husband's secret swinging. Sometimes the lobbyist provides a woman for the congressman whose company he keeps.

To the casual observer the Gaslight Club is an amiable, low-lit place where men like to drink and talk. Some eyebrows were raised shortly after the 1976 election, however, when a lawyer prominent in then-President Ford's reelection campaign committee gave a bachelor dinner for a friend about to be married, an evening that featured an attractive nude blond (by day she worked in a dentist's office) who sat next to the groom. But that, after all, was a private party of men so well-connected that the Gaslight staff was told the party was a gathering of executives from a major computer firm.

In Maryland's suburban Prince Georges County, there are supper clubs and bars known as favorite hangouts for Washington's organized crime figures (the action is generally bookmaking), and some of the men and women who frequent those nightspots work hard to make the big leagues by developing friendships with political figures. Elizabeth Ray, for example, spent time in a Prince Georges County after-hours club with small-time businessmen friends before she became a familiar figure on Capitol Hill. In those circles, status symbols for women are Corvettes with personalized license plates. For men, women are the status symbols, and no one asks the men how they make their living or if they are married.

In other parts of America, men and women can frolic with less concern about their image than can the public people in Washington. A man's reputation is usually his best currency in the political world and should private indiscretions become public knowledge, a career can be wrecked.

And people are watching.

The polite phrase is "opposition research," but, in fact, digging dirt on politicians is as much a part of Washington as the Jefferson Memorial. Private eyes hire out to comb the past of a candidate, sometimes paid by the candidate's opponent, other times paid by an organization that has reason to want to thwart an individual's election.

Prior to the 1972 election, every senator received a letter from a suburban Washington private detective firm that began this way: "Dear Senator, I cordially invite you to utilize the services of our firm which is a general agency capable of meeting your investigative needs in the national capital area."

Private eyes don't have to look hard for trouble. In Washington even a domestic case can have severe political repercussions. Just after Lyndon Johnson's reelection, Washington private eye Richard Bast was assembling evidence for a divorce case against Washington socialite and Johnson confidante Barbara Howar. When Bast crashed through the door of Howar's sixty-dollar-a-day hotel room in Montego Bay, he found (and photographed) her in bed with a senior White House official who was married.

The President's assistant eventually left Washington to find employment in private industry. Howar returned distraught to Washington and was temporarily frozen out of Washington society. Both the White House aide and the married senator with whom Barbara Howar had another affair, Birch Bayh of Indiana, were spared the political embarrassment of being named correspondents in a divorce case because the Howars reconciled. Although Bast had monitored Howar's conversations with Bayh, the senator's name did not surface in print as her lover until years later. Two years after the Montego Bay incident, the Howars divorced.

The research staffs of both political parties maintain confidential files on congressmen from the opposition party. At the right time, a damaging bit of informaton leaked to the right reporter might prove advantageous. J. Edgar Hoover's files on congressmen were so sensitive he kept them in his own office, using them to titillate Presidents such as Lyndon Johnson, who loved to hear dirty little secrets about his former colleagues in the House and Senate. More than one congressman has wondered aloud just what Hoover's files might say about him. And any lobbying group in Washington, whether it's a high-powered special interest group or a modestly funded "do-gooder" group, stays briefed on the politics and personalities of the legislators who preside over their interests.

The experienced Washington watcher sometimes gathers information by cultivating the trust of the men close to those in power, the highly paid aides who labor in the shadows of politicians, men with entrée to the sanctums of power but who share none of the fame. Resentment can build in those men—there is little glory and sometimes even less self-respect in serving as a forty-thousand-dollar-a-year errand boy—and sometimes they grow bitter and talkative.

Reporters and political operatives searching for scandal often go to a public figure's opponents, or to an interest group with an ax to grind; those sources often know the unflattering parts of a person's history and, if protected, don't mind sharing their information. (Not all damaging information in Washington is lurid. In Senator Thomas Eagleton's case, which produced more public sympathy than voyeuristic delight, a tipster's calls to a Midwest newspaper with hints of Eagleton's mental treatments started a chain of events that dashed his chances of being a vice-presidential candidate in 1972.)

The public record also holds useful information if examined carefully. To whom does a congressman owe money? Who are his big contributors? What is his voting record? Has he introduced many special "private bills?" What is the background of his staff? Does he belong to any clubs that discriminate in the choosing of members? If he is a lawyer, who were his clients before he was elected to Congress? From whom does he receive lecture fees? Does he maintain an office account? Does he like to junket?

A suspicious answer to just one of those questions can spell political trouble for a representative or senator with aggressive enemies.

Politics and sex, like politics and money, have always gone together well in Washington. In 1901 a congressional wife,

Mrs. John Logan, produced a formidable book called *Thirty Years in Washington* in which she attempted to describe the entire city, from the Secretary of State who "very largely holds in his hands the national honor" to the lazy "colored people" who were always "out at elbow, loose all over, and content whenever the sun shines on them."

(About seventy-six years later Gerald Ford's agriculture secretary, Earl Butz, would modify that canard somewhat and be forced to resign. Mrs. Logan, however, included the line in a chapter called "The Omnipresent Negro.")

She didn't call it powersex, turn-of-the-century prose being what it was, but Mrs. Logan made her point: "It is a noticeable fact that the [Senate] waiting room is frequently thronged with women," she wrote. "A number of them are conversing with senators; others are gazing towards the doors which lead to the Senate. Some seem to be waiting with eager eyes and anxious faces; others are leaning back upon the sofas in attitudes of luxurious listlessness. Do you ask why they are here? Are they studying the stately proportions and exquisite finesse of the anteroom? Not at all. It is not devotion to the aesthetic arts nor the inspiration of patriotism which brings these women here, but necessity, whether real or imaginary. Sometimes it is their only way to success in securing employment or a hearing of their grievances and claims."

Even earlier, in the 1830s, a woman writer named Anne Royall took great glee in skewering Congress with her pen: "But of all sights that ever disgraced a city, a house of Legislation, I mean, and one which most astonishes a stranger, is the number of abandoned females which swarm in every room and nook in the capitol, even in daylight. . . . I have seen these females with brazen fronts, seated in the galleries listening to the debates."

For congressmen the state of the art of meeting women has become more sophisticated, though some Hill staffers' most vivid recollection of Elizabeth Ray was of her standing just off the floor of the House, buttonholing congressmen with a come-hither smile when she was in need of employment. In the 1970s the safest way for a congressman to procure a woman for sex is to depend on a trusted male aide. Oftentimes the staffer serves as a go-between for the congressman and a woman, both of whom then avoid any misunderstanding or complications. And the congressman maintains some freedom to deny everything.

A former Senate employee sometimes arranged the meeting place for congressmen and their girlfriends. One of the most frequent spots for trysts: the Quality Inn at the foot of Capitol Hill, which features underground parking with an elevator that serves all ten floors. Which allows a congressman to bypass the lobby of the motel. The Hill employee would visit the motel earlier in the day, register under his name and then pass the room key to the congressman. The latter and his girlfriend could then drive directly into the parking garage and ride the elevator to their room. No muss, no fuss, no evidence.

Later the Senate employee would be reimbursed for the rental of the motel room and, generally, be given a handsome tip for his trouble. The only person not always delighted with the arrangement was the man's wife, who was sometimes suspicious of the numerous motel room charges found on her husband's monthly credit card statement.

If sex was to be purchased some congressmen relied until the middle of 1976 on the discretion of a man we'll call Howard Gardner, who left Washington not because business was bad but because he disliked the city's summer humidity.

Gardner came to Washington in 1974 to begin a high-priced escort service, a trade he had learned several years before while studying law at night at a Midwest university. During the day he sold insurance. But Gardner's life changed when he filed suit on behalf of some local massage parlor owners under attack by the city fathers.

"I was making about twenty-five thousand dollars a year

but I saw these massage parlor owners sleeping until noon and making about seventy thousand," Gardner recalled, "and I thought, hey, I'm in the wrong business."

So he moved to Chicago and later New York. When he arrived in Washington he met an old friend who worked on the Hill. When Gardner told him he had been earning a living running escort services, his friend was enthusiastic about local prospects. He encouraged Gardner to give him some of his business cards because, he said, Congress was filled with older men who made no secret of the fact that that they were on the prowl for attractive and available young women.

"So I ran ads for models, hostesses and escorts, which is really the hardest part of the business. You talk to forty women on the phone. Maybe you talk in person to ten of those and out of that ten, only one works out," Gardner said. "I didn't want average-looking women. In most cities I'd tried to get your nurse or school teacher with education but not much money. They don't consider themselves hookers, you know. But in Washington I met so many really talented, beautiful, mainly southern women that came to D.C. with intelligence and brains but just couldn't get any other job and had no desire to do anything but screw their brains out with powerful men.

"Poise. They had a lot of poise. I found that one of their main reasons for being in D.C. was that they just dug being around politicians and powerful people—they would have done it for free. It was just too good to be true, which is why I'm thinking of returning to Washington even though I can't stand the summers there."

Gardner's business was entirely by word of mouth, no advertisements. His rates were one hundred dollars an hour (which he would split with the woman) or three hundred dollars a night (he would receive two hundred of that). Besides liking the women he recruited in Washington, Gardner said he enjoyed a steady clientele. Once a politician began using his service, Gardner said, he would stay with him because the fewer people who knew his sexual predilections, the better. He said he was mildly surprised to find his biggest customers were not the young, single' congressmen but the older, more conservative ones from rural states.

Gardner accepted American Express cards under the name of a messenger service, itself a handy ruse that enabled his women to visit clients at their offices. They would arrive with an oversized envelope and enjoy access to offices and apartment buildings with a minimum of questions.

Gardner acknowledged being asked by third parties to provide prepaid sex for men.

"People said to me, 'I want a girl who Senator XYZ would not know and who could pass herself off to the senator for free,'" Gardner recalled. He generally refused such deals because "I suspected something a little funny was going on and if it blew up, the senator would see to it that I lost business. That's the problem with Washington—if you piss someone off, you can really get hassled."

Others, such as the hundred-dollar-an-hour Capitol Hill call girl Dolly, had no hesitation providing sex for someone even if it was paid for by another person, a situation she said was not uncommon in Washington.

"Getting laid is considered kinky sex in Washington," Nancy Collins, a *Washington Post* reporter, once observed.

By and large the generalization is correct. For all the furtive sex that goes on in official Washington, it is made to seem daring and sometimes sinister largely because the stakes are so high, because the pressure is so great for public officials to conform to an impossible moral standard.

Certainly there are interesting exceptions. One congressman is fond of mixing a capsule of amyl nitrate with his extramarital lovemaking. And one congressman's mistress gave him a present of lacy, peek-a-boo black lingerie and underwear just so he could hand it back to her for use in their favorite motel room at Christmas, 1975. But usually official Washington's sexual proclivities are no more interesting than those of men and women anywhere. Except that instead of affection, gifts or even memorable lovemaking, the Washington woman is expected to be satisfied with the mere presence of an important man. *Post* reporter Sally Quinn wrote of a woman friend who received a pair of American eagle bookends from her congressional lover, a gift the senator handed out routinely to constituents. And the women Clark and Maxa talked with about congressional sex had few stories of exquisite lovemaking; the women said they found legislators rather selfish in bed.

The romances of Capitol Hill do not always have happy endings. One woman told Clark and Maxa a common story of powersex: A young woman becomes dazzled by a congressman, loves him, is left by him. Except this young woman was left with something more than memories: a son by the congressman, who had a family of his own in his home district.

In 1963, on Delores Craft's eighteenth birthday, she was arrested during a raid on a Waldorf, Maryland, gambling club in the company of Mafia figures. She was at the club as the date of Washington restaurateur Duke Zeibert, who would become famous thirteen years later as Elizabeth Ray's frequent escort. Craft, a brunette model, was a long way from home.

She had come to Washington from a small town in West Virginia, and she made money in the nation's capital by acting in trade association movies and modeling for such things as the sculpture of Jacqueline Kennedy at Washington's wax museum. She spent her evenings at the after-work haunts of men of power: Duke Zeibert's restaurant, or the high-priced restaurant at the foot of Capitol Hill called The Rotunda, or assorted congressional receptions.

She was an attractive woman, wise beyond her years, and when she was arrested in suburban Washington—as Zeibert frantically crammed his gambling winnings down a toilet—no one suspected she had just turned eighteen. The newspapers said she was twenty-three.

Two months after her arrest Craft left for a vacation in

Europe with a girlfriend. In Paris, while she waited in the lobby of the posh Georges V Hotel for an operator to place a long-distance call, a charming American gentleman struck up a conversation. He was a lanky, pipe-smoking southern congressman.

The congressman spent that night with Craft, she said, after a grand dinner at Maxim's. They were together during most of the congressman's junket, too, and she said that an hour before he was to leave from Orly Field for Washington, he persuaded her to accompany him. She still has a copy of his House of Representatives check made out to Pan American Airlines, a memento she has kept along with a cache of letters from him.

In Washington, Craft said she moved in with the congressman at his Hill apartment. For nine months, Craft said, they lived together, from October, 1963, to June, 1964. In June, she became pregnant and she left to live with her mother in Virginia. She said she paid a near-stranger to marry her so her child would not be illegitimate.

Although Craft was never on the public payroll, her younger sister (seventeen years old) was employed for three months in the congressman's office soon after Craft left to have her child. The sister was paid fifteen hundred dollars, according to Craft, for doing little work; it was understood that the money was meant for her older sister.

In December of 1965 the congressman, while not admitting he was the father of Craft's son, paid her sixty-five hundred dollars to release him from any future claim of paternity, according to an agreement on file with the D.C. Corporation Counsel.

The congressman, now retired from Congress, told Clark and Maxa he saw Craft socially during his years in Washington but only gave her the sixty-five hundred dollars because "a lot of times when you're in public life the better part of valor is to avoid noise."

In another, very different case, a woman who had worked part-time for a senator received a year's worth of paychecks in the mail, guilt money she told Clark and Maxa, from her employer who had wanted to have an affair with her but didn't.

It had started routinely enough. She was in her forties, divorced, with children. It was 1969. He was a young, exciting new face on Capitol Hill, a senator with great plans. He had seen her at a political meeting and asked an aide to call her about joining his staff. She only wanted to work part-time. He agreed to pay her nine thousand dollars a year and, at her request, permitted her to work out of her Washington home.

"I was the first and only person not from his state who he hired," she said later. "I realize in retrospect there must have been some fatal attraction I didn't know about."

There was. The senator repeatedly asked her to come to his office to chat. They "talked about everything under the sun—nothing I could take much offense to, but I couldn't get much work done," the woman would recall later.

"One evening we were in New York and the whole staff was sitting around a room, and it became apparent to me that he was giving me an inordinate amount of attention. He talked freely about his poor marriage. He said he had a medium who told him he was going to be divorced by April."

Then, after she had been working for the senator for six months, he asked her to meet him somewhere alone. She refused. He asked her to set up two committee hearings in out-of-the-way locations because he wanted to consult with two mediums in those places. She said no.

"He was a very attractive man," she said, "I won't deny that. And I was certainly turned on by him but I realized it was very inappropriate . . .

"Then one night he and one of his aides came to my house to do some mystical thing. They put cloths on the windows but by then I thought the whole thing was so bizarre it had to end. I needed the job but he was beginning to show his feelings to me quite openly. So I agreed with the administrative assistant that they'd send my work to me at home. For the next year the paychecks kept coming.

"I had enough of the old Puritan ethic in me that I didn't like this but his A.A. said we'd get things straightened out and I'd be able to do some work. After three months I stopped asking for work."

The checks kept coming. She cashed them, guiltily. Sometimes the senator's A.A. would accept her calls, sometimes he would not. She wrote letters; no answers. Then, one year after she stopped working, the A.A. called to say there would be no more checks.

"I said, 'fine, it's about time,' and I chided him for not returning my calls," she said.

Later she and the senator appeared together on a panel in whose topic they had a mutual interest. The senator didn't mention their past dealings. She couldn't be certain he even knew that she had received a year's pay for not working. She knew the moral of the lesson: There is very little accountability on Capitol Hill.

Powersex lends a very literal meaning to the cliché that "politics makes strange bedfellows." Several weeks after the Hays-Ray story, Representative Robert Leggett (D-California) walked into Ben Bradlee's office to tell an incredible story of the twists and turns a congressman's personal life can take.

Leggett had been prompted to make his confession to *The Post* by a Bradlee column he had read days before. In a signed column on *The Post*'s op-ed page, Bradlee had explained why *The Post* decided not to run a Jack Anderson column alleging Senator Harry Byrd (Ind.-Virginia) had made sexual demands on a female constituent who needed his help in locating her husband, who had left her with two children and no support. (Byrd denied the allegations in the Anderson column.)

Leggett had been happy to read Bradlee's denunciation of

the column and the accompanying statement by Bradlee that "public persons' private lives tend to be their own business unless their personal conduct is alleged to violate the law or interfere with performance of a public job." He was happy to read those words because for months a *Post* reporter, Maxine Cheshire, had been investigating Leggett's relationship with the Korean-born secretary to House Speaker Carl Albert, Sook Nai Park Thomson, known in Washington as Suzi Thompson.

Leggett began an affair with Thomson in 1973. She was known in Washington as an attractive woman who managed to stretch a modest salary far enough to entertain members of Congress lavishly. She had been very close to Albert and had often introduced South Korean diplomats to congressmen, sometimes escorting legislators on grand trips to South Korea. Eventually she became a prime figure in a federal investigation of South Korean influence peddling in Washington.

Leggett began introducing statements of support for South Korea into the *Congressional Record,* and in February of 1976 Cheshire reported that he, along with Representative Joseph Addabbo (D-New York), was under investigation for accepting bribes from the South Korean government.

When he walked into Bradlee's office in July of 1976, Leggett apparently wanted to tell the newspaper the details of his complicated private life in the hope Bradlee would realize his problems were strictly personal, not deserving of newsprint. So as a tape recorder ran, with the congressman's permission, Leggett told Bradlee, Cheshire and another reporter working on the South Korean story, Scott Armstrong, about his life since he was elected to Congress in 1963. In later interviews he elaborated for Armstrong.

His first affair had been with a Capitol Hill secretary (not Suzi Thomson). She became pregnant. She turned down Leggett's suggestion that she have an abortion. She had the baby and Leggett bought a modest home for his girlfriend.

She quit her job and, within a year of having her first child, she became pregnant again.

Leggett bought her a larger home in a Washington suburb. He discussed divorcing his wife, but he continued to live with her and their three children. He began to grow apart from his mistress; he was a liberal, she was becoming a Goldwater Republican. Though they stopped seeing each other, he continued to support her with about twenty thousand of his annual fifty-thousand-dollar income. She insisted on title to her house; he signed his wife's signature to effect transfer of the property.

In 1975 Leggett's wife learned of her husband's second family. They considered divorce, but Mrs. Leggett stayed with her husband, though she asked him to sign over his interest in *their* home to her.

Leggett bet incorrectly. On July 18 *The Post* ran all of the foregoing, and more, in a front page story headlined "Robert Leggett: Life of Immense Complications." It was an unusual story, beginning with its soft news lead: "When Rep. Robert Leggett came to Washington in January, 1963, the lyrics and score of the musical 'Camelot' resounded often through the residential quarters of the White House."

The story went on to describe the life Leggett had made for himself in Washington, the town to which he had come with so much hope and promise. One paragraph in the story gave a clue to why *The Post* felt Leggett's tale should have been published: In a philosophical aside, Leggett said, "I was always under the impression that what you did in your private life, albeit I've stretched the point a bit . . . as long as it didn't affect the way you handled the people's business, was really not the people's concern."

The Post's editors felt Leggett's complex and costly personal life might have had an effect on his legislative life. He was a natural target for bribery because of his poor financial position; Cheshire had reported earlier that the Justice Department was investigating Leggett on just that subject. And he was also under suspicion of having been involved in "the illegal transmission of classified information," though the story made clear no conclusions of illegality could yet be drawn. As a member of the House Armed Services Committee, Leggett had access to confidential material, some of which he could have kept in his office safe. The combination to that safe, which his staff and several friends knew, was kept on the bottom of his desk calendar. Considering that one of his closest friends was Suzi Thomson, Leggett was the subject of curiosity for investigators piecing together the picture of South Korean influence peddling on Capitol Hill.

For his part, Leggett said he had never had a breach of security in his office. And he said if *The Post* ran the story of his personal life, he would probably be forced to retire from Congress.

He was reelected to Congress in November of 1976.

One of Suzi Thomson's friends also played the powersex game and may have had a hand in delivering a Senate seat to former Representative Don Riegle, a Michigan Democrat. Days before the November 1976 election, in the final weeks of a closely contested senate race in Michigan, the *Detroit News* reported that as a married congressman in 1969, Riegle had had an affair with a young woman who tape recorded some of their intimate conversations. ("I . . . I . . . God, I feel such super love for you. By the way, the newsletter should start arriving," Riegle said at one point.) The story was of questionable journalistic merit. Reporters around the country, including two of the *Detroit News*'s columnists, attacked the paper's decision to run the story.

The woman behind the tapes, though she was identified only as "Dorothy" in the first news reports, was Bette Jane Ackerman, a delicate brunette with pretensions of being a writer. She had come to Washington in 1968 to attend a conference of Young Republicans while still a student at Boston University. She fell in love with Riegle and taped their phone calls so she could listen to his voice when he was not with her. When she returned to Washington following a post-graduation trip through Europe, Ackerman found Riegle was no longer interested in seeing her. (It gets very complicated: Ackerman said her go-between was a woman on Riegle's staff who would eventually become his second wife, the same woman who announced plans to divorce Riegle early in 1977.)

Ackerman decided to stay in Washington. She got a job with the Library of Congress. She began attending parties hosted by South Korean millionaire Tongsun Park. She lunched on the Hill with Suzi Thomson. She began writing an uninspired food and wine column for a small publication circulated free to Washingtonians in upper-income neighborhoods. Then, when writer Robin Moore arrived in Washington in the wake of the Hays-Ray scandal, Ackerman accepted five hundred dollars to help him meet women with Capitol Hill sex stories to tell. Somehow the tapes made their way to the *Detroit News* after Ackerman entrusted them to Moore, who was planning a paperback book about Washington sex.

"I didn't wish him (Riegle) any harm," Ackerman said after her identity became known. "I am not that type of person. That was a long time ago."

Some political observers in Michigan thought the lurid exposé created a sympathy vote for Riegle. When the story appeared he enjoyed only a one-point lead in the polls; three weeks later he won his Senate seat by a six-point margin.

Several weeks before the Hays-Ray story broke, a psychologist and psychiatrist research team, Dr. Samuel Janus and Dr. Barbara Bess, reported to the American Psychiatric Association the results of a study of top-level call girls in New York, Las Vegas and California.

Their findings: About 60 percent of the women's clients were either "political figures of significance or influential executives in public monopolies such as telephone, power and light companies." It is not an unreasonable expectation that had the researchers included Washington call girls in their study, the percentage would have been higher. Janus and Bess stated that "often these clients will provide prostitutes as companions for political and business associates to get favors" and that "call girls are often kept on the payroll at the taxpayer's expense." The politicians and power brokers, concluded the study, preferred kinky sex from the call girls, a viewpoint that differs from that of some Washingtonians, such as *Post* reporter Nancy Collins, who considers Washington sex a yawn.

Much of the press and public take great delight in such reports, as well as in the news of a Washington scandal, especially if a dollop of sex is involved. Political escapades offer hints of lust, money and intrigue that many Americans believe (or want to believe) are lurking below the surface of all political activity in Washington.

But powersex is hardly the exclusive affliction of the elected. Consider, for example, the press. A well-known syndicated political columnist frequently irritated the residents of one block in Georgetown by arriving drunk, banging loudly on the door of his mistress' home. His curses only multiplied when he was sometimes refused admittance.

Capitol Hill police still chuckle over the congressional correspondent who invited two streetwalkers to his apartment for a midnight dinner of tuna salad and wound up the victim of one of the oldest games in town: a shakedown in which each woman began accusing the other of having received money with such ferocity that the hapless reporter finally paid them to leave his habitat quietly.

One Washington reporter who covers the city's courts is a student of pornography—he keeps his collection locked in the drawer of his desk at the local courthouse—while a city desk reporter of some repute finds peep shows more to his liking.

How many Elizabeth Rays work on Capitol Hill? Dozens of legislators have affairs with members of their office staff. But not many have the power or gall to hide a mistress in an obscure office with no work duties. And not all aspects of powersex are as clear as the relationship between Wayne Hays and Elizabeth Ray. For example, gay congressmen still must wrestle with their sexuality, fearing discovery and political ruin. They are not concerned about the question of hiring staffers for sex (though some are said to have affairs with male staffers); the gay politician has enough problems operating in a straight society where a political brand of macho is still very much a way of life. At least two senators and eight representatives are known by their colleagues to be gay. They have their own subculture, including at least one well-known gay prostitute. As a cover he works as a hairdresser in a fashionable Washington department store, but he told Clark and Maxa the major part of his income is from entertaining men, one of whom he knows is a congressman.

In one respect the devilish question of sex, power and politics has been made complicated by elected officials themselves. They have spent so many years impressing the voters with their devotion to family and a high moral standard that they have created a climate which offers scant forgiveness to the wayward politician. Add to that the insinuation of power that pervades official Washington, and sex becomes a volatile subject in the capital Charles Dickens once called, with a sneer, "the City of Magnificent Intentions."

ELEVEN

GOSSIP OR JOURNALISM?

IF YOU WANT to have an affair in Washington, go to Baltimore.

That is the counsel given Washington newcomers, and
it is good advice. Baltimore and one particular Maryland
county in suburban Washington, Prince Georges County,
were historically the places frequented by important Washingtonians who would rather not have been seen by their
neighbors as they patronized striptease houses, gambling
dens and gay bars. In the last two decades both areas, especially Prince Georges County, have managed to shed much
of their naughty reputation, but they still offer a measure
of anonymity to the politician who doesn't want to take his
girlfriend to a Washington restaurant his friends may frequent.

Never mind that nearly three million people live in the
metropolitan area; Washington is one of the smallest towns in
the country when it comes to gossip—personal or professional
—about its famous residents. The reason is simple: Talking
politics is everything in Washington. New York has its
theater, art, business and publishing circles; Washington is
a government town. There is no heavy industry, and most
private businesses are in the capital because that's where the
federal government is located; if the bureaucracy decided to
move to Cleveland, Washington's major public relations
firms, news bureaus, law firms and lobbying groups would

be right behind in the next moving van. That kind of single-mindedness gives the nation's capital an intimate feeling that is comfortable to some, stifling to others. It also makes for precious few secrets.

There is a deceptive air of certainty about the famous *New York Times* motto, "All The News That's Fit to Print." In fact, the *Times,* as well as most other newspapers, frequently has trouble deciding just what is fit to print, and nowhere is the problem more difficult than in Washington, where the public's right to know can conflict with personal privacy and government secrecy.

Richard Nixon's administration gave prominence to the question of "national security," as when, for example, Daniel Ellsberg provided the press with the classified Pentagon Papers in 1971, or when word leaked about the CIA's secret efforts to raise a sunken Soviet submarine in 1975. Decisions to go public with those stories caused difficulty for the editors involved. Just as hotly debated is the issue of when a public figure's private life should become news.

Unfortunately there is no immutable yardstick by which reporters can measure the wisdom of publishing a delicate story, but it has become clear that no newspaper can police the private lives of politicians; there must be a hook, a kicker that elevates a politician's indiscretions beyond the realm of the ordinary failings and weaknesses of other men and women. In Wilbur Mills's case, it took reckless driving on a stretch of road near the Tidal Basin to bring his nighttime cavorting and boozing with Fanne Foxe to the public's attention.

Shortly after the Mills incident CBS correspondent Mike Wallace asked several reporters how they covered a public figure's private life, how they determined when gossip was news. Eileen Shanahan, a Washington reporter for *The New York Times,* said she hadn't reported Mills's swinging before the Tidal Basin mishap "because my paper, like most respectable papers, doesn't engage in a lot of what people consider to be 'gutter reporting.' I knew that there would be no interest. As long as it appeared that this was just a purely private sexual escapade that didn't affect his work, it was not considered news. I personally disagree with that. I think the character of our public officials is important."

Shanahan said she had covered Senate Banking Committee hearings when the junior senator from New Jersey, Harrison Williams, was drunk at ten o'clock in the morning, "asking rambling questions that didn't make a lot of sense, and the witnesses were trying to answer as if they made a lot of sense —I saw that dozens of times."

"Did you write about it?" asked interviewer Wallace.

"I did not," Shanahan replied.

"Why?"

"I think . . . because I knew that my paper—there was no point in fighting about it. I'd had a titanic fight sometime before that over a story where Russell Long was drunk on the Senate floor, where it really affected the outcome of a major Johnson administration tax bill, and was unable to get into the paper that Russell Long was visibly drunk on the Senate floor. Having lost that fight, I didn't try again on Williams."

"I think," Shanahan added, "the problem is that editors all over this country tend to require a higher standard of proof from reporters when we're dealing with what they regard as personal matters. When I say Russell Long was visibly drunk on the Senate floor, they say to me, 'How do you know he didn't suddenly have a terrible high fever and get sick?' "

Not all publications have the same standards, of course. Joan Kennedy's fondness for liquor after her husband's accident at Chappaquiddick was known in Washington, but it was the supermarket tabloid, the *National Enquirer,* that finally decided the world should share the sad secret. The weekly newspaper paid two patients in a New York alcoholic rehabilitation center to tell all about their fellow patient, the wife of Ted Kennedy, in the spring of 1976. Apparently for the *Enquirer,* Joan Kennedy's fame was reason enough to publish the two-part story that began, "'I am a lush,' beautiful Joan Kennedy quietly confessed." Later that year the *Enquirer* tried to prepare a story on the "Ten Biggest Drunks In Congress," but fear of libel suits doomed the assignment. (Said one Capitol Hill aide: "Why just limit it to ten?")

When does a public figure's boozing become news? Generally a drunk driving charge against a politician is reported. If someone with a history of heavy social drinking is involved in an accident, a newspaper might give the story bigger play than otherwise. Such was the case with former Speaker of the House Carl Albert. Washington reporters knew of his drinking and included broad hints of it in some of their stories as Albert neared the end of his career, but when Albert was involved in a fender-bender, newspapers gave the story prominent display. On December 17, 1976, Jack Anderson and Les Whitten reported seventy-one-year-old Representative Robert N. C. Nix (D-Pennsylvania) had "a drinking problem." (Nix denied the charge.) The justification for the embarrassing story: Nix was in line to assume the chairmanship of the important House Post Office and Civil Service Committee, a post the columnists reported some congressmen felt might be better handled by a more sober member of the House. Like most stories about Capitol Hill drinking, the decision to run with the report was largely a judgment on the part of the columnists and the editors who subscribe to the Anderson column, but it also pointed to a subtle trend toward more aggressive reporting of hitherto unmentionable topics.

Sex is an even more difficult area for a Washington journalist to evaluate. Alcohol would obviously impair a politician's performance, but sex is another matter. For Clark and Maxa it was easy to become jaded by the people who called them after the Hays-Ray story to tell of wayward congressmen. But one particular call reminded Maxa that no matter how bold the Washington press corps had become after Watergate and the Wilbur Mills affair, it was still blasé about sexual habits that outraged a good part of America.

The caller said he was standing in a phone booth in North Carolina. As he fed quarters into the phone, the caller told Maxa a woman in his hometown was having an affair with a congressman.

"She goes to Washington every weekend and has been for the last six weeks," the man said in a tone of moral outrage. He gave the woman's name, address and phone number.

"Is this woman on the congressman's staff?" Maxa asked.

"No."

"Is she—would you have any way of knowing?—traveling to Washington at the taxpayer's expense?"

"No, I don't think so."

Maxa explained that he didn't think the romance would be of any concern to *The Post,* that it sounded like a routine affair with no overtones of illegality.

"But this congressman is *married!*" the caller said.

The intensity of the caller's protest made it clear he thought the fact his congressman was straying was reason enough for a news story. Later that day, over lunch with conservative columnist John Loftin, Maxa repeated the conversation. Loftin, who loves nothing more than a session of verbal sparring, immediately sided with the North Carolina tipster.

"Oh, I think I'm beginning to understand," said Loftin with a smile. "A congressman cheats on his wife with one of his employees and that's a story. A congressman simply cheats on his wife and that's not a story. In other words, a politician violates the D.C. Code or some congressional regulation and you'll happily write about it. But a politician simply"—and Loftin dismissed the thought with an exaggerated wave of his hand—"simply *violates one of God's Ten Commandments* and you just shrug it off."

Loftin overstated the case slightly, but one school of journalistic thought holds that the press shouldn't wait until a politician's wenching and drinking have a direct effect on his work to report his excesses. A politician's behavior, this opinion holds, in regard to women, alcohol and other personal matters is an indication of both his character and the attitude he might bring toward legislation touching on those areas.

Furthermore, if a politician takes a simon-pure stance in public that his personal life belies, some reporters argue his private life is fair game for aggressive, candid reporting. One elderly senator, for example, has a reputation in his home state for hiring young women and sometimes a man to engage in the sexual art of bondage and domination with him. His national reputation and public speeches, on the other hand, establish him as a tough conservative strongly opposed to prostitution and gay rights. The reason his rumored private life has not been made public (and the reason his name is not used here) is that no one has accumulated sufficient proof to withstand the test of a libel suit, though one person who says he procured various partners for the senator volunteered to sign an affidavit for Clark and Maxa because the senator still owes him $350 for services rendered.

While the press gropes for guidelines about reporting such stories, gossip flourishes. One *Washington Post* reporter, Sally Quinn, has made her career watching Washington's shakers and movers whisper to one another and once wrote an article describing only half in jest etiquette for gossip in Washington.

"You must establish ground rules," Quinn advised. " 'You mustn't tell a soul' and 'don't breathe a word' means it's O.K. to tell but don't connect the person. 'Disguise the source' means you can tell it but intimate it came from somebody else. 'Pass this along carefully' means really keep it in the group and don't let it get out of hand. 'This is dangerous' means you could get in trouble. 'This is really dangerous' means we both could get in trouble."

To impress a friend with the strictness of a particular confidence, Quinn wrote, it is necessary to invoke religion, as in "You must swear on the Bible you'll never tell" or "Jesus Christ, don't ever let this get out."

The game is not as ludicrous as it might appear; reporters and sources play by similarly arcane rules on sensitive stories. Probably in no American city other than Washington do reporters have to deal with so many admonitions of "off-the-record," "for background only," "for deep background only," "not for attribution" and modifications of those arrangements. Failure by a reporter to honor his word can lead to the loss of a source, not to mention the possibility of a source losing his job.

Some Washington gossip is as regular as national elections. Most presidential candidates seem to have fathered an illegitimate child somewhere during their lives, it is rumored every four years, though 1976 gossip about Jimmy Carter went one step further: Carter's mother, this rumor alleged, had once worked for Joseph Kennedy, who was really Jimmy Carter's father. Working from that erroneous premise, the story grew with the contention that details about Carter's deceased father were vague and wasn't that toothy smile reminiscent of the Kennedy look . . .

In 1962 right-wing hate sheets began a rumor that alleged President Kennedy had once been secretly married to a two-time divorcée. Although the White House was receiving close to five hundred letters a day on the subject and Washington reporters for respectable publications were familiar with the report, no one in the mass media would touch the story. Finally *Newsweek* debunked the rumor in a press section piece that detailed how the false report had spread through fringe publications. (*Newsweek*'s bureau chief in Washington then was Ben Bradlee, who wrote the story with the help of FBI documents provided by the White House in exchange for Kennedy's right to review the story prior to publication, an uncomfortable arrangement that Bradlee later detailed in his book, *Conversations With Kennedy*.)

Nothing improves the gossip landscape as much as the death of a famous Washingtonian.

It only took a few months after J. Edgar Hoover's death for rumors that he had been gay to emerge from Georgetown salons and into print. It took nearly ten years, but after Judith Campbell Exner revealed her past relationship with JFK, newspapers and magazines rushed to print long stories describing Kennedy's womanizing. Even Dwight Eisenhower's former World War Two aide, Kay Summersby, wrote a memoir, published in 1976, which described her wartime romance with Ike.

Legend has it that Washington reporters knew all those stories and more but refused to share them with their readers. Sometimes that is true. For some public figures whose personal conduct is egregious, it is a happy coincidence that they are the same sex as most reporters—a kind of male clubbiness has protected them from public scandal. Further, both professions have their share of alcoholics and philanderers. And both rely on each other. Reporters need the cooperation of news sources to write stories, the newsmakers need reporters to make them newsmakers; to offend one another disturbs that relationship.

On the other hand, had Washington reporters in the 1960s known John Kennedy was having an affair with a woman acquainted with Mafia figure Sam "Momo" Giancana, who was, in turn, plotting with the CIA to assassinate Fidel Castro, it would have been a major news story regardless of how cordial a relationship Kennedy enjoyed with the Washington press corps in the days of Camelot.

Not all Washington gossip is frivolous. Sometimes Washington table talk can lead to front page stories, as happened to Representative James R. Mann, a South Carolina Democrat, in February, 1977.

Mann became something of a national figure when, in the summer of 1974, he served on the House Judiciary Committee during its televised impeachment proceedings. Mann, who had been an Army lieutenant colonel at age twenty-five during World War Two and was a former prosecuting attorney, spoke up boldly for the Constitution during the impeachment inquiry. "If there is no accountability, another President will feel free to do as he chooses," Mann said. "But the next time there may be no watchman in the night."

Mann is a congressman who, by his own admission, just

can't say no to a friend. And he has plenty of friends. The list of contributors to his 1976 primary race is a quick primer on the range of interest groups that can fatten a politician's campaign chest.

Among Mann's contributors: the Tobacco People's Public Affairs Committee ($200); the Recording Arts Political Action Committee ($100); the American Textile Industry Committee for Good Government ($500); the Transportation Political Education League ($500); Truck Operators Non-Partisan Committee ($200); Committee Organized for the Trading of Cotton ($100); the American Medical Practice Action Committee ($100); the Non-Partisan Committee for Good Government (Coca-Cola Company, $100); the Banking Profession Political Action Committee ($300); Southern Railway Tax Eligible Good Government Fund ($200); Non-Partisan Political Support Committee (General Electric Company, $200); Manufacturing House Institute ($100); the Lumber Dealers Political Action Committee ($100); the American Optometric Association Political Action Committee ($100); Gas Employees Political Action Committee ($200); Independent Bankers Political Action Committee ($300); the National Rifle Association ($100); the Life Underwriters Political Action Committee ($400); and the Texaco Employees Political Involvement Committee ($100).

It is an extraordinary list, the likes of which few other congressmen with only eight years of Hill service can boast. But if his campaign chest was well filled, Mann had not been so fortunate in his personal financial dealings, despite the best efforts of his congressional staff to help him prosper. Those efforts led to a *Washington Post* story about Mann. His office staff, grumbling in 1975 and 1976 about running personal errands for Mann, talked too much. The gossip began making Capitol Hill rounds: What kind of strange business had Mann become involved in that his congressional staff had to perform such unlikely tasks as, in one case, sticking thirteen-cent stamps on thirty thousand dollars' worth of two-dollar bills?

In the summer of 1976 Maxa heard that working on the staff of James Mann sometimes meant performing a variety of strange chores, most of which seemed related to the coin business of someone named Ben Gause. A businessman in Greenville, South Carolina, Gause had invested in real estate with Mann. He used Mann's congressional offices for some of his other businesses. In 1974, Maxa learned, Mann carried bags of pennies to Gause in Greenville. In 1975 he carried thousands of dollars' worth of quarters and half dollars to Gause. In 1976 the errands continued. A young attorney working as a legislative research assistant for Mann went shopping for twenty thousand dollars' worth of mint-condition two-dollar bills, the denomination reissued by the government in the hope of saving money by easing the demand for one-dollar bills.

The attorney, Ashley Thrift, took over twenty thousand dollars in cash from the congressman and obligingly made two trips on separate occasions to Washington banks. Each time Thrift bought ten thousand in two-dollar bills and five thousand regular postage stamps. Then, with the assistance of other staffers in Mann's office, the thirteen-cent stamps were affixed to the crisp bills and taken to a post office where the bills were postmarked "First Day of Issue—Washington, D.C." The bills were then packed neatly for Mann, who would carry them to his home district in South Carolina for Gause. Thrift later admitted he wasn't delighted with his assignment and, in fact, refused to make the trip a third time. Mann had to buy the stamps and another ten thousand dollars in two-dollar bills himself.

During that same spring and summer, a college-age intern who eventually joined Mann's payroll for a short time, performed other favors at Mann's direction. David Kimpel, working in his first job since he graduated from college, drove the congressman's car to a downtown office building, picked up sacks of mail and returned them to the congressman's office. Kimpel admitted that Mann had instructed him to say, if asked, that he was doing a favor for a friend, that his connection with Mann's office was strictly coincidental.

Once Kimpel detoured to make a stop at the Treasury Department. Mann had given him eight hundred dollars in cash to purchase some sets of Presidential Medals issued by the government as well as a large number of small plastic boxes used by collectors to display coins. Kimpel's freight was then sent to the House folding room that is supposed to package official congressional mail. There the boxes and sets of medals were packaged for easy carrying by the congressman. Mann's cargo was then driven by a staffer to National Airport where it was loaded on an airplane as Mann's personal baggage.

When Maxa heard the stories of the coin running, he wondered what was in it for Mann. House ethics forbade a congressman from operating a business out of his office, and it appeared Mann had some personal interest in Ben Gause's business. First Maxa asked the postal service about Gause's companies. He learned that Gause was about to be indicted because one of his firms, the U.S. Coin Company, had failed to deliver $250,000 worth of bicentennial coins ordered (and paid for) by customers. With the help of James Mann, Gause had arranged to share a mailing address with a personnel agency in downtown Washington for another of his companies, the Federal Currency Corporation. The address was used in national advertisements that read, in part: "UNITED STATES MINT STRIKES 1976 COPPER CENT. This is the only penny that the United States Mint will strike during the Bicentennial Year that is dated 1976 and has Lincoln seated in the Lincoln Memorial Chair on the reverse side and Lincoln's bust in relief on the obverse side; both sides struck by the United States Mint from official engraving."

The design sounded familiar. A postal investigator explained to Maxa why: It was the same design printed the year before and the one that would be stamped on pennies the year after 1976, too. In short, it was your average penny —the only difference was the date, 1976. But the advertisement made this coin sound special. And the price certainly indicated it was: One dollar bought a customer a shiny 1976 "Bicentennial" penny mounted in a small plastic case. (The bags of mail and plastic boxes Mann had asked Kimpel to pick up stemmed from this promotion.) It didn't take long for customers to complain that one dollar was too much to pay for a common penny they thought was a collector's item. Postal investigators agreed, and in mid-1976 they closed down Gause's penny selling operation on the grounds that its ads were misleading.

Maxa reached Mann the evening of October 21, 1976, while the congressman was campaigning for reelection in South Carolina. During a telephone conversation, Mann assured Maxa several times that he had no financial interest in Gause's coin companies. He and Gause, Mann admitted when pressed, had owned some property together, but his extraordinary efforts to supply Gause's companies with coins and two-dollar bills was purely a constituent service, he said.

"You'd be surprised what I do for people," Mann said. "I've even picked up Chinese sausages for constituents. You've got to remember the time frame. I had sympathy for their problem [Gause's default on about $250,000 worth of orders], and they were trying to do some business to pull out of it. I had no financial interest in it. There's a line beyond which constituency service may or may not go but, well, we just don't like to say no."

When Maxa hung up the telephone he was convinced Mann was not telling the whole truth. No congressman would go to so much trouble, he thought, unless he stood to gain from the effort.

Maxa checked the records of contributors to Mann's primary campaign at the Federal Election Commission for evidence of donations by Ben Gause.

Nothing.

He talked to several of Mann's staffers. Ashley Thrift, at about thirteen thousand dollars a year undoubtedly one of Capitol Hill's better paid deliverymen for a brief period, said, "I assumed it was a normal constituent type of service."

Asked if as an attorney he did not find it odd to be detailed to buy thousands of dollars in two-dollar bills and then to spend time affixing stamps to them, Thrift said, "Looking back on it, I think when you look at it like that, that might be true. But at the time it really didn't occur to me as something unusual."

In fact, Thrift, Kimpel (the other gofer) and several other of Mann's staff had sometimes discussed the propriety of their assignments and wondered what they would say if the press ever got word of them. But except for Thrift, who finally refused to make a third trip for two-dollar bills, Mann's staff generally carried out the congressman's orders soon after Gause called with his requests. In a congressman's office, after all, the boss's interests are his staff's interests.

But if there was a news story in Mann's actions, Maxa knew he didn't have it yet. One of *The Post*'s Capitol Hill reporters, Mary Russell, was working on a feature article about favors staffers performed for congressmen. Maxa told the Mann story to Russell but changed his mind and asked her not to use it. He wanted a little more time to see if Mann had been telling the truth.

Maxa called Lee Bandy, the Washington correspondent for a Columbia, South Carolina, newspaper. Sometimes a reporter from a congressman's state can supply the missing pieces to a puzzle, and Bandy had been highly recommended as an astute newsman. The name Gause rang a bell with Bandy. He searched through his files and found that he had received a tip months earlier, something about Mann and Gause being in some money deal together. It wasn't much, but it offered some hope to Maxa that his hunch was correct.

A reporter's time is money to a newspaper, and *The Washington Post* had spent a lot of money chasing false leads since Watergate had made it a clearing house for rumors of scandal. The paper's managing editor, Howard Simons, sometimes told his reporters that the newspaper's early lead on the Watergate story was a mixed blessing; the favorable publicity about the newspaper had been accompanied by story tips that too often led down blind alleys. And a five-hundred-dollar-a-week reporter could spend days checking out vague or false information.

While Maxa felt the information he had gathered about Mann was accurate, he wondered if the story was worth pursuing. Election day was only two weeks away; to write a fast story about Mann so near the election might appear to be an effort by the newspaper to sabotage Mann's reelection. And even if Maxa's suspicion was correct, if Mann did have a financial involvement in the coin operations, the story would be a good one but certainly not a blockbuster. No one else was working on it and it could wait, Maxa decided, until the December mail fraud trial of Gause and two of his business partners for failure to deliver the sets of coins for which they had received payment. Mann's name was not in the indictment, but perhaps something would surface during the trial that would show he had some interest in the troubled companies for which he and his Washington office had done so much.

On December 14, 1976, in a Columbia, South Carolina, courtroom, a bank officer linked Mann to the officials of U.S. Coin Company. It was merely a footnote to the trial: The banker testified that a ten-thousand-dollar company check had been made payable to Mann to repay a loan. But it was enough to convince Maxa that he should visit the congressman's South Carolina hometown.

In Greenville, Maxa learned that Mann's business enterprises had stretched from a leather company in Chad to extensive local real estate holdings. There was some question about how much money he had actually made, but it was evident he was trying hard. In 1975 Mann had been questioned about a *Charlotte Observer* story that alleged Mann was involved in business deals featuring worthless stock, phony mortgages, almost nonexistent corporations and bad checks. The congressman conceded to the press that while some of his financial arrangements may have seemed peculiar, he was a soft touch for business deals and said he neglected his personal finances because of his congressional workload. In fact, the evidence Maxa was beginning to accumulate indicated just the opposite: The congressman not only paid a considerable amount of attention to personal business, he felt it necessary to involve his congressional staff in his efforts, too.

A former twenty-seven-thousand-dollar-a-year staffer, Thomas Poteat, had carried coins from Mann's Washington office to Greenville during his visits there until he refused to do it any more, according to a close friend. (Poteat had died earlier in 1976, so Maxa had to take the friend's word for it.) On the last day of December, 1974, U.S. Coin Company had transferred title of its building to a companion corporation, Roosevelt Mint. The witnesses to the transfer were Mann's two secretaries in his district office. Then there were the interviews Maxa had conducted in October with four of Mann's staffers who admitted they had, in varying degrees, performed chores for U.S. Coin Company in the course of their business days on the Hill.

Most importantly, a bank officer in Greenville told Maxa off-the-record that Mann had endorsed a loan of over thirty thousand dollars for U.S. Coin in 1973 or 1974. And Mann had a reputation in local banking circles for having cash flow problems; his bank account had been "flagged," which meant no overdrawn checks would be honored. If the banker was telling the truth, Mann had lied to Maxa before the election about the extent of his dealings with Gause and U.S. Coin.

The next move was to confront Mann, that point in the pursuit of a story when a reporter's heart beats fastest. A good reporter tries to give an individual the opportunity to refute any charges against him before writing a story. It is generally an awkward moment for all concerned, each person wondering how much the other knows, each choosing his words carefully.

Congress was recessed during December, and Mann's staff

made it clear to Maxa that the congressman was going to be difficult to reach. One day Mann's Washington office said he was in South Carolina; minutes later his district office reported he was in Washington. When Maxa called the Washington office back and reported the confusing news, Mann's secretary replied sweetly, "Well, how about that?"

Finally, on January 11, 1977, Mann's secretary called Maxa to arrange an appointment with Mann for the next morning in the Rayburn House Office Building. Mann is a gray haired man with soft features, younger looking than he had appeared on television when his voice had broken as he explained why, as a member of the House Judiciary Committee, he was compelled to vote for the impeachment of Richard Nixon.

Perhaps it was because he had been safely reelected two months earlier, perhaps it was because his name had been mentioned in the mail fraud trial, or maybe it was because he had heard through the Greenville grapevine that Maxa had been asking questions, but on the cold morning of January 12, Mann greeted Maxa with a smile, a handshake and a quick retreat from his statements of the previous October.

"I want to talk to you primarily about your finances and Ben Gause and U.S. Coin Company," Maxa began. "We talked last October if you recall—you were right in the heat of a campaign and you called me from South Carolina—and you had said you had no financial relationship with him and U.S. Coin except that, and I quote, 'We had owned some property together.'"

"No," Mann said quickly, "that isn't what I said and I hope you have a good record of it. I said I had no *ownership* relationship—I distinctly remember using the word 'ownership.' I did have a financial relationship—"

"—now I asked you that several times—"

"No, no, no, I'm sorry—I hope you made a recording of it?"

There's the thrust, Maxa thought to himself. Mann wanted to establish quickly whether his voice had been recorded so he could see how firm his denial could be. For a moment Maxa cursed himself for not having taped the October conversation.

"No," Maxa said, "I didn't."

Mann didn't miss a beat, his easy-going lilt picking right up on the end of Maxa's sentence.

"Well, that's too bad," Mann said, "because I was very, very careful to use the word ownership because that's the way it is—I had no ownership relationship. My Lord, at that time I had clearly told several people that I had loaned some money to Ben Gause."

You didn't tell me, Maxa thought to himself as he pulled out his typewritten notes of their October phone conversation. They were clear and to the point since Maxa had had no trouble keeping up on his typewriter with Mann's short answers to his questions. There was the flat assertion: "I had no financial interest."

It was a point of disagreement between the two men that would remain unresolved; Mann had his memory, Maxa had his notes. One point was undisputed: What had begun as gossip about the way a congressman ran his office had developed into a public question about the ethics of a congressman using his staff and office to benefit a company in which he was a principal financial backer.

Later that day at *The Post,* Maxa told the deputy managing editor for national news, Richard Harwood, that he and Mann agreed on the basic facts about Mann's errand running for U.S. Coin, agreed that Mann had a substantial financial stake in the company, but disagreed about the meaning of it all. Mann argued that making his money back was as far from his mind "as the man on the moon," he was only trying to aid a constituent in trouble. Maxa thought a reasonable, objective person might reach a different conclusion.

"Write it," said Harwood.

Gossip does not become news unless someone ups the ante by whispering into the ear of a reporter. Good sources, like rose gardens and star quarterbacks, must be cultivated, and good sources—the kind who know when gossip should be leaked to the press—are a reporter's best asset. The most famous Washington source in recent history was the mysterious Deep Throat, the well-connected *basso profundo* who kept Bob Woodward and Carl Bernstein hot on the Watergate story.

A source like Deep Throat is rare. The most common kind of information leaker in Washington calls for one reason: He wants to stab someone else in the back. He was denied a promotion; the other guy got the girl; he lost his job; he didn't get cut in on a deal as someone had promised. Revenge is his motive.

While there is nothing strictly wrong with that motive, it behooves a reporter to understand why someone is handing him sensitive information. Fortunately, in Washington enough people are so adept at leaking that inside information comes from all sides. Daniel Ellsberg dumped boxes of secret Pentagon papers into the laps of the eastern press. At the White House in 1971 Charles Colson, in turn, plotted to leak damaging information about Ellsberg. (Earlier Colson had tried to peddle fake cables to a *Life* magazine reporter, cables that implicated President Kennedy in the 1963 assassination of South Vietnam's President Ngo Dinh Diem.)

After the Hays-Ray story appeared, *The Post* was deluged with calls and letters telling of crimes by government officials. Some callers left their names, most did not. Some whispered. Some laughed. One caller from a federal agency phoned Maxa from the Southwest to report that his boss in Washington traveled with his secretary (at public expense) just so they could spend nights away from the boss's wife. The caller was clearly uncomfortable in his role. "Listen," he said in a quavering voice, "the only reason I'm calling you is that we drew straws in the office and I got the shortest one."

In the 1950s two *Confidential* magazine writers authored a scorching book called *Washington Confidential* that noted Washington "is a city of wistful people with adding machine minds. Overall a feeling of fear pervades it. People become conditioned to talking in whispers. Senators will walk you to the middle of the room, then mumble, even when what they have to say is inconsequential. The main indoor sport is conspiracy."

The description could have been written in 1977. Washington has become even more a town of conspiracy, and no longer is it a sport confined to the indoors. For fear of eavesdroppers, Bob Woodward and Deep Throat met in empty underground parking garages. Other reporters meet sources in parks, away from crowded restaurants where tables are within easy earshot of one another. Sensitive business is rarely conducted on the telephone.

One prominent member of the House meets his mistress (who is on his payroll, too) aboard his boat docked in Annapolis, Maryland. When they arrive together at the harbor, she walks about five hundred feet ahead of him on the dock, seemingly two strangers who happen to be going in the same direction.

In May, 1974, shortly before he walked into a federal courtroom to enter a plea of guilty to a charge of obstructing justice, Nixon aide Charles Colson visited Richard Bast, a Washington private investigator, to confide that he felt the CIA had masterminded the Watergate break-in and subsequent exposure to discredit the Nixon White House. Colson poured out his bizarre tale to Bast as the two sat in the backyard of the detective's expansive suburban Virginia home. It was summer; the fountain in the middle of Bast's pool tinkled softly in the background. And every once in a while bees would hover around the landscaped hill that provided the backdrop near Bast's patio. Hidden in the bushes was a microphone attached to a tape recorder that preserved for posterity Colson's darkest fears. The tapes also provided the details for a story in *The Washington Post* several weeks later about Colson's revelations.

If they were writing today, the seasoned authors of *Washington Confidential* might not be startled to learn what has become of their city of paranoia. After all, in the 1950s a park bench in Lafayette Square across from the White House was bugged, according to their chapter titled "Wiretappers, Snoops and Spies." At the time the downtown park was a favorite gathering place for men the authors termed "semi-boys," "pansies" and "faggots." Of the bugged bench they wrote: "You ought to hear some of the gay conversations. We did. Then we squirted penicillin in our ears."

TWELVE

LEGACY OF A SCANDAL

WHEN GERALD FORD gave his last State of the Union address in January, 1977, his voice quavered as he surveyed the House of Representatives in which he had served. "It is not easy," he said, "to end these remarks in this chamber where, along with some of you, I have experienced many of the highlights of my life. It was here that I stood twenty-eight years ago with my freshman colleagues as Speaker Sam Rayburn administered the oath. I see some of you now."

Ford mentioned the names of several remaining members who, like him, had been elected to the House in 1948.

One of the men the President did not mention was the fresh-faced school teacher and young politician from Ohio who had stood with him on January 3, 1949, as Sam Rayburn charged the freshman class of that year with the responsibility of supporting and defending the Constitution. In one of those curious footnotes history sometimes provides, if Gerald Ford had had his way as a congressman, Wayne Hays might have been spared disgrace. It was Hays's wide-ranging authority as chairman of the House Administration Committee that gave him the power to hire Elizabeth Ray and other women and to tuck them in obscure columns of the House payroll. But in 1971 it was then-Representative Gerald Ford who had argued against vesting so much authority in the housekeeping committee whose chairmanship Hays had just inherited.

"Once this authority is given to this committee, twenty-five members out of four hundred and thirty-five, it will never be retrieved by the House as a whole until and unless there is a scandal," Ford prophesied. "I think the better way to avoid that scandal is to require those additional benefits be voted on in the House by each and every member of the House."

Ford's colleagues rejected his plea because they were eager to shift the power to award increases in fringe benefits from their shoulders to those of Wayne Hays. So Hays went about the business of accumulating and exercising power until, as another House member had predicted in 1974, he violated "one amenity too many."

In November, 1976, the Justice Department announced it would not prosecute Hays on criminal charges because of lack of sufficient evidence. One reason given in some news accounts was the refusal of the attorney general to approve a subpoena that would have ordered Clark and Maxa to testify before a grand jury. Justice Department prosecutors apparently felt the two reporters would make "better witnesses" than Elizabeth Ray, at least in recounting the substance of the phone conversations they had heard between Hays and Ray.

The reporters' reluctance to appear before the grand jury stemmed from fears that cooperation by the press with the government might have a chilling effect on future relationships between reporters and their sources. Had Clark and Maxa told Ray the first day they met that on some future date everything she said to them might be repeated before a federal grand jury, the story of Wayne Hays might never have been written.

It is generally a reporter's refusal to identify a confidential source that brings him to a confrontation with a prosecutor. In the Hays case that was not the issue—Clark and Maxa had no confidential sources of information; Elizabeth Ray had permitted her name to be used in their stories. Since there was no unnamed source involved, had the Justice Department pressed the question, attorneys for *The Post* feared they might not be able to convince a court that the interests of a free press would be better served by excusing Clark and Maxa from the subpoena. But *The Post* felt strongly enough about the issue to try to persuade the attorney general to refuse the requests of his prosecutors and to quash the effort to subpoena the reporters. For whatever reason, Attorney General Edward Levi did just that. And his prosecutors, wary of launching a case that depended on Ray as the principal witness, declined to press criminal charges against Wayne Hays.

On May 14, 1977, one day after Wayne Hays's sixty-second birthday, Elizabeth Ray had her thirty-fourth birthday, thereby ending "the year our Lord died," number thirty-three. It hadn't been a smooth year for Liz either.

For starters, she'd been fired after that newspaper story had come out. Then Wayne Hays, who'd just gone off and married someone else, got on national TV and told the whole country Liz was crazy. Then some wise guy down in North Carolina had looked up her birth certificate, and now everybody knew she wasn't really twenty-seven years old and that her real name was Betty Lou. How was she ever going to get into movies in Hollywood and into *Playboy*, much less find a husband, now that the whole world knew she was over thirty, right smack in the throes of Gail Sheehy's "Deadline Decade"? Was there any rock left unturned?

Yes. The terrible press dug up her mother in the "stovepipe-topped trailer" in North Carolina and made fun of her, and now the whole country knew Liz was low class. Then they tried every police blotter east of the Mississippi, trying to pin her down as a prostitute. They wrote about her nose job and her double chin. Then that photographer she'd once posed for nude in another life sold all the pictures, even the bad ones, to *Hustler*, "the dirtiest, filthiest magazine there is," and so everybody in the whole world had seen what she looked like . . . bending over.

She was notorious. Horrible telegrams came in the night asking her to strip at burlesque houses. Horrible phone calls came from breathers. Her best girlfriend's husband decided Liz couldn't visit anymore. He didn't want his son exposed to her. Duke Zeibert, her old dear pal, told her he didn't want to be seen in public with her. The press had her sleeping with everyone from President Ford to Mickey Mouse. The Justice Department was forever grilling her. Normal men were frightened of her. She couldn't find a date. The women on Capitol Hill despised her. She had damaged their image. Mothers wrote her long letters with hate-filled messages. Perverts wrote her mash notes. Guys in prison wrote her wanting signed nude photographs. Her own aunt, whom she had always depended on to be strong and sensible, could only cry on the phone. Her mother didn't know why Betty Lou had done this to her.

Her book got rip-roaring terrible reviews. Ditto for her acting job in the Chicago production of *Will Success Spoil Rock Hunter?*. The man she fell in love with, her director in the play, turned around and told *Time* magazine she was loony. The movie she was supposed to star in—finally, her silver screen dream come true—fell through because the low-budget producer couldn't get any backing for it. The country and western hit record she was supposed to cut fizzled out. The little dog she'd bought for companionship barked all the time and drove her wild. Her new chin job looked . . . weird. Her plants all died. And on top of all that, she didn't even get the centerfold in *Playboy*. So much for "the year our Lord died."

"I have been through hell," she said. "No one can know what it's been like. They can't know. Unless they were me, they couldn't know what hell means." So much for the Calendar Girl.

"I can't type, I can't file, I don't even know how to answer the phone," she had said in print that Sunday morning at the beginning of her thirty-third year. And then her boss lost his job too. And Congress rewrote some rules. "Me! A little girl from the South," she told Maxa and Clark, "a Dumb Blond, going after a great big congressman all by myself. Who would have ever thought it?" So much for . . . Dumb Blonds.

And now that the hoopla is over and the Star Spangled Rodeo has bitten the dust, the Rhinestone Cowgirl has some small regrets. "Poor guy," she is still saying, "I didn't want to hurt him. If he just hadn't been so mean . . . so damn mean . . . none of this would have ever happened."

Wayne Hays had intended to mark the start of his fifteenth consecutive term in Congress the evening Gerald Ford said farewell to Congress. Thirty years was long enough, he had told friends. In 1978 he would see if the Ohio governorship was within his grasp or he would settle into life at Redgate Farms as Belmont County's elder statesman. There he would tend his cattle and horses, sometimes making the ninety-minute drive to Columbus to attend Ohio State football games.

But like so many politicians before him, Hays will not be remembered the way he would have liked. His legacy is a sex scandal; the memory of him for most Americans will be the image of an aging playboy with a weakness for large-breasted blonds. The day after Hays announced he would not seek reelection, secretaries in his office stopped answering the phone with his name.

"Hello," they said instead, "Eighteenth District of Ohio."

One of the men who drove the electric subway cars between the House buildings and the Capitol asked a friend if he was attending the Hays going-away party. "They're holding it upstairs in a phone booth and all his friends are invited," he said without a smile.

Three weeks after he began quietly moving to Ohio, Hays suffered rib bruises when the new pickup truck he was driving crossed the center line of the road and struck an oncoming small truck. In mid-November, 1976, Hays was to attend a gathering in Williamsburg, Virginia, of the North

Atlantic Assembly, the parliamentarians' association in which he had been active since 1955. But he was gored by a bull on his farm and could not go, an unkind fate that did not disappoint some of the members of the conference who were worried that Hays's presence would create embarrassing publicity.

Wayne Hays's yearly retirement pay from Congress is almost $30,700. He is financially secure. If he lives into his seventies he will become, along with Elizabeth Ray, the subject of "Whatever happened to" articles in newspapers and magazines that will send reporters to his Belmont County farm to see what the passage of time has done to Wayne Hays. He will draw strength from the fact that the Justice Department declined to prosecute him. He will probably not talk about what would have happened had the ethics committee held public hearings about his hiring practices.

When former Senator Everett Dirksen was once asked about the chances of passing a certain congressional reform, he replied, "Ha, ha, ha, and I might add, ho, ho, ho." But when the Congress with the first billion-dollar budget arrived in Washington in 1977, it found that the Hays-Ray scandal had produced some immediate changes. The House had voted, six weeks after the Clark-Maxa story, to strip the House Administration Committee of its authority to increase members' allowances without a floor vote. Gerald Ford had been right in 1971; it had taken a scandal to remove that power from the committee and to return it to the House members.

The Democratic leadership, anticipating Republican criticism in the November elections, had also instituted quarterly reporting of all expenditures as well as regular reports of staff hiring and performance. Furthermore, for the first time members were forbidden to withdraw cash from such accounts as the House stationery allowance. And the elevator operators whose seats Wayne Hays had removed were once again allowed to sit on the job.

Despite fears by many House incumbents that the scandals

of 1976 would cost them their seats in the 95th Congress, most returned safely to Washington.

California Democrat Robert Leggett—who admitted to *The Post* that he had taken a mistress years ago, supported her two children and purchased a home for her with a deed on which he had signed his wife's signature—was reelected.

So was Representative John Young, the Texas Democrat accused by Colleen Gardner of paying her a handsome salary in exchange for sex in suburban Washington motels.

Representative Allan Howe, the Utah Democrat convicted of soliciting police decoys for prostitution, was defeated by his heavily Mormon constituency.

Florida Democrat Robert Sikes was reelected despite his reprimand by the House. However, on January 26, 1977, the Democratic Caucus—which two years earlier had ousted three senior committee chairmen but let Hays retain his seat—flexed its muscles again and repudiated the House leadership by removing Sikes from his chairmanship of an Appropriations committee's subcommittee on military construction.

And Representative Frank Horton (R-New York), who served a week in jail in 1976 for drunk driving, was reelected, some said, because he rejected his lawyer's advice to fight the charge and instead admitted his mistake and accepted the sentence of the court.

But as the 95th Congress opened, members found themselves in the middle of a burgeoning scandal that threatened to involve as many as sixty members who had accepted cash, travel, gifts or women from the well-oiled South Korean lobby based in Washington.

According to newspaper accounts, the State and Justice departments believe Korea's lobbying efforts began in the 1960s when businessman Tongsun Park was arrested by Korean intelligence agents in Seoul for reportedly claiming he was a relative of South Korean President Park Chung Hee. Tongsun Park subsequently met with the president, an aide to the evangelist Reverend Sun Myung Moon, and members of the Korean CIA in the president's "Blue House" to discuss a plan for creating a favorable climate of opinion in the United States for South Korea, which has received more than twelve billion dollars in military and economic aid from the United States since the end of the Korean War.

In 1969 South Korea correctly perceived a shift in the way foreign policy was being set in Washington. No longer was it the exclusive domain of the executive branch; Congress was becoming involved in decisions regarding overseas troop strength, foreign aid and import-export regulations. The South Korean dictatorship, fearful of the designs of the North Koreans, wanted to make certain its government had friends on Capitol Hill, friends who would not balk at providing money and moral support to South Korea. President Nixon's decision in 1970 to withdraw one third of America's military force from South Korea added urgency, South Korea felt, to its cause.

Tongsun Park, with the alleged blessing of his government, established himself in Washington as the middleman between American suppliers of federally financed grain and South Korean purchasers of rice. With the commissions he earned from this business, Park launched a dazzling program of entertaining in official Washington. South Korean politicians visiting Washington would pay courtesy calls on members of Congress and often leave behind expensive gifts. Employees of the South Korean embassy were dispatched with envelopes of cash to Capitol Hill.

Lest American rice sellers misunderstand Park's role, the South Korean agency that oversees foreign trade wrote a letter to major rice exporters in 1972 that read in part: "In order to insure more satisfactory transactions for our rice trade, we are pleased to inform you that Mr. Tongsun Park, president and chief executive officer of Miryung Moolsan Co. of Seoul, has once again, as in the past, agreed to serve as an intermediary. In fact, his service will be required for all of our rice trade with the United States in the future."

The message was not subtle and the two Post reporters who wrote the initial stories about the Korean influence in

Washington, Scott Armstrong and Maxine Cheshire, said government investigators estimated Park earned as much as five million dollars per year in rice sale commissions. With the help of those funds he decorated an expensive home in Washington, hosted elaborate parties and gave jewelry, silver trinkets, Oriental antiques and vacation trips to dozens of congressmen and other United States officials.

Among the incidents that came to light:

—A White House aide under Richard Nixon, John Nidecker, was given ten thousand dollars in cash in an envelope marked "bon voyage" after a visit to Seoul in May, 1974. He quickly returned it to the Korean government.

—Senator Ted Stevens (R-Alaska) received a check for at least twenty-five hundred dollars from an American fish processing company during his 1972 election campaign. When Stevens' staff inquired about the unsolicited donation, they were told that the senator's "friends in Korea" had asked that the check be sent to him; it was returned.

—Representative John Rhodes (R-Arizona) returned a vase a South Korean parliamentarian left him after a visit to his office. "Even to my uncultured eye it was valuable," Rhodes said after he returned it to the South Korean embassy.

—At an embassy reception a South Korean aide handed Representative Larry Winn, Jr. (R-Kansas) an envelope stuffed with hundred-dollar bills. "We'd like to help your office," the gift giver said; Winn refused the cash.

—A South Korean assistant naval attaché left a topaz pin for the wife of Representative Phillip Burton (D-California) after an office visit; Burton returned the pin.

One family that didn't return gifts from Tongsun Park was that of former Representative Edwin W. Edwards of Louisiana who went on to become governor of his state. Newspaper reports forced him to admit his wife accepted ten thousand dollars in cash from Park in 1971. But he denied the gift played any part in his central role of arranging for South Korea to get subsidized federal loans to buy most of Louisiana's unsold rice surplus in 1971, a move that aided

Edwards considerably in his gubernatorial campaign.

A former press attaché at the South Korean embassy in Washington, Jai-Hyon Lee, defected as the Korean scandal began to unfold in 1976. He told prosecutors he had witnessed the Korean ambassadors stuffing hundred-dollar bills into white envelopes that Lee said would be delivered to Capitol Hill.

Other plans called for the South Korean government to pressure American businesses that had vested interests in South Korea to exercise their influence with the American government on behalf of the Park Chung Hee regime. "Wine, women, song, gifts, cash—you name it," said Jai-Hyon Lee.

Lee also said on the CBS News program *60 Minutes* that he saw a letter from the president of South Korea to his ambassador in Washington that read, in effect, "Do not quarrel, but give full cooperation to Tongsun Park."

In 1975 and 1976 South Korea also extended all-expense-paid invitations to members of Congress to visit that country. The Korea-U.S. Economic Council insisted the trips were privately funded, but State Department officials suspected the council's operating funds came from the South Korean government. Members of Congress are not allowed to accept free trips from foreign governments. Among the congressmen who sampled the hospitality of the Korea-U.S. Economic Council were Representative Thad Cochran (R-Mississippi), Representative Dawson Mathis (D-Georgia) and Representative David Bowen (D-Mississippi). Their trip to Korea in 1975 included a lavish dinner party in Seoul hosted by the ubiquitous Tongsun Park.

Such generosity on the part of the South Koreans provided Park with entrée to the biggest names in Washington. At his members-only Georgetown club in late 1973, for example, Park hosted a birthday party for then-House Majority Leader Tip O'Neill. Guests included numerous congressmen, Vice President Gerald Ford, presidential assistant Melvin Laird and the secretaries of the departments of Housing and

Urban Development and Health, Education and Welfare.

How intent Congress is on shunning such lobbying in the future is an open question. During a December 12, 1976, appearance on *Face the Nation,* Representative James Wright (D-Texas) was asked if he thought Congress could discipline itself in light of the fact some of its leaders had been linked in news accounts to the Korean lobby in Washington. The new House Majority Leader said he wasn't concerned "about their having been connected in the press—I am concerned about the degree, if any, and I hope it's none, to which any of these gifts may have been made in the anticipation of some selfish return. I should like to suggest that Tip O'Neill has never received any monies or campaign contributions. Now, if someone contributed to a party, on a birthday or in his honor, how is he to know that? If someone invites me to a reception in my honor, I don't say, oh, oh, wait a minute, are there some Koreans helping to pay for this?"

(Six weeks later Wright was the subject of embarrassing publicity about commingling campaign funds with personal funds; he used excess political contributions to pay off personal debts. Only a loophole in the House code of ethics saved him from possible disciplinary action by his colleagues.)

As the House ethics committee requested $530,000 to begin an investigation of the Korean influence on Capitol Hill, it became clear that the day-to-day rules by which Congress had been living needed to be changed. The new Speaker of the House, Tip O'Neill, called for a more stringent code of ethics. In the wake of the Hays-Ray scandal, Representative David Obey (D-Wisconsin) was appointed to head a commission to recommend House rule changes.* Pre-

* The Republican minority in Congress, it should be pointed out, never was satisfied with the aftermath of the Hays-Ray affair. While Democrats moved quickly to assign Obey the task of suggesting a stronger code of ethics and tougher House rules, the Republicans said they wanted the same standards that had applied to Watergate to apply in 1976. They demanded an accounting of past abuses of hiring practices, including an audit of every member's

liminary suggestions for changing the code of ethics were made by the commission in late January of 1977. The proposed code would for the first time limit outside earned income by members, abolish slush funds and office accounts, forbid gifts of more than one hundred dollars from a single contributor and end travel by lame duck congressmen. Most significantly, the new rules, if adopted by the House, would require public disclosure of income, holdings, debts and other financial transactions, including real estate dealings. The dramatic disclosure requirements would apply not only to a member of Congress but also to a member's spouse.

In the Senate, the body that had been spared much of the harsh publicity that had attended the House in 1976, the push for change was being accomplished more quietly. Just as Speaker of the House Carl Albert retired in 1976 before the influence of the Korean lobby in his office (through Tongsun Park's occasional date and Albert's secretary, Suzi Thomson) could be explored, so did Senate Minority Leader Hugh Scott retire after one of the kindest "probes" ever conducted. A former Gulf Oil lobbyist had said he had paid Scott five thousand dollars each spring and fall for a number of years from corporate funds, an illegal practice. The Senate ethics committee, which makes its counterpart in the House look aggressive, voted in a closed meeting in September, 1976, to drop its "investigation" of the Scott-Gulf Oil matter.

Scott's sealed financial statement (each senator is required to file one annually with the committee) was never opened. Nor was it given to the Internal Revenue Service. Gulf Oil officials, one of whom had said in a court deposition that large amounts of company funds had been given to Scott and other senators, were not called to testify before the committee. In short, there was no investigation.

The Senate ethics committee doesn't even like to tell the

---

staff by the General Accounting Office. The suggestion was received coolly by the Democratic majority, who said they were more concerned with future abuses.

public about itself. NBC Washington newswoman Linda Ellerbee found that the ethics committee in 1976 was no more active than it was in 1964 when it was formed to avoid a stronger measure—a bill which would have required senators to disclose the sources of their income. Except for a vote to censure Senator Thomas Dodd in 1966 (Dodd himself had asked to be investigated), the committee, whose staff director receives thirty-eight thousand dollars a year, has not suggested any action against any senator.

When Ellerbee decided she would try to learn more about the committee, she discovered that the time and place of the ethics committee meetings were secret, despite Senate rules that forbid such a practice. Then she found that none of the six senators on the committee would agree to be interviewed "in general" about the ethics committee. It was not the kind of response that engendered trust in the Senate's willingness to vigorously police itself.

Jerry Landauer, a *Wall Street Journal* investigative reporter, took an even closer look at the Senate ethics committee and hypothesized that the members were reluctant to scrutinize Scott because some of the committee members themselves benefited from corporate gifts.

"For example, Ashland Oil has reported it unlawfully contributed $5,000 for the reelection of ethics committee member Carl Curtis (R-Nebr.)," Landauer wrote, "and $3,500 for the benefit of committee member Milton Young (R-N.D.)."

Landauer also reported that the committee's chairman, Howard Cannon of Nevada, accepted four free airplane trips from Northrop Corporation, including a Christmas visit to the British West Indies with his family. Why didn't Cannon file an official disclosure report? Cannon explained that the ethics committee, in an unannounced and handy policy, had decided unsolicited airplane rides on a "space available" basis did not have to be disclosed.

In the Senate, Wisconsin Democrat Gaylord Nelson chaired a committee assigned in 1977 to toughen the Senate's code of ethics, just as Representative Obey was trying to do in the House. But neither the Senate nor the House distinguished itself as 1977 began, even as both legislative bodies made much of their Clean Up Congress drive. Tip O'Neill said the stronger code of ethics should be linked to the thirteen-thousand-dollar pay raise a special presidential commission had recommended for congressmen, federal judges and government executives. But in February, 1977, both the House and Senate worked hard to thwart a floor vote on the raises. Which meant no congressman had to vote on his own pay raise.* Which meant the pay raise would take effect without being tied to the new code of ethics, a clear case of Congress "taking the sugar without the pill," as one editorial writer phrased it.

Congress cannot afford to continue enjoying only the sugar. A Harris poll commissioned by the House revealed that Americans rated the ethics of Congress lower than eight other institutions, including the press, the White House, local government and consumer groups. If legislators ever doubted there was a national sentiment for making Congress a more open and accountable institution, Congress' own survey put those doubts to rest.

In the last decade Congress has made moves toward change, but the task, as Representative Morris Udall (D-Arizona) often notes with an Oliver Wendell Holmes quote, is "no sport for the short-winded." Congress has improved its budgeting procedure, reduced the absolutism of the seniority system, made its leadership more responsive to individual members. And the Senate began in 1977 to reorganize its cluttered committee system. But as of this writing, the codes of ethics of both the House and Senate are flabby. Enforcement is uneven. Reporting of member junketing is still an obscure process that demands diligence on the part of anyone

---

* "This is one of the better-known conspiracies. The fix is in," Representative Robert E. Bauman (R-Maryland) told a House Post Office and Civil Service subcommittee February 8, 1977, as he testified about the well planned effort that allowed congressmen to simply accept the commission's recommended pay raise without a floor vote.

who wants to learn when, where and at what cost his congressman traveled. Congress has not moved to extend to its employees the same measure of protection against sex (and other) discrimination it had mandated to other parts of the nation's work force years earlier. As women began shopping for jobs at the start of the 95th Congress, they began hearing some of the same old songs.

One attractive divorced woman visited her congressman from Florida, who quickly made it clear he had a very personal interest in hiring her. Over a long lunch he described his private apartment, where he and his friends sometimes hosted sex parties. Which focuses attention on the cause célèbre that began the season of congressional reform: sex.

The Hays-Ray affair did not alter the passions of the people of Capitol Hill. Shortly before the Hays-Ray affair, and days before he announced his retirement, House Speaker Carl Albert bolted the door to his office as he prepared to show some scrapbooks of his years in Congress to an attractive blond reporter. He confided to the woman that he intended to announce his retirement. Then he put his arm around her and, as she moved from couch to chair to desk, Albert pursued her until she finally left his office, shaken and embarrassed. The woman, a friend of Clark and Maxa's, said she was startled to see Albert's son waiting patiently in the outside office to see his father. She did not miss the irony when Albert declared in his retirement announcement that he wanted to spend more time with his family. She also thought that had Elizabeth Ray made her revelations earlier, she might have been spared the scene in Albert's office.

Capitol Hill sex can have a more subtle, long-range effect on the quality of government. Interviews with numerous women on Capitol Hill indicated an office girlfriend exercises an inordinate amount of influence on her boss's professional life. Because many congressmen do not have the time (or don't take the time) to get to know their employees well, a woman who has her boss's ear in bed can be instrumental in the hiring and firing of staff. And a new employee who is bright, attractive and talented can be perceived as a threat by a mistress, who can work to exclude better-skilled employees from a congressional office.

In at least two House offices—one representing a district in the West, another representing a district in Indiana—the congressmen's girlfriends have achieved such positions of power that they are, in effect, gatekeepers who can insulate their congressmen from anyone they think they should not see.

In the office of former Representative Andrew Hinshaw (R-California), one woman's alleged romance with the congressman engendered staff bitterness because of resentment toward her casual approach to work. Two women kept a log of her work days. During one 204-day period between August, 1975, and May, 1976, she was absent over half of the time: 94 full days and 28 half days. Her salary was about twenty-three thousand dollars a year. And her daughter, hired for seven thousand as a "congressional aide," had an equally unexceptional attendance record. It wasn't until Jack Anderson mentioned both of these facts in a May, 1976, column that the mother and daughter began showing up each day for work.

(Hinshaw retired from the House in disgrace in 1976. He was convicted in January of that year on two counts of taking bribes from a company that had a matter pending before him while he was Orange County, California, tax assessor in 1972. A fellow California Republican, Charles Wiggins, urged the House to expel Hinshaw in July because the House ethics committee had refused to take action while Hinshaw was appealing his conviction. Apparently out of courtesy, the House refused to do so in a vote in October, even though Hinshaw had spent little time in Congress after his conviction.)

In the final analysis, of course, Congress is an institution of mostly men and a few women who arrive in Washington with the votes and best wishes of constituents around the country. Their assignment of governing the nation frequently conflicts with their individual concerns about the people and places they represent. Sometimes they embroil themselves in personal situations or financial dealings that reflect poorly on their integrity. Occasionally the most unlikely politician distinguishes himself while others stumble and trip through their careers. They are expected to offer wisdom and leadership in jobs that, as one member who retired in frustration put it, are mainly "glorified social work." (Representative Bill Stuckey, a Georgia Democrat who retired in 1976, said he once received a call from a constituent in Macon, Georgia, who said her garbage hadn't been picked up. Stuckey asked her why she hadn't looked up the department of sanitation in her phone book and called the director to complain. "Well, congressman," she replied, "quite frankly I didn't want to go up that high.")

The Hays-Ray scandal was symptomatic of the kind of abuse power encourages. Pampered by fawning staffs, financed by seekers of favor, feted by special interest groups, and lulled by fringe benefits, some congressmen have little difficulty cultivating a sense of self-importance that bears little resemblance to the image they attempt to project at election time.

Shortly before he left the House, Representative Thomas Rees (D-California) told Clark and Maxa he recommended congressmen limit themselves to twelve years on Capitol Hill. "After that," he said, "you become oriented toward Washington—life becomes very comfortable here because it's part of the Washington syndrome. Maybe they should put the Capitol in Chicago or New York, where there are real people doing other things. Most senior members believe if they left Congress the government would collapse. I remember one who said to me, 'Well, Tom, the longer you're here the more you'll like it.' My answer was not very polite. I've always had the feeling to get out when you're hitting three hundred for the Dodgers, not when you're hitting one twenty-seven for Albuquerque."

Rees's philosophy enjoys little support among many of his

colleagues who consider the twelfth year in office the beginning of the prime of a congressman's life. It is just about that time that a member of the House can look forward to moving into a spacious office in the Rayburn Building. His committee assignments improve. He knows his way around Congress, he settles in for the duration, perhaps fixing a sharp eye on a leadership post.

That comfortable congressional way of life could be—and should be—in jeopardy. Believers in the American political cliché which holds that "the voters get what they deserve" never considered this: most voters simply don't know what they're getting. For the first time in the history of Congress, members may have to give the voters more than empty campaign promises and political banalities. They may have to tell the public their private sources of income. They may have to publish their travel expenditures in an easily readable manner. They will have to answer for their office staffs' work and pay. They will have to once again vote on their own fringe benefits.

Since 1970 the aggressiveness of some congressmen, particularly those who worked through the Democratic Caucus, has led to a perceptible change in Congress. More votes are recorded, subcommittee chairmanships are limited to one per member in the House, and committee chairmen no longer can expect to enjoy absolute rule until death or retirement removes them from Congress.

The public and press interest in Congress that accompanied the Hays-Ray scandal continues with the piecemeal revelations of South Korean influence-peddling on Capitol Hill. For all its intractability, Congress understands and responds to pressure from the voters. An electorate that ignores Congress encourages an atmosphere that allows special-interest groups to prosper, permits venality and corruption to flourish, and insures a mediocre legislature.

The campaigns of 1974 and 1976 were marked by calls for a new style of open government. The post-Watergate morality of 1974 and, two years later, the reaction to the congressional scandals of 1976 held the promise of better government in Washington: campaign speeches everywhere were filled with pledges of a new political morality. It is not unreasonable to expect that Congress itself demand only the highest ethical standards of its members, nor is it asking too much of Congress that in the future its members provide an increased measure of forthrightness and accountability.

INDEX